Worlds of Women

Susan M. Socolow, Samuel Cano,
Latin American History, Emory University
Series Editor

The insights offered by women's studies scholarship are invaluable for exploring society, and issues of gender have therefore become a central concern in the social sciences and humanities. The Worlds of Women series addresses in detail the unique experiences of women from the vantage points of such diverse fields as history, political science, literature, law, religion, and gender theory, among others. Historical and contemporary perspectives are given, often with a cross-cultural emphasis. A selected bibliography and, when appropriate, a list of video material relating to the subject matter are included in each volume. Taken together, the series serves as a varied library of resources for the scholar as well as for the lay reader.

Volumes Published

Judy Barrett Litoff and David C. Smith, eds., *American Women in a World at War: Contemporary Accounts from World War II* (1997). Cloth ISBN 0-8420-2570-7   Paper ISBN 0-8420-2571-5

Andrea Tone, ed., *Controlling Reproduction: An American History* (1997). Cloth ISBN 0-8420-2574-X   Paper ISBN 0-8420-2575-8

Mary E. Odem and Jody Clay-Warner, eds., *Confronting Rape and Sexual Assault* (1998). Cloth ISBN 0-8420-2598-7 Paper ISBN 0-8420-2599-5

Elizabeth Reis, ed., *Spellbound: Women and Witchcraft in America* (1998). Cloth ISBN 0-8420-2576-6   Paper ISBN 0-8420-2577-4

Martine Watson Brownley and Allison B. Kimmich, eds., *Women and Autobiography* (1999). Cloth ISBN 0-8420-2701-7 Paper ISBN 0-8420-2702-5

Women and Autobiography

Women and Autobiography

Edited by
Martine Watson Brownley
and
Allison B. Kimmich

Worlds of Women

Number 5

A Scholarly Resources Inc. Imprint
Wilmington, Delaware

Scholarly Resources Inc.
104 Greenhill Avenue
Wilmington, DE 19805-1897

Library of Congress Cataloging-in-Publication Data
Women and autobiography / edited by Martine Watson Brownley and
    Allison B. Kimmich.
        p.   cm.—(Worlds of women ; no. 5)
    Includes bibliographical references.
    ISBN 0-8420-2701-7 (cloth : alk. paper).—ISBN 0-8420-2702-5
(pbk. : alk. paper)
        1. Women's studies—Biographical methods. 2. Autobiography—Women
    authors. 3. Autobiography—Women authors—History and criticism.
    I. Brownley, Martine Watson. II. Kimmich, Allison B., 1968–   .
    III. Series.
    HQ1185.W65   1999
    305.4 ' 07—dc21   99–10956
                                                                                                CIP

♾ The paper used in this publication meets the minimum requirements of the American National Standard for permanence of paper for printed library materials, Z39.48, 1984.

About the Editors

MARTINE WATSON BROWNLEY is Goodrich C. White Professor of English at Emory University. From 1992 to 1996 she served as the director of the Emory Institute for Women's Studies. In the field of eighteenth-century English literature she is the author of *Clarendon and the Rhetoric of Historical Form* (1985), an edition of Clarendon's *Dialogues* (1984), and numerous articles. In the field of women's studies she coedited the collection *Mothering the Mind* (1984) and has published essays on women writers ranging from Aphra Ben to Christina Rossetti.

ALLISON B. KIMMICH is the assistant director of the Women Involved in Living and Learning (WILL) program at the University of Richmond. She has published essays on autobiography and feminist pedagogy. She is currently revising a feminist analysis of four twentieth-century American autobiographies.

Contents

Introduction

Over the last two decades, literary critics have increasingly focused on autobiographies as objects of serious scholarly inquiry.[1] Interest in lifewriting has not been limited to academic circles, however. Americans regularly read enough autobiographies by literary figures, politicians, sports heroes, journalists, and Hollywood celebrities to place such works on bestseller lists. Why do autobiographies succeed in capturing the attention of such a diverse audience?

We can find both scholarly and commonsense answers to that question. Recent academic theories have offered new ways to think about how people define themselves. For example, poststructuralist theories suggest that identity is not a stable entity, but a fluid process.[2] People change dramatically over time, for example, or when their surroundings alter. New scholarship in areas like women's studies, African-American studies, and Asian studies has also contributed to the growing body of work on identity. Scholars in these fields have focused both on the ways people are socialized to fulfill certain roles, thus constrained by their identities, and on the ways in which particular identities may offer people a sense of strength and community. Not surprisingly, autobiographies serve as ideal resources for scholars to apply and expand their ideas about identity.

We can arrive at even more fundamental explanations for why autobiographies appeal to a wide audience. Reading an autobiography is an act of voyeurism; it allows us to look in on the high and low points of another person's life. At the same time, reading an autobiography is an act of self-discovery. Learning how others live, think, and feel can teach us about ourselves.

Autobiographies have not always enjoyed such widespread attention. For a long time, many critics viewed lifewriting as a subliterary genre, ranking it far below such works as novels and poetry. They reasoned that autobiographies required much less skill to create than novels or poetry because the writer could easily draw on real life for the subject matter. At the same time, the creation of fictional works seemed to require greater mastery over language, making them more complex and interesting objects for study. Those biases began to shift in 1980, however, when James Olney published *Autobiography: Essays Theoretical and Critical*. That collection is generally credited with revitalizing and legitimizing the study of autobiography as a field.[3]

However, the selections in this volume indicate that generalizations about autobiography change substantially if we examine renewed interest in the genre with gender in mind. Carolyn Heilbrun notes in "Women's Autobiographical Writings: New Forms" that James Olney's acclaimed text contained only one essay on lifewriting by women. Its author described the seventeenth-century texts under consideration as "early prototypes," thus implying that those narratives were not legitimate—or at least not full-fledged—autobiographies.[4] Heilbrun's example reveals much about how critics have traditionally defined autobiography. First, they typically assumed that "autobiographer" was a synonym for "man." Second, scholars did not treat works by women as "real" autobiographies, especially if women wrote life stories that diverged from the textual models established by their male counterparts.

The pieces included here provide a historical overview of trends in feminist autobiography criticism. *Women and Autobiography* includes essays by critics who have been central to establishing women's autobiography as a field of study and a number of additional analyses that show contemporary approaches in the treatment of women's lifewriting. The contents of the essays reflect a similar variety. Some critics provide critiques of key autobiographical texts, such as Harriet Jacobs's *Incidents in the Life of a Slave Girl*, while others address lesser-known writings, including those by women diarists. The final section of the volume contains selections from texts by women autobiographers themselves, both classic pieces and works that may be difficult to find or rarely studied. The excerpts suggest in miniature the scope and variety of modern autobiography. Beginning with Margaret Cavendish in the seventeenth century, the first Englishwoman to publish her autobiography, they offer an example from each subsequent century through the present.

Readers of this volume will notice that some of the same terms appear in a number of different critical selections. For example, several contributors use the words *subject* and *self* to refer to the author of an autobiography. By choosing "subject," the critics draw on a term that first came into use after the seventeenth-century philosopher René Descartes posited a split between an individual's body and mind. In this context, *subject* refers to one's capacity to think or reason. That early usage resonates for today's autobiography critics because it suggests that the autobiographical "I" is a product of the writer's mind, one deliberately constructed by recording certain details about the past and omitting others.

Self typically denotes a person's inner being, identity, or essence. However, many of the selections dispute this definition and refer to the mythical or fictive self. These critics reason that if identity is a fluid process, we cannot discover an individual's one true self but rather the individual's many selves. The concept of multiple selves has been a liberating one for many feminist critics because traditional ideas of selfhood go hand in hand with unity, and the notion of a unified, essential self has historically been more appropriate for a man's life than a woman's. Several critics included in this volume argue that women see their lives as fragmented or contradictory as they attempt to fulfill the impossible expectations society places on them and as they fashion self-understandings separate from those oppressive norms.

Other terms that recur in the critical selections focus on language. Shari Benstock, for instance, writes about the "symbolic order." The phrase is roughly synonymous with spoken or written language, and it also suggests issues of power and control. Men have typically had the greatest access to and control over language, and some would argue that women cannot enter into that language with much authority or success. Thus, language not only describes or communicates but also orders or organizes the world into groups with varying degrees of power. "Symbolic order," in other words, makes reference to the gendered nature of language. The term "voice," in turn, describes the autobiographer's ability to negotiate the symbolic order and make herself heard. Many critical selections address the woman autobiographer's struggle to find a voice and claim selfhood in a world that repeatedly devalues all things feminine.

Part I, "Women's Lifewriting and the (Male) Autobiographical Tradition," examines the field of autobiography as it has been traditionally defined and raises questions about how, or if, women writers fit into that framework. In the opening selection, the feminist scholar Shari Benstock challenges the theories male critics have proposed to define autobiography and notes that such theories, driven by the desire "to know, define, and sum up," frequently overlook works by women writers. Additional critical selections in this section build on the theme of women's exclusion from the tradition of autobiography, such as Winifred Morgan's analysis of slave narratives by male and female writers.

Early feminist criticism focused on distinguishing women's and men's autobiographical writing. Part II, "Theorizing the Female Subject: Who Writes, How, and Why?" develops logically out of such arguments. Once larger questions about the tradition of autobiography have been addressed, more specific consideration of the unique challenges faced by the woman writer becomes the salient issue. The selections identify a range of obstacles that the woman autobiographer must overcome, including women's subordinate status in relation to men along with their alienation from male-dominated discourse and the masculinist concept of authorship itself.

The third section, "Rethinking Genre: Autobiography in Other Forms," points to new directions emerging in autobiography criticism.

The authors included here advocate a broader understanding of the genre, suggesting that its traditional aesthetic focus on formal patterns tracing an author's life from youth to adulthood is too limited. The selections argue that such approaches reflect a gender hierarchy that excludes much of the writing that women typically produce. The final section, "Women's Autobiography from the Early Modern Period to the Present: Sample Texts" offers four examples of women's lifewriting. Thematically the excerpts address issues that feminist critics argue are unique to women's texts, from Margaret Cavendish's emphasis on relationships to Barbara Webster's honest commentary about the physical and psychological effects of multiple sclerosis.

The ten critical essays and four excerpted autobiographies included in *Women and Autobiography* suggest that women have long produced evocative, engaging life stories in spite of the many obstacles they have faced as writers. The selections also suggest that women's experiences—though tremendously varied over time and from one individual to another—produce some thematic and structural similarities among their narratives. Taken together, however, these scholars' and autobiographers' contributions also warn us against making sweeping claims about women's lifewriting because they reflect a diverse range of critical opinions and autobiographical styles. Indeed, to generalize too broadly about women's autobiography might lead to the same exclusions that arose when many scholars assumed that "autobiographer" and "man" were synonyms.

Notes

1. For an excellent analysis of trends in autobiography criticism, see Lynn Z. Bloom and Ning Yu's "American Autobiography: The Changing Critical Canon," *a/b: Auto/Biography Studies* 9 (1994): 167–80.

2. Many theorists have published texts that discuss postmodern theories of the subject as a process. For a particularly thought-provoking feminist analysis of postmodern subjectivity, however, see Judith Butler, *Gender Trouble: Feminism and the Subversion of Identity* (New York: Routledge, 1990).

3. James Olney himself understands why some literary critics have little regard for autobiographical writing. He explains that "autobiography is the least 'literary' kind of writing, practised by people who would neither imagine nor admit that they were 'writers'" (4). Olney's remarks appear in *Autobiography: Essays Theoretical and Critical* (Princeton: Princeton University Press, 1980), 3–27.

4. See Mary G. Mason, "The Other Voice: Autobiographies of Women Writers," in Olney, *Autobiography*, 209.

I   Women's Lifewriting and the (Male) Autobiographical Tradition

Taken together, these selections develop two common themes. They explain how critics have typically understood autobiography as a genre, then proceed to show how women's writings differ from that standard model and thus dispute the descriptive power of such definitions for women autobiographers. Indeed, women writers have a conflicted relationship with the autobiographical tradition. Through much of history (and even today) women have not been treated as legal, political, religious, or social subjects. During colonial times in America, for example, married women could not own property and any wages that a woman might earn belonged to her husband. Women, in other words, quite literally belonged to their husbands and so were socialized to view themselves as objects.

Autobiography, in contrast, requires that the writer lay claim to subjectivity. Typically, autobiographers also have regarded themselves as autonomous individuals in control of themselves and their lives. At a purely practical level, to produce an autobiography—or any text—the writer must have the time and space to write and enough money to live. In this context, it might seem surprising that women have written autobiographies at all. These selections show, however, that women imagine new ways to write autobiographies that reflect their experiences. For example, women write autobiographies that emphasize relationships because they are accustomed to thinking of themselves in relation to others, as somebody's daughter, wife, or mother. The focus on relationships also means that women's lifewriting typically concentrates on private, or home, life in contrast with men's texts, which often foreground the authors' activities in the public sphere.

These selections also demonstrate that women's autobiographical innovations are not without negative consequences. Unlike the male autobiographer, whose narrative may suggest that he alone deserves recognition for his accomplishments, the typical woman writer acknowledges that her life is part of a larger social fabric. However, the woman autobiographer may also refuse to take credit for her successes by bowing to the social norms that link femininity and self-effacement, thus reinforcing the very ideologies that make it especially challenging for women to imagine themselves as the authors of their own life stories.

1

The Female Self Engendered: Autobiographical Writing and Theories of Selfhood*

~

Shari Benstock

This selection by Shari Benstock echoes many of the issues she addressed in her introduction to The Private Self *(1988), a collection of essays on women and autobiography. Here and in that text, Benstock questions whether contemporary academic theories of autobiography offer satisfactory treatments of the richness and variety of women's autobiographical practices. She argues that autobiography is difficult to define as a genre, and cultural complexities highlight the inadequacies of attempts to define it. In addition, theory depends on drawing firm distinctions, which autobiographies by women subvert in many different ways. For example, Benstock explains that autobiography critics have characterized the typical autobiographer as one who draws clear boundaries between himself and others and between the conscious and the unconscious. Women autobiographers, however, rarely represent themselves and their lives in such either/or terms, and their texts indicate that many scholars need to rethink their understanding of autobiography.*

Most autobiography theories treat identity and subjectivity as givens, taking them for granted. In contrast, women's autobiographies raise numerous questions about what identity actually means and how the self can be defined. Three brief examples from autobiographical texts by Zora Neale Hurston, Maya Angelou, and Jamaica Kincaid suggest how their representations bring into question prevailing cultural notions of the self.

*From Shari Benstock, "The Female Self Engendered: Autobiographical Writing and Theories of Selfhood," *Women's Studies* 20 (1991): 5–14. Reprinted by permission of *Women's Studies*.

Shari Benstock is the director of Women's Studies and professor of English at the University of Miami. She recently published "No Gifts From Chance": A Biography of Edith Wharton (1994). *Benstock is currently the senior editor for a two-volume project entitled* A Handbook of Literary Feminisms: An Anthology of Literary Feminisms *(2000).*

Here I come to one of the memoir writer's difficulties—one of the reasons why, though I read so many, so many are failures. They leave out the person to whom things happened.

—Virginia Woolf, "A Sketch of the Past"

THE ACADEMIC DISCIPLINE of autobiography studies, itself rather newly engendered, focuses attention on its own identity: what *is* autobiography? What texts belong to the genre autobiography? Following recent work in French philosophic and psychoanalytic theory, we have tried to construct a theory (or theories) of autobiography, to articulate the "system of assumptions or principles" that guides autobiographical writing. We search for "models" of autobiography whose complexity could encompass the richness of diversity of our cultures, including in their dizzying sophistication places for racial or ethnic "otherness," for marginal voices, for *le grain de la voix* of gender. You hear a grain of skepticism in my own voice. This mark of doubt leads me—by way of women's autobiographies—to consider academic theories and practices, our collective desire to know, define, and sum up. The very possibility of autobiography repeats this desire and puts it into question, raising all sorts of specters: self/other, private/public, center/margin, genre/gender, reading/writing, etc. We all know this, but what we may not know—or cannot bear to acknowledge—is the way autobiography refuses to admit our academic research practices.

The first impasse is genre. We do not agree—by "we" I mean the international academic institution—about whether autobiography is a separate, definable genre with its own laws and aims (and if it is a genre unto itself, what kind of autobiographical writing forms the "model"); or, whether autobiography is a subset of some other kind of writing (history, biography, fiction). In order for autobiographical studies to have claimed the attention of the scholarly community and have found places on academic programs, we have had to treat it as though it were a genre, something we could examine in the realm of theory as well as at the level of practice. Once Georges Gusdorf proclaimed autobiography to be a genre, then it became safe to question his premises, especially as his genre of autobiography specifically denies women, ethnic minorities, those who are not Christian and heterosexual, those who do not live within northern American and western European culture, those who do not employ traditional narratives of action, adventure, and tests of manhood as the driving force of their autobiographical plots. Gusdorf does not deny that these groups write, he just denies that what they write can be called "autobiography."

The question of genre has implications for notions of culture. Either genre definitions deny that there is any culture other than White-Male-Western-Bourgeois; or cultural complexity throws into relief the impossibility of such a definition. But if genre tries to incorporate all the multiplicities of cultural difference, then what kinds of assumptions can it make, what norms can it postulate? How can it explain itself? On this question we return to ground zero, the zero degree of Western philosophy, the ground of cultural definitions that *by definition* operate through exclusion. One dictionary definition of "culture" is: "the totality of socially transmitted behavior patterns, arts, beliefs, institutions, and all other products of human work and thought characteristic of a community or population." (Parenthetically I note that we must at some time come back to at least two terms in this definition, "totality" and "characteristic," but there is not space enough here to do so.) Perhaps we should look beyond cultural explanations—beyond the cultural custodianship that is the heavy mantle of academic citizenship—to see culture in the ways we have recently learned to see texts, as "woven things." Woven, intertwined, a working together of parts without privileging one over the other (no "center," no "margin"), individual strains and colors still available within the larger pattern. Isn't this the answer to our problem of providing a "model" for autobiography that acknowledges the diversity of culture, that resists privileging the center and raveling the edges?

Theoretically speaking, what I have just described, and you could further elaborate its intricacies, is not possible. Because definition—*by definition*—must display self-sameness in order to be recognizable; definition can acknowledge difference, but only difference outside its own mode, not within the warp and weave of its fabric. The texts I have sketched are texts precisely because they do not share properties of sameness, not with other texts, not with themselves. In practice, however, this is precisely what confronts us in autobiographical studies: individual texts that quite individually elaborate lives that exist, for instance, at what Nellie McKay calls "the intersection of race and gender." This argument moves away from theoretical generalities and toward specificities within cultures and histories, within languages and family groups. We confront enormous obstacles when we try to "theorize" autobiography outside the brutally hegemonic generic terms (terms of "self-sameness") outlined by Georges Gusdorf where the "individual"

life or text reflects a social subset that claims for itself the right to define
the entire text of culture. And yet we *must* theorize outside Gusdorf's
terms because they are unacceptable: they begin from a notion of cultural orthodoxy in the hands of a few. There is no such thing as a "theoretical margin." If theory, in the sense of a "systematic statement of
principles or rules to be followed," is working properly, it draws firm
border lines. Can theory only elaborate an essentialism, as it seems to
have done with the terms "Woman," or "Self"?

I grappled with these problems recently in writing an introduction to
The Private Self, a study of theory and practice of women's autobiographical writings. I must repeat this gesture of grappling because it discloses—
still, even today—my discomfort with the terms in which we speak of
autobiographical writing and the uses to which we put literary theory and
practice. So, to cite myself (which is its own form of the autobiographical):

> I think that recent work on autobiography has fallen into the theoreti-
> cal trap in which American criticism now finds itself—that is, this ges-
> ture [of repeating the priority of "theory" over "practice"] suggests
> that theory and practice are separate from each other, each with clearly
> defined interests and borders, and that when they come together (as in
> the cliched coupling "theory and practice") theory always takes prece-
> dence as that which can make clear the implications for a blinded prac-
> tice. For autobiography, this blind enthrallment to theory has serious
> (and for the most part overlooked) implications; it assumes that autobi-
> ographical writings can only be taken seriously when they are taken
> theoretically to mean something more than a critical practice can elu-
> cidate. And it often means that the implications of theory for certain
> practitioners (women, blacks, working classes, the nonliterary) are
> deadly: theory is taken up and added on to practice without a rigorous
> (that is, a theoretical) examination of the effects of that theory. The
> study of autobiographical writings has often repeated the worst sins of
> academic criticism in order to legitimate the autobiographical. (3)

To say this is not to say that we should return to antediluvian notions of
"value-free" critical practices that divorce texts from cultural and historical contexts or privilege aestheticism at the expense of what is often
termed "sociology."

The relation between theory and practice rests on the notion of "relation," which is often the first casualty of a discussion that insists that the
two terms remain distinct, their borders intact. The little word "and"
smudges their borders, creating a territory that is not "neither/nor" but
"both/and." Any "separate and opposed" claim is, in fact, a misreading of
theory. Theory and practice are not separate from each other, nor are they
necessarily opposed, nor is it certain that practice must bow to the claims

of theory or that theory comes first in some kind of ontological reading of the histories of theory and practice. The arbitrary division between theory and practice attempts to clarify what is vague and arbitrary. But this relationship is *by definition* often vague and fragmentary, its articulation a shifting one, its boundaries never entirely clear or its premises secure. Like auto/bio/graphy, theory and practice are defined in relation to each other, and these definitions change depending upon the subject of the discourse.

The interrelation of theory and practice in analysis of epic poetry or the modern novel is quite different from the interrelation of letters to the epistolary novel or film *noir* to the "woman's film." The relation shifts even within generic boundaries: is "autobiography" something different from "autobiographical writings"? Is it assumed to be self-conscious, directed toward an external reading audience, bound to aesthetic principles and a certain kind of rhetoric? Is this what Gusdorf means by a genre of autobiography? What do we do then with letters, memoirs, diaries? Are these merely notes on the way to autobiography, an interim stage of a process? If we substitute the word "novel" or "poem" for "autobiography" in my question, then maybe letters, memoirs, and diary entries are something extraneous to the genre. Which brings us round to the old question of autobiography and genre, and this is really a question of legitimacy that rests, according to Gusdorf, in the sanctity of "self."

In the word "autobiography," writing mediates the space between "self" and "life." One definition suggests that autobiography is an effort to recapture the self—in Hegel's claim to know the self through "consciousness." This claim presumes that there is such a thing as the "self" and that it is "knowable." This coming-to-knowledge of the self constitutes both the desire that initiates the autobiographical act and the goal toward which autobiography directs itself. Thus the place to begin our investigation of autobiography might be at the crossroads of "writing" and "selfhood."

For Gusdorf, autobiography "is the mirror in which the individual reflects his own image" (33). In such a mirror the "self" and the "reflection" coincide. But this definition of autobiography overlooks what might be the most interesting aspect of the autobiographical: the measure to which "self" and "self-image" might not coincide, can never coincide in language—not because certain forms of self-writing are not self-conscious enough but because they have no investment in creating a cohesive self over time—they do not name self. Indeed, they seem to exploit difference and change over sameness and identity: their writing follows the "seam" of the conscious/unconscious where boundaries between internal and external overlap. Such writing puts into question the whole notion of "genre" as outlined by the exclusionary methods of Gusdorf's rather narrow definition of the autobiographical.

Psychic health is measured in the degree to which the "self" is constructed in separateness, the boundaries between "self" and "other" carefully circumscribed. From Gusdorf's perspective, autobiography is a reerecting of these psychic walls, the building of a linguistic fortress between the autobiographical subject and his interested readers: "The autobiography that is thus devoted exclusively to the defense and glorification of a man, a career, a political cause, or a skillful strategy . . . is limited almost entirely to the public sector of existence," he writes (36). Gusdorf acknowledges that "the question changes utterly when the private face of existence assumes more importance" (37), but he suggests that "the writer who recalls his earliest years is thus exploring an enhanced realm that belongs to him alone" (37). In either kind of autobiography, the writing subject is the one presumed to *know* (himself), and this process of knowing is a process of differentiating himself from others. The chain-link fence that circumscribes his unique contributions is language, representative of the very laws to which the writing subject has been subjected. That is, language is neither an external force nor a "tool" of expression, but the very symbolic system that both constructs and is constructed by the writing subject. As such, language is both internal and external, and the walls that defend *me* are never an entirely adequate defense network against the multiple forms of *I*.

If the linguistic defense networks of male autobiographers more successfully keep at bay the discordant "I," it may be because female autobiographers are more aware of their "otherness." Like men, we are subjected to the phallic law, but our experience of its social and political effects comes under the terms of another law—that of gender. Ellie Ragland-Sullivan comments that "the early mother is internalized as the source of one's own narcissism, prior to the acquisition of individual boundaries, while the father's subsequent, symbolic role is that of teaching these boundaries—he is a limit-setter. As a result, the father is later both feared and emulated, since his presence has taught the infant about laws and taboos" (42). Language itself, as Jacques Lacan has shown, is a defense against unconscious knowledge (Sullivan, 179). But it is not an altogether successful defense network, punctuated as it is by messages from the unconscious, messages that attempt to defeat this "fencing-off" mechanism. Indeed, there is no clearly defined barrier between the conscious and the unconscious, certainly not hierarchical ordering (conscious is "up"; unconscious is "down" or below). Fenced in by language, the speaking subject is primordially divided.

This division is apparent as well in writing, and especially in autobiographical writing. Denial of the division on the part of some theoreticians of autobiography, however, is itself a symptom of autobiographical writing—a repeated but untranslated, unconscious message. This message is directed at culture from the position of the Other, by those who occupy positions of internal exclusion within society—by women, blacks, Jews, homosexuals, and others who exist at the ever-widening margins of society. The relation of the conscious to the unconscious, of the mind to writing, of the inside to the outside of political and narrative systems, indicates not only a problematizing of social and literary conventions—a questioning of the Symbolic law—but also the need to reconceptualize form itself.

In definitions of autobiography that stress self-disclosure and narrative account, that posit a self called to witness (as an authority) to "his" own being, that propose a double reference for the first-person narrative (the present "I" and the past "I"), or that conceive of autobiography as "recapitulation and recall," as James Olney does, the Subject is made an Object of investigation (the first-person actually masks the third-person) and is further divided between the present moment of the narration and the past on which the narration is focused. These gaps in the temporal and spatial dimensions of the text are often successfully hidden from reader and *writer*, so that the fabric of the narrative appears seamless, spun of whole cloth. The effect is magical—the self appears organic, the present the sum total of the past, the past appears as an accurate predictor of the future. This conception of the autobiographical rests on a firm belief in the *conscious* control of artist over subject matter; this view of the life history is grounded in authority.

It is perhaps not surprising that those who cling to such a definition are those whose assignment under the Symbolic law is to *represent* authority, to represent the phallic power that drives inexorably toward unity, identity, sameness. And it is also not surprising that those who question such authority are those expected to submit to it, who line up on the other side of the sexual (or cultural) divide. The self that would reside at the textual center is decentered—often absent altogether—in women's autobiographical texts. The very requirements of the genre are put into question by the limits of gender—which is to say, because these two terms are etymologically linked, genre itself raises questions about gender. Stated differently, autobiographical studies shine a bright light on questions of identity and subjectivity, and autobiographical theory often takes these questions for granted, as the ground on which autobiography stakes its claims. There is a danger in assuming that *we*, the interpreters of autobiographical texts, are the measure of the "self" that autobiography studies so meticulously examine.

I want to shift the grounds of this "self," to complicate its construction by looking briefly at two autobiographical texts by African-American women writers and one by a Caribbean writer. I will place emphasis less on the writing practice that engenders these texts [but] than on the reading practices that interpret and try to account for their narrative alignments.

The most scrupulous reading practices move with the rhythms of the text, submit to the life of the text, feel the weight of each word, experience the effect of each mark of punctuation, notice the shifts in pronouns, respond to the white spaces as well as the print on the page. This kind of reading resists the impulse to dismember and colonize; "re-members" the text, as the writer of autobiography "re-members" the life and in so doing weaves self, culture, life into a textual relation of which language is the fabric itself—not a tool of communication.

Over the past several months my students have been helping me to be a better reader, a reader who resists the need to summarize, theorize, and colonize (although reading always leads us into these traps). We have been reading together Zora Neale Hurston's *Their Eyes Were Watching God* and Maya Angelou's *I Know Why the Caged Bird Sings*. The initiatory gesture of each text is one of remembering, and without making any grand claims I want to cite these gestures as suggestions of the possible relations between women's autobiography, culture, and self. I cite these two passages from Hurston and Angelou in full knowledge that I am dismembering their texts, and I apologize for this act.

Hurston's novel opens in contemplation of the differences between men's wishes and women's dreams. The language of this section is philosophic, its opening sentence very nearly a maxim:

> Ships at a distance have every man's wish on board. For some they come in with the tide. For others they sail forever on the horizon, never out of sight, never landing until the Watcher turns his eyes away in resignation, his dreams mocked to death by Time. That is the life of men.
>
> Now, women forget all those things they don't want to remember, and remember everything they don't want to forget. The dream is the truth. Then they act and do things accordingly.
>
> So the beginning of this was a woman and she had come back from burying the dead. (9)

Men and women are distinguished here in their relation to time. Men's dreams are "mocked to death by Time," while women forget what they do not want to remember. But for this particular woman, remembering (that is, telling her own story) begins in the burial of the dead, a re-membering of the "sudden dead." There is much I am forced to overlook in this passage: the relation of dream to truth, of life to death, of spatial distances (the shoreline, the horizon) and time's movement, of eyes (turned away in resignation) to the eyes of the sudden dead "flung open in judgment."

But I must pass quickly to the opening gesture of Maya Angelou's story. It opens with a quotation:

"What you looking at me for?
I didn't come to stay . . ."

I hadn't so much forgot as I couldn't bring myself to remember. Other things were more important.

"What you looking at me for?
I didn't come to stay . . ." (1)

Here the relation of forgetting to remembering marks the moment the story begins. That is, the origin of this story (and for Hurston's character, Janie, as well) is remarked by the *loss* of its origins. The young girl in Angelou's novel cannot remember the rest of the poem as she stands on Easter Sunday in the children's section of the Colored Methodist Episcopal Church in Stampes, Arkansas. When Hurston's Janie begins to tell her story to her friend Phoebe, she says (in the dialect Hurston uses to mark the oral culture and history of her black protagonists), "Ah, know exactly what Ah got to tell yuh, but it's hard to know where to start at. Ah ain't never seen mah papa. And Ah didn't know 'im if Ah did. Mah mama neither" (20).

The autobiographical fictions begin in a loss of beginning, sources, authority, cultural and social legitimacy. They are initiated by the simultaneous movements of forgetting and remembering. The visual and aural presences of the texts make this available to us in such a way that the "content" or meaning of the work cannot be separated from its "style" or dialect. Further, the relation of forgetting to remembering is specifically gendered and coded by class and race. These texts prevent me—the white, first-world, bourgeois critic—from being at ease with my stockpile of critical terms (self, autobiography, culture) and my bag of reading tricks (a quotation here, a paraphrase there). Indeed, I am incapable of quoting Janie's speech, which is rendered with phonetic care so that we "hear" her as we "read" her. To try to read her speech as it is written forces a gesture of white-woman-mimicking-black-woman. It forces a racist gesture as it crosses racial-cultural boundaries. To read the quotation as I did erases Janie's black presence, it translates *her* self into my white idiom. This moment of discomfort, of cultural dismemberment and throwing into question of selfhood, is a moment that resists theory precisely because it represents what our autobiographical theories have left unsaid—that reading places us, as Gayatri Spivak argued so cogently in the introduction to her translation of Mahaveta Devi's "Draupadi," in the position of the first-world colonialist with regard to the text we elucidate. This should make us think twice about our cultural, critical practices.

Bella Brodzki and Celeste Schenck have recently remarked, speaking of Jamaica Kincaid's *At the Bottom of the River*, that there are "aspects of identity that are outside even race, class and gender, and that cannot be explained by even that recent opening up of critical categories to broader political concerns." Kincaid poses her subject above a basin of water, regarding her self-image as though in a mirror: "I saw myself clearly," she writes, "as if I were looking through a pane of glass" (79). Brodzki and Schenck comment that the subject speaks from a place she cannot yet name, even though her "self" is reflected in the image. Kincaid writes:

> I stood up on the edge of the basin and felt myself move. But what self? For I had no feet, or hands, or head, or heart. It was as if those things—my feet, my hands, my head, my heart—having once been there, were now stripped away, as if I had been dipped again and again, over and over, in a large vat filled with some precious elements and were now reduced to something I yet had no name for. I had no name for what I had become, so new was it to me. . . . I stood as if I were a prism, many-sided and transparent, refracting and reflecting light as it reached me, light that could never be destroyed. And how beautiful I became. (80)

Fragmented by the light, unnamed even by herself, this "self" escapes any prefabricated notions of itself imposed by cultural definitions—even those of gender, race, ethnicity, historical moment, or social context.

My point, very simply, is that autobiographical writing—whatever form it takes—questions notion of selfhood rather than taking self for granted. The coordinates of self cannot be graphed or plotted. Like autobiography, which slips in and out of genre definitions, self is both culturally constituted *and* composed of all that culture would erase—rather like a fishnet, composed both of string and empty spaces between the fibers. Or a skein of tangled yarn that cannot successfully be untangled—where knots and frayed elements remain.

Works Cited

Angelou, Maya. *I Know Why the Caged Bird Sings.* New York: Bantam, 1985.

Benstock, Shari, ed. *The Private Self: Theory and Practice of Women's Autobiographical Writings.* Chapel Hill: University of North Carolina Press, 1988.

Brodzki, Bella, and Celeste Schenck, eds. "Criticus Interruptus: Uncoupling Feminism and Deconstruction." In *Feminism and Institutions*, edited by Linda Kauffman. Oxford: Basil Blackwell, 1990.

Gusdorf, Georges. "Conditions and Limits of Autobiography." In Olney, *Autobiography*, 24–48.

Hurston, Zora Neale. *Their Eyes Were Watching God.* Urbana: University of Illinois Press, 1978.

Kincaid, Jamaica. *At the Bottom of the River.* New York: Random House, 1984.

Olney, James, ed. *Autobiography: Essays Theoretical and Critical.* Princeton: Princeton University Press, 1980.

Ragland-Sullivan, Ellie. *Jacques Lacan and the Philosophy of Psychoanalysis.* Urbana: University of Illinois Press, 1986.

Woolf, Virginia. *Moments of Being.* Edited by Jeanne Schulkind. New York: Harcourt Brace Jovanovich, 1976.

2

Woman's Autobiographical Writings: New Forms*

~

Carolyn G. Heilbrun

This selection was first published in 1985, and it contains many of the same themes that literary critic Carolyn Heilbrun would return to three years later in her landmark volume Writing a Woman's Life. *In this essay and in the bestselling book, Heilbrun argues that much of women's autobiographical writing has not revealed the truth of the writers' lives. Such narratives typically downplay the autobiographers' accomplishments, rarely contain expressions of anger, and avoid discussing either platonic or sexual love between women. Heilbrun points to the women's movement of the sixties and seventies as a pivotal event that changed the ways in which women thought and wrote about themselves and argues that an impressive honesty emerges in women's autobiographical writings published during and after that time.*

She identifies the publication of May Sarton's Journal of a Solitude *(1973) as a watershed moment in women's autobiography, because Sarton's text records the anger and despair that accompanied buying a house, living alone, and writing. Heilbrun also discusses Adrienne Rich's poetry and prose writings in detail. She admires the frankness with which Rich acknowledges the frustration she feels as a mother in* Of Woman Born *(1976) and the poet's struggles to understand her relationship with her father. Accounts like Sarton's and Rich's point to new directions for women's autobiographies where the writers will seek to recount the full range of their experiences, both positive and negative.*

*From Carolyn G. Heilbrun, "Woman's Autobiographical Writings: New Forms," *Prose Studies* 8 (1985): 14–28. Reprinted by permission of *Prose Studies*.

Carolyn Heilbrun retired in 1992 from Columbia University, where she was a professor of English. Her recent work, The Last Gift of Time: Life Beyond Sixty *(1997) examines her own life and the aging process. Heilbrun also writes mysteries using the pseudonym Amanda Cross.*

The man who takes delight in thus drawing his own image believes himself worthy of a special interest. Each of us tends to think of himself as the center of a living space: I count, my existence is significant to the world, and my death will leave the world incomplete. . . . The author of an autobiography . . . looks at himself being and delights in being looked at—he calls himself as witness for himself; others he calls as witness for what is irreplaceable in his presence.

—Georges Gusdorf on autobiography

IN EARLIER TIMES, Gusdorf points out, in those periods and places where "the singularity of each individual life" has not yet evolved, there was no autobiography. Men have been writing autobiographies shaped by the contemplation of their own singularity at least since the time of Saint Augustine. It is my intention in this paper to argue that women's self-writings were, until very recently, radically different from men's, and if the contemplation of one's own singularity is critical, scarcely deserve the name of autobiography, but that in the last decade women's autobiography has unmistakably found its true form.

Here's how Gusdorf describes what we might call the preautobiographical era in human history: "The individual does not oppose himself to all others; he does not feel himself to exist outside of others, and still less against others. . . . The important unit is never the isolated being." And again: "Each man thus appears as the possessor of a role," and not as an individual.[1] Until very recently women lived in such a preautobiographical era, and though they occasionally wrote about their own lives, singularity was hardly to be boasted of. Even in the twentieth century, before the current women's movement, women had only what Patricia Spacks has called "selves in hiding." Their narratives of self were strictly bound in by convention and scarcely to be compared with those of the male autobiographer expressing, as Gusdorf puts it, "the wonder that he feels before the mystery of his own destiny." Autobiography in that sense has been possible for women only in the last two decades, and then probably not in what theorists of the genre would call its true form.

Only since 1980 in America have critics even bothered to speak of women's autobiography, and then in less than confident tones. As in academic departments of literature before the age of "equal opportunity" there had been an "honorary man," or "token woman" already on the premises, so in autobiography there had been Gertrude Stein. Apart from the obvious qualification that her autobiography was an account within the male norms of destiny, its indirect mode of discourse (it was presented as *The Autobiography of Alice B. Toklas*) doubtless provided a comfortable and "literary" angle from which to approach it. James Olney's collection: *Autobiography: Essays Theoretical and Critical*, published in 1980, included only one essay on the autobiographies of women, in this case four women dating from before 1700, whom its author, Mary G. Mason, called "early prototypes." The dialogue of these women was with God; thus they manifested Christian virtue, "an excellent thing in woman."

For secular women there was only one plot, though we have lately diversely named it: the erotic plot, the marriage plot, the romance plot, all the plots ending, as Nancy Miller has pointed out, with marriage or death: the euphoric or dysphoric plot.[2] The labels change, the outcome is the same. Henry James's words from *The Portrait of a Lady* suffice for the story of women's lives: "She was intelligent and generous; it was a fine free nature; but what was she going to do with herself? This question was irregular, for with most women one had no occasion to ask it. Most women did with themselves nothing at all; they waited, in attitudes more or less gracefully passive, for a man to come that way and furnish them with a destiny."[3] And as we know, Isabel Archer, for all her intelligence and generosity, is provided with a destiny by a man. What other story could there be?

James Olney, in a book published in 1972, took the maleness of autobiography for granted. "Autobiography," he wrote, "seems to mean the most to us because it brings an increased awareness, through an understanding of another life in another time and place, of the nature of our own selves and our share in the human condition."[4] Olney is interested, he goes on to tell us, in "why men write autobiographies, and have written them for centuries." It did not occur to him that half the human race did not share, in the way he described, in "the human condition." For women, their "condition" was female rather than human.

Albert Stone writes that "black autobiography vividly re-creates links between the singular self, the immediate community, and a wider world of sympathetic readers and fellow human beings." For women there were no such links to be re-created: their only "immediate community" were their family or neighbours to whom no doubts about their condition could easily be expressed. There were no sympathetic readers, at least none readily identified, and women were inevitably "other" to those "fellow human beings" whom Olney and everyone else referred to simply as "men."

But if the lack of any community or audience for their scarcely defined condition of storylessness was a hamper to women's autobiography, their own internalization of patriarchal standards operated more force-fully still. So, in the words of Patricia Spacks, writing of eighteenth-century women's autobiographies, a fantasy of feminine strength, even if that were achieved, "transformed itself mysteriously into one more con-fession of inadequacy."[5] Spacks continues: "The nature of public and pri-vate selves . . . is for women, in some ways, the reverse of what it is for men. The face a man turns to the world . . . typically embodies his strength," while the only acceptable models for women "involve self-deception and yielding."[6]

By the time Spacks came, four years later, to publish her essay enti-tled "Selves in Hiding," she had extended her observation of women's au-tobiographical disabilities to our own century. The women whose autobiographies she discusses are Emmeline Pankhurst, Dorothy Day, Emma Goldman, Eleanor Roosevelt, and Golda Meir, each a profoundly radical individual, responsible for revolutionary acts and concepts, and possessing a degree of personal power unusual in men as well as women. But, Spacks notes, "although each author has significant, sometimes daz-zling accomplishments to her credit, the theme of accomplishment rarely dominates the narrative." "Indeed," Spacks continues, "to a striking de-gree they fail directly to emphasize their *own* importance, though writing in a genre which implies self-assertion and self-display."[7] The women ac-cept full blame for any failures in their lives, but shrink from claiming ei-ther that they sought the responsibilities they ultimately bore, or were in any way ambitious. Day, for example, has what Spacks calls "a clear sense of self—but struggles constantly to lose it." All of these autobiogra-phies "exploit a rhetoric of *uncertainty*."[8] And in all of them the pain of the lives is, like the successes, muted, as though women were certain of nothing but the necessity of denying both accomplishment and suffering.

All of these modern autobiographies, Spacks observes, "represent a female variant of the high tradition of spiritual autobiography."[9] One must be called by God or Christ to service in spiritual causes higher than one's own poor self might envision, and authorized by that spiritual call to an achievement and accomplishment in no other way excusable in a female self. So Florence Nightingale, in her desperate desire for an oc-cupation worthy of her talents and desires, four times heard God calling her to his service. But if, for men, spiritual autobiographies resulted in personal satisfaction deriving from their spiritual achievement, this was not the case for women. As Mary Mason writes, "Nowhere in women's autobiographies do we find the patterns established by the two prototyp-ical male autobiographers, Augustine and Rousseau; and conversely male writers never take up the archetypal models of Julian, Margery Kemp, Margaret Cavendish, and Anne Bradstreet." On the contrary, Mason writes, "the self-discovery of female identity seems to acknowledge the real presence and recognition of another consciousness, and the disclosure of female self is linked to the identification of some 'other.'" Identity is grounded through relation to the chosen other.[10] Without such relation, women did not feel enabled to write openly about themselves: even with it, they did not feel entitled to credit for their own accomplishment, spiritual or other.

The claim of achievement, the admission of ambition, the recognition that accomplishment was neither luck nor the result of the efforts or generosity of others, all continued, well into the twentieth century, to be impossible for women to admit into their autobiographical narratives. Jill Conway, in a study of the accomplished women of the progressive era in the United States (women born 1850–65), has remarked upon the narrative flatness with which, in their autobiographies, they have described their exciting lives. Their letters and diaries are quite different, reflecting ambitions and struggles in the public sphere and strong personal feelings; in their published autobiographies they portray themselves as intuitive, nurturing, passive, never managerial which, to have accomplished what they did, they inevitably had to be.

The autobiography of Jane Addams (who founded Hull House in Chicago, and was a prominent social worker and pacifist), Conway points out, is sentimental and passive: her cause finds her, rather than the other way around. Not so in her letters, where she takes over the family business and fights for her due. The money for Hull House, in the autobiography, fell in off the street: her letters reveal the truth. This same pattern, Conway demonstrates, is true of the autobiographies of Charlotte Perkins Gilman and Ida Tarbell. There is a wholly different voice in the letters on the one hand and the autobiographical narratives on the other. All of the autobiographies begin confessionally, and, except for Gilman, report the encounters with what would be the life's work as occurring by chance: this was, in every case, quite untrue. Each woman set out to find her life's work, but the only script for women's life insisted that work discover and pursue them, like the conventional romantic lover. As Conway points out, there is no model for the female who is recounting a political narrative. There are no recognizable career stages in such a life, as there would be for a man. Nor have women a tone of voice in which to speak with authority. As Natalie Davis has said, women up to the eighteenth century could speak with authority only of the family and religion. These women had no models on which to form their lives, nor could they themselves become mentors since they did not tell the truth about their lives.

Ida Tarbell, for example, one of the most famous of the muckrakers, author of the history of the Standard Oil Company, reports that the subject just "happened to be there," and, as Conway shows, Tarbell credits the idea of her work to others. This is wholly belied by her letters. Where anger is expressed in these autobiographies it is not, Conway believes, used creatively, as by black authors. The expression of anger has always been a terrible hurdle in women's personal progress. Above all, the public and private life cannot be linked, as in male narratives. This prevents women from writing exemplary lives: they do not dare to offer themselves as models, but only as exceptions chosen by destiny or chance.

What these women could least express in their autobiographies, Conway shows, is their love of other women. Jane Addams loved her college classmate and hated her stepmother, but none of this can be expressed. The unspoken law that women who "make it" must not identify themselves as women, nor dare to annoy men by their self-identifications as women, serves to erase from the record these women's love of one another, and their support of each other. Conway demonstrates that the only lively sections of the autobiographies she discusses are the accounts of childhood.[11] For girls, childhood is often the happiest and freest time. As Spacks has written: "For women, adulthood—marriage or spinsterhood—implied relative loss of self. Unlike men, therefore, they looked back fondly to the relative freedom and power of childhood and youth."[12] It is not only that in childhood girls were allowed to play with boys with a freedom later restrictions on female activity would prevent ever recurring, but that accounts of childhood were somehow freed from the terrible anxieties induced by adult female ambition and encounters. One notes, therefore, that in *The Autobiography of Alice B. Toklas*, Stein does not recount her childhood, but achieves a narrative of frank, mature accomplishment.

Eudora Welty's recent *One Writer's Beginnings*, a charming and popular re-creation of her childhood, on the other hand, beautifully exemplifies this pattern. As a highly skillful writer, long and justly renowned for her ability to evoke pain and conflict in accounts of apparently ordinary events, Welty is able to suggest her parents' anguish; her own suffering is never recalled, nor are any facts mentioned that might spark such a recollection. She writes that "Of all my strong emotions, anger is the one least responsible for any of my work. I don't write out of anger." She has earlier dismissed her youthful anger as "all vanity. As an adolescent I was a slammer of drawers and a packer of suitcases. I was responsible for scenes."[13] But these outbursts of anger are mentioned no more.

A clue to the female displacement of anguish may be found in a sentence of Margaret Mead's, which Welty's memoir exemplifies. "There is much to be said," Mead wrote, "for the suggestion that the true oedipal situation is not the primal scene but parents talking to each other in words the child does not understand."[14] This, which is likely to be true for girl children especially, accounts for the sense that there is a secret to the world that has, because of one's inferiority, been withheld from one. It is far likelier that the girl child, like Welty, has witnessed, not the sexual intercourse of the parents, but their whispered consultations which suggested adult discourse. This is a condition experienced by children of both sexes, but likelier to result, in women, in the profession of writer, interpreter of that whispered, hard-to-perceive adult world.

Another point: Welty was clearly, like Charlotte Bronte and George Eliot, a plain, unpretty child. So was Catherine Drinker Bowen, who has written: "I sometimes wonder why women do not write more about the condition of being born homely. It is something that colors a woman's life, almost from the moment of consciousness. . . . Every girl who lacks beauty knows instinctively that she belongs to an underprivileged group, and that to climb up and out she will have to be cleverer and stronger and more ruthless perhaps than she would choose to be."[15] Bowen goes on to say that many successful (and married) women have told her of this, and that many of them grew beautiful in their later years. But, like Welty, most women do not write of this, nor do they observe that not having been a natural sex object in youth may have turned out to be a very good thing. Childhood may be a happy time but, even as a writer like Welty recalls it, anxiety and unhappiness are not analyzed. The desire to remember only the good things is perhaps not unconnected with Freud's ultimate conclusion that memories of childhood sexual assault were merely the fantasies of the women who recounted them: the women patients themselves may have conspired in Freud's desire to absolve parents from the charge of cruelty and sexual aggression.

In 1962, Lillian Smith, a revolutionary white novelist of the South, analyzed the reasons why no woman had "as yet written a great autobiography." Women, she wrote, "dare not tell the truth about themselves for it might radically change male psychology. So—playing it safe—women have conspired to keep their secrets."[16] Smith was right, but she missed, perhaps, what was most important, the degree to which women had internalized the "facts" dictated to them by male psychology. And when Albert E. Stone asserts, in *Autobiographical Occasions and Original Acts*, that there has been a remarkable outpouring of autobiographies by American women since 1962,[17] he fails, perhaps from gallantry, to notice that the outpouring is more remarkable than the quality or courage or originality of the autobiographies. The two women Stone chose as exemplars of female autobiography from this period are Margaret Mead and Anaïs Nin: regrettable examples in many ways. Nin's diaries are, of course, diaries, and not "autobiography" at all. But even apart from this, Nin, while she has rebelled against the value and limits placed on those qualities defined as "feminine," has made no attempt to free herself from them, nor to redefine the possible "non-feminine" strengths of women.

As Betty Friedan wrote in 1963 of Mead's autobiography *Blackberry Winter*, Mead confirmed all the then dominant Freudian prejudices in her "glorification of the female sexual function. Those who found in her work confirmation of their own unadmitted prejudices and fears ignored not only the complexity of her total work, but the example of her complex life."[18] In a similar way, Helene Deutsch, the prime orchestrator of Freud's theories of female masochism and the dangers of female intellectuality and achievement, wholly ignored her own experience as an achieving, professional woman when laying down the law for other members of her sex. Norman Holland has written that "the basic difference between our experience of fiction and our experience of nonfiction stems from the difference in the amount of reality-testing each asks from us."[19] Yet here, as with so many other statements from the male establishment, the opposite is true for women. It is likely that the amount of "reality-testing" women applied to nonfiction, that is, women's autobiographies, was much less than that they applied to fiction by and about women, precisely because the autobiographies confirmed them in their internalized patriarchal attitudes, and were therefore "real," while some of the fiction challenged these attitudes and could, therefore, be "reality-tested." It is interesting to note that even so "unwomanly" an autobiographer as Simone de Beauvoir is not, Alice Schwarzer observes, a "particularly introspective person."[20] But even had Beauvoir been able to view herself as the ground of profound struggle, rather than as an especially endowed individual who opted out of the usual female destiny, her account would not have changed the general picture. For, as Estelle Jelinek has observed, "As long as women were willing to operate within the system of female subjugation, to see evidence of their own excellence as exceptional, individual marks of courage or intelligence did not threaten the social fabric and perhaps even reinforced it."[21] Without class consciousness, and with few friends among women, Jelinek goes on to observe, women who recorded their own achievements were quick to express their reservations about other women, and men "were quick to foster this separation." For a classic example of this, Jelinek points to Swift, who observed that he "never yet knew a tolerable woman to be fond of her own sex."[22]

Extraordinary women's autobiographies have indeed been written in recent years, though not going back to 1962, Stone's watershed. These remarkable autobiographical accounts have, moreover, been tucked away into other forms, other genres, most of them new. The woman's autobiography as such has probably not changed greatly in recent years, though biographies of women certainly have. The remarkable breakthrough in women's life stories has come in the form of the "confessional," as it is often called with scorn, referring to a work in which the woman critic or writer refuses to adopt an Olympian stance on the male model, instead of offering her own experience as example and evidence of commitment to other women. Especially important is the fact that women found a frankly autobiographical, "confessional" mode for their poetry and, for the first time in an extended way, discovered a form for their uninhibited autobiographical impulses.

Two generalizations appear to be valid concerning recent women's autobiographical writings, whether these writings are in the form of poetry or are embedded in other genres, such as social or literary criticism, the interview, or the essay focused on a particular element of women's life history. The first is that the poet is likely to have reached middle age before beginning upon a clearly autobiographical work. The second is that the autobiographical efforts are clearly outspoken, offering details of personal rebellion and sudden, dazzling recognition of too-easily accepted female servitude with a forthrightness unthinkable two decades ago. In the past, as Sandra Gilbert and Susan Gubar have observed, women writers have created concealed plots, the story of "the woman writer's quest for her own story."[23] Now, women have begun to seize upon their own stories, and to tell them with a directness that shocks as it enlightens. This transformation can be seen clearly in the American poet, novelist, and memoirist May Sarton. Her *Plant Dreaming Deep*, an extraordinary and beautiful account of her adventure in buying a house and living alone, eventually dismayed her as she came to realize that none of the anger, passionate struggle, or despair of her life was revealed in the book. She had not intentionally concealed her pain: she had written in the old genre of female autobiography and then lived into a period which allowed the realization that she had, unintentionally, been less than honest. In her next book, *Journal of a Solitude,* she deliberately set out to recount the pain of the years covered by *Plant Dreaming Deep.* Nineteen seventy-three, when *Journal of a Solitude,* was published, may be accounted the watershed in women's autobiography.

If women's writing until the last decade has been secretive, either wholly disguising the personal struggle, or encoding it in another story or form, readers have been no less unable to read or understand women's hidden stories. We, those taught by the patriarchal world, have not learned to read women's writings because, as Annette Kolodny put it, "we read well, and with pleasure, what we *already know* how to read; and what we know how to read is to a large extent dependent upon what we have already read (works from which we've developed our expectations and learned our interpretative strategies)." Nancy Miller, after quoting Kolodny, has pointed out that, for example, Henry James could not read Georges Sand, as opposed to Balzac, because he was not able to *re*-read Sand; he had not learned to read her in the first place.[24]

If women's writing was, in essence, dismissed as a female, and therefore valueless, art, if women had neither the skills nor the courage to represent their own brutalization and dehumanization, their own despair and secret hopes, then the break into autobiographical expression which occurred in the last decade is the more astonishing and, of course, the more threatening, the more easily dismissed as "confession." It is, also, inevitable that the writers who made this break into the autobiographical mode should have been middle-aged when they did so. (We remember that Virginia Woolf recorded in her diary that she had at last, at forty, found her own voice.) Erik Erikson has said that autobiographies "are written at certain late stages of life for the purpose of re-creating oneself in the image of one's own method; and they are written to make that image convincing."[25] As is usual with Erikson's observations about life histories, this applies more easily to men. Women do not look back to re-create themselves in keeping with some finally perceived ideal; rather, they look back toward the moment at which they found the courage to move forward into as yet unnarrated and unexplored ways of living; they have no "image of one's own method."

In a recent collection of essays, *The Voyage In: Fictions of Female Development*, the bildungsroman is newly examined as a female form. Obviously, it differs from the male form, heretofore accepted as universal: the male pattern, for example, is that of apprenticeship, essentially chronological; for females, the pattern is often that of awakening, "deferred maturation." What is clear is that the male "evolution of a coherent self" has now become possible also for women, but in different ways, and at a different time of life. Women move "from introspection to activity," not the other way.[26] Women must recognize that their spiritual conformity is often a "death warrant," signed in the name either of marriage or other personal sacrifice. As Marianne Hirsch succinctly puts it, the "story of a female spiritual *Bildung* is the story of the potential artist who fails to make it."[27] Spiritual conformity for women is slavery; for men, it can be release into activity and moral revolution. And, in their fictions of female development, women often observe, as did Doris Lessing's Martha Quest, that "there was no woman she had ever met she could model herself on."

Small wonder, then, that it is only past youth that women begin to write the first uncoded, clearly expressed autobiographies. Virginia Woolf, in fact, was in the last months of her life when she wrote "A Sense of the Past," her first wholly open autobiographical sketch; Quentin Bell had not seen it when he published his biography of her. It is a remarkably honest, almost searing memory, and, as with many such recollections in the past, it was disbelieved: Ellen Moers, to take but one example, regarded the memories of childhood sexual assaults upon

Woolf as probably fantasy.[28] What is important, however, is that, exhausted, living in a country fearful of invasion, Woolf wrote her first outspoken autobiography, and then only for intimate friends in the Memoir Club. She was in her late fifties.[29] An American poet like Maxine Kumin did not begin writing poetry "as a woman" until she was middle-aged: her autobiographical prose came even later. In 1975, when she was fifty, she said in an interview: "I didn't really begin to be able to write womanly poems until, let's say, my consciousness was raised by my daughters. . . . I was programmed into one kind of life, which was to say: get a college degree, get married, and have a family. . . . And I came to poetry as a way of saving myself because I was so wretchedly discontented, and I felt so guilty about being discontented."[30]

Within the last two years, two volumes of essays have appeared, one in England and one in America, that present women in their new autobiographical mode with a sharpness and clarity suggesting that, for the first time, women's autobiographical writing has become an exploration of painful experience rather than a denial of pain and struggle. The volumes are: *Fathers: Reflections by Daughters*, edited by Ursula Owen, published by Virago in England in 1983, and *Between Women: Biographers, Novelists, Critics, Teachers and Artists Write About Their Work on Women*, edited by Carol Ascher, Louise DeSalvo, and Sara Ruddick, published by Beacon Press, Boston, 1984. There have, during this time, been other women's autobiographies that recount personal histories with the new honesty women have required. Of these, Ann Oakley's *Taking it Like a Woman* is a fine example. But because I can speak with more assurance of American autobiography, and because it happens that in the English collection on Fathers and Daughters, the essay by Adrienne Rich is the most searing and the most explorative, I shall limit my discussion to American autobiographers.

It must first be noticed, however, that for women examining with new awareness the hitherto mutely accepted constraints of their lives, their parents and other male and female figures are seen with sharp distinctions. One can generalize from these essays with only minor if any exaggeration that fathers, as representatives of patriarchy, are the pivot on which, usually in memory, the new awareness turns. Mothers have no obvious role in this change, but some other female mentor or figure, often not even known personally, operates in the new female plot to enhance the reaction from the father and encourage or inspire the awakening. Mothers may come to be recognized with a new, loving perception, but it is not mothers who free women from their fathers. Not, at any rate, as recounted in autobiographies.

Fathers have so clearly represented patriarchy to newly awakened feminists that, in 1983, Sheila Rowbotham felt the need to defend the individuality of fathers: "Because we were not dealing with abstractions of a vaguely defined 'patriarchy' but talking about actual men, a complex picture began to emerge of 'manhood' and 'fatherhood' and our contradictory needs and images of both. Because these were men with whom we were connected passionately and intimately, however painfully, it was impossible to settle for an oversimplified stereotype in which they could be objectified as 'the enemy' or even 'the other.'"[31] Yet a statement such as this, amounting to forgiveness of the father, or at least an understanding of him, which almost all women autobiographers, except those who have been actually brutalized or sexually assaulted by their fathers, seem eventually to reach, must not be allowed to obscure the great difficulty women have in coming to terms with this figure. As Maxine Kumin has said, the poem about her father was "the hardest poem I ever wrote." She wrote it originally in syllabics and rhyme, using these as a defense between her and the material of the poem: "That's how terrified I was of writing it."[32]

This terror of analyzing one's relation to the father, as Kumin describes it, in no way denies, however, that until recently such analysis was the only way to female self-realization. Ellen Moers in *Literary Women* describes the influence other women's writing had in the past upon lonely and exceptional female creators. But for the ordinary woman, or the gifted woman who was not able, like Emily Dickinson or Madame de Staël, to become in herself a one-woman revolution, the father held the only possible key to female achievement, and the only available encouragement. Bell Gale Chevigny's essay in *Between Women* on Margaret Fuller clearly sets forth the conflict within a gifted woman like Fuller of the male example provided by the father, the female example provided by the mother, and the unbearable conflict between them for the daughter. As Adrienne Rich has observed: "It is a painful fact that a nurturing father, who replaces rather than complements a mother, *must be loved at the mother's expense*, whatever the reasons for the mother's absence."[33] The essays in *Between Women* demonstrate further that when the woman sought a female model for self-realization and achievement, she had to find it in a woman already dead (this is true of almost all the essays in the book), and she was enabled to find it, as the ages of the contributors testify, only with the encouragement of the current feminist movement. Without these dead women, and above all the feminist current bearing the lonely female swimmer along, the discovery and use of a female model would have been impossible.

Only two living women, May Sarton and Simone de Beauvoir, provided courage and inspiration for female achievement and are the subjects of essays in *Between Women*.[34] The latter is, of course, French, and Carol Ascher's essay is entitled "On 'Clearing the Air': My Letter to

Simone de Beauvoir." Her letter, which attempts to clarify her own problems and does not set out to change Beauvoir's views, suggests the same relation between essayist and model as do the other essays. May Sarton provides the only other living mentor or model, and it is significant that Sarton has served so many women this way: she has done so not only through her writings in three genres, but by her life about which she has written in great detail. Her life devoted steadily to writing, lived for many years in solitude but encompassing a love for women, makes her a model both unique and available. Among the other essays for this volume, from Alix Kates Shulman's on Emma Goldman to Alice Walker's on Zora Neale Hurston, the dead woman as recorded in her own and others' writings seemed to replace the mother in affirming the daughter's right to her own destiny and her own opinions. It is now without question that these essayists will, in their turn, provide their daughters, or other young women of the age of daughters, with that encouragement that was denied them. Future women's autobiographies cannot but change profoundly in the light of this.

Side by side with the new examination of the influence of fathers, a widely represented group, and of accomplished women, a frighteningly small or hidden collection of rare individuals, went the new need to identify oneself, claiming, in a new multiple identification, a new freedom for seeking selfhood. Sheila Rowbotham, for example, would write: "Changes outside our immediate family have worked upon our lives. . . . I am a townswoman, educated at Oxford, part of the educated middle class, a Marxist, a feminist."[35] She defines herself as having undertaken a journey formerly inconceivable in one generation. But the multiple identification was not, in itself, enough. It matters whether the identifications are asserted or merely assented to. So Maxine Kumin wrote: "I began as a poet in the Dark Ages of the fifties with very little sense of who I was—a wife, a daughter, a mother, a college instructor, a swimmer, a horse lover, a hermit—a stewpot of conflicting emotions."[36]

Adrienne Rich, who more than any other woman has revolutionized women's autobiographical writing, has recorded how she sought again and again to identify herself in new ways, ways guaranteed to be upsetting to the neat, orderly world from which she came. Her most fundamental struggle was to recognize herself as a poet, and to mean by this that the quality of what she felt impelled to say in poetry was not diminished because it was thought to be female, political, and offensive. Rich, like all of us, grew up with anthologies of poetry we were convinced represented a "universal vision." "I still believed that poets were inspired by some transcendent authority and spoke from some extraordinary height." Although she had been born a woman, she "was trying to think and act as if poetry—and the possibility of making poems—were a truly universal—that is, gender-neutral—realm. In the universe of masculine paradigm, I naturally absorbed ideas about women, sexuality, power, from the subjectivity of male poets." Of course she was told that her sort of poetry, "that is, writing from a perspective which may not be male, or white, or heterosexual, or middle-class," was grinding a political axe, that what she was writing was "bitter," and "personal."[37]

Rich has written, in both poems and essays, of many women who preceded her, from Emily Dickinson to the Russian women's climbing team which perished. But while in the creation of her autobiography, which, it must be emphasized, is, except for the essay in *Fathers: Reflections of Daughters*, always either a poem or part of some other not chiefly autobiographical work, Rich writes with loving attention of her female predecessors, it is her father with whom she has had to come to terms: it is her father who is the pivot upon which her autobiography ultimately turns. And, like Woolf, she is over fifty when she finally comes to terms with him in print, and identifies herself: she knows that in the rest of her life, "every aspect of her identity will have to be engaged. The middle-class white girl taught to trade obedience for privilege. The Jewish lesbian raised to be a heterosexual gentile. The woman who first heard oppression named and analysed in the Black civil rights struggle. The woman with three sons, the feminist who hates male violence. The woman limping with a cane, the woman who has stopped bleeding, are also accountable. The poet who knows that beautiful language can lie, that the oppressor's language sometimes sounds beautiful."[38] One can scarcely imagine a woman so identifying herself in print two decades ago: it is Rich who best demonstrates, in her writings, the new autobiographical form which permitted, indeed demanded, such a statement to be openly made.

Rich began her prose writings in the autobiographical mode in her profoundly important and shocking book *Of Woman Born*. Her honesty in this book, her admission that women might at times hate their children, might even have murderous thoughts about them, so shocked the women who were its first reviewers that the book was denied much publicity and exposure that had, before the reviews, been offered.[39] Rich wrote at the beginning of her book: "It seemed to me impossible from the first to write a book of this kind without being often autobiographical, without often saying 'I.' Yet for many months I buried my head in historical research and analysis in order to delay or prepare the way for the plunge into areas of my own life which were painful and problematical." Rich asserted here, as she had previously, her belief that it is only the willingness of women to share their "private and often painful experience" that will enable women to achieve a true description of the world, and to free and encourage one another.[40] Feminist theoreticians like Elaine Showalter have, since then, defended this female mode, despite efforts to dismiss it by calling it confessional. "In comparison to this flowing confessional criticism," she wrote, "the tight-lipped Olympian intelligence" of such writers as Elizabeth Hardwick and Susan Sontag "can seem arid and strained."[41] They can also seem self-protective, and too readily conforming to the male model of distance and apparent disinterest.

Therefore, in *Of Woman Born*, Rich spoke many hidden truths: that only when visibly pregnant did she feel, in her whole adult life, not-guilty. That like so many women with "male" dreams in childhood, she had set her heart on a son, and had felt triumphant over her mother, who had brought forth only daughters, at the birth of her "perfect, golden, male child." That her husband was unusual in the fifties in "helping," but there was no question that the major career was his, all the initiative for domestic responsibilities was hers. She reports what she wrote in her journal in those years, the despair, resolutions, self-hatred, anger, weariness, bouts of weeping characteristic of so many women's journals. Nor was she willing to dismiss her despair during her children's early years as "the human condition." As she noted, "those who speak largely of the human condition are usually those most exempt from its oppressions—whether of sex, race, or servitude."[42]

By the date of this book (1976), Rich's poetry had already broken through the barriers of impersonality, and the propriety of autobiography in women's poetry. Contemporary male poets, principally Robert Lowell and W. D. Snodgrass, had chosen the same path. But it is chiefly in Rich's generation of women poets—Plath, Sexton, Kumin, Kizer, Levertov—that the T. S. Eliot ban upon the personal fell. These same women—certainly Plath, Sexton, and Kumin—began, like Rich, to explore in other genres their previously hidden resentments and experiences, guilts and sufferings. Novels, interviews, letters all served this impulse. But it is Rich alone who, in writing the essay devoted to her father, practiced the new female autobiography directly, in prose.

The writing of this essay, "Split at the Root," seemed to her "so dangerous an act, filled with fear and shame," but nonetheless necessary. It is well to take these words at their face value. If women's autobiography has taken a great leap, it has not done so without great pain and courage on the part of women like Rich. What became central to Rich's account of her father was not only what was denied her as a woman, but what was denied her as a Jew. Her father's devoted belief in "passing," in making it into the gentile world by being so like gentiles that they would forgive him his Jewishness, is what she chiefly remembers and resents about him: "With enough excellence, you could presumably make it stop mattering that you were Jewish; you could become the *only* Jew in the gentile world." "I had never been taught about resistance," Rich wrote; "only about passing." And to pass meant to be the right sort of Jew, one who exemplified "achievement, aspiration, genius, idealism. Whatever was unacceptable got left back, under the rubric of Jewishness, or the 'wrong kind' of Jews: uneducated, aggressive, loud."[43]

To disconnect herself from her family, Rich married a "real Jew." Perhaps she was simultaneously rejecting her Protestant mother and attempting to transform, to humanize, her father. But it is not really evident that her departure from her marriage, which followed her identification with the women's liberation movement, had a great deal to do with her father's Jewishness, although the essay is so finely written that one does not notice this. Yet there may be an indirect connection. Because in trying to state, to reveal, the truth about everything, particularly the fear of "seeming," let alone "being," Jewish, Rich suggests how profound is the feminist revolution, how it matters that one rethink everything once one has begun to think anew as a woman. She suggests, further, that the efforts of fathers to be accepted in the male world they do not question or challenge are vitally connected with their efforts to imprison their female children, however talented and encouraged, in the conventions of femininity.

The sense one has, in this essay, and in many of the others in this volume, is that in finding both themselves and their fathers these women have come home, have, in the concluding words of Rich's essay, cleaned up their act. The problem of mothers, except to forgive and understand them, is harder, perhaps impossible to solve. The new women autobiographers will probably be the first real mothers of achieving, self-realized women in the history of the world. It is a sobering thought, and one which reveals how new and revolutionary a form we are considering.

NOTES

1. Georges Gusdorf, "Conditions and Limits of Autobiography," in *Autobiography: Essays Theoretical and Critical*, ed. James Olney (Princeton: Princeton University Press, 1980), 28–48.

2. Nancy K. Miller, *The Heroine's Text* (New York: Columbia University Press, 1980).

3. Henry James, *Portrait of a Lady* (London: Oxford University Press, 1947), vii.

4. James Olney, *Metaphors of Self* (Princeton: Princeton University Press, 1972).

5. Patricia Spacks, *Imagining a Self* (Cambridge: Harvard University Press, 1976), 59. The reference in the previous paragraph is to "Introduction," *The American Autobiography*, ed. Albert E. Stone (Englewood Cliffs, N.J.: Prentice Hall, 1981), 4.

6. Spacks, *Imagining a Self*, 88.

7. In *Women's Autobiography*, ed. Estelle C. Jelinek (Bloomington and London: Indiana University Press, 1980), 113–14.

8. "Selves in Hiding," 131.

9. Ibid.

10. Mary G. Mason, "The Other Voice: Autobiographies of Women Writers," in Olney, *Autobiography: Essays Theoretical and Critical*, 207–8, 210.

11. Jill Conway, Paper on Autobiographies of Women of the Progressive Era. Delivered at Workshop in "New Approaches to Women's Biography and Autobiography," Smith College Project on Women and Social Change, June 12–17, 1983.

12. Patricia Spacks, "Stages of Self: Notes on Autobiography and the Life Cycle," in Stone, *American Autobiography*, 48.

13. Eudora Welty, *One Writer's Beginnings* (Cambridge: Harvard University Press, 1984), 38.

14. Margaret Mead, *Blackberry Winter* (New York: Morrow, 1972), 211.

15. Catherine Drinker Bowen, *Family Portrait* (Boston: Little Brown, 1970), 127–28.

16. Quoted in Albert E. Stone, *Autobiographical Occasions and Original Acts* (Philadelphia: University of Pennsylvania Press, 1982), 194.

17. Ibid., 195.

18. Ibid., 200.

19. Ibid., 320.

20. Alice Schwarzer, *After the Second Sex*, trans. Marianne Howarth (New York: Pantheon, 1984), 20.

21. Jelinek, *Women's Autobiography*, 24.

22. Ibid, 34.

23. Sandra Gilbert and Susan Gubar, *The Madwoman in the Attic* (New Haven: Yale University Press, 1979), 76.

24. Nancy K. Miller, "Arachnologies: The Woman, the Text, and the Critic," in *The Poetics of Gender*, ed. Miller (New York: Columbia University Press, 1986), 270–95.

25. Erik H. Erikson, *Life History and the Historical Moment* (New York: W. W. Norton, 1975), 125.

26. Elizabeth Abel, "Introduction," in *The Voyage In: Fictions of Female Development*, ed. Elizabeth Abel, Marianne Hirsch, and Elizabeth Langland (Hanover: University Press of New England, 1983), 11, 13.

27. Marianne Hirsch, "The Beautiful Soul as Paradigm," in Abel et al., *The Voyage In*, 26, 28.

28. Ellen Moers, *Literary Women* (New York: Doubleday, 1976), 105.

29. See my "Virginia Woolf in her Fifties," in *Virginia Woolf: A Feminist Slant*, ed. Jane Marcus (Lincoln: University of Nebraska Press, 1984), 236–53.

30. Maxine Kumin, *To Make a Prairie* (Ann Arbor: University of Michigan Press, 1979), 31–32.

31. Sheila Rowbotham, "Our Lance," in *Fathers: Reflections by Daughters,* ed. Ursula Owen (London: Virago, 1983), 213.

32. Kumin, *Prairie*, 27.

33. Adrienne Rich, *Of Woman Born* (New York: Norton, 1976), 245.

34. Elizabeth Kamark Minnich's essay on Hannah Arendt, written after Arendt's death, recounts Minnich's meetings with her in life. The subject's death offers distance and freedom.

35. Rowbotham, "Our Lance," 215.

36. Kumin, *Prairie*, 106.

37. Adrienne Rich, "Blood, Bread & Poetry: The Location of the Poet," *Massachusetts Review* 24 (1983):521–40.

38. Rich, "Split at the Root," in *Fathers*, 186.

39. See Kathleen Barry, Reviewing Reviews: *Of Woman Born* in *Reading Adrienne Rich: Reviews & Revisions, 1951–81*, ed. Jane Roberta Cooper (Ann Arbor: University of Michigan Press, 1984), 300–303.

40. Rich, *Of Woman Born*, 15–16.

41. Elaine Showalter, "Feminist Criticism in the Wilderness," in *The New Feminist*, ed. Showalter (New York: Pantheon, 1985), 252

42. Rich, *Of Woman Born*, 26, 193, 223, 27, 30, 34.

43. Rich, "Split at the Root," 170, 178, 175, 179.

3

Construing Truth in Lying Mouths:
Truthtelling in Women's Autobiography*

~

Sidonie Smith

Sidonie Smith's scholarship on women and autobiography has been important in both defining and advancing the field of feminist autobiography criticism. She has written and edited several books that focus on women's lifewriting. Here she draws on a number of poststructuralist and feminist theorists to explore the contradictory status of "truth" in women's autobiography. Almost all autobiographies claim to be honest self-depictions. But autobiographers' self-understandings are shaped by the language that they use to express themselves. Particularly difficult for women autobiographers are the historical and linguistic limitations that have shaped concepts of what a "woman" is at any given point in time. In writing her life, the autobiographer must choose whether to reproduce or to contest dominant views of femininity in her culture, views that, historically, have been misleading, unfair, or insufficient.

Smith outlines three strategic moves possible for women autobiographers. Although each of these moves involves "lies" of one kind or another, these ostensible lies are so closely related to "truth" that they become a way to get at a kind of truth, however partial and elusive. The first method, "excessive storytelling," mimics traditional autobiographical paradigms, all of which presuppose a white middle-class male writer. By precisely adhering to these norms of self-representation, the "lie" of their insufficiency for women writers is revealed. In the second move, masquerade, overidentification with the ostensibly feminine, operates to show the gap between femininity

*From Sidonie Smith, "Construing Truth in Lying Mouths: Truthtelling in Women's Autobiography," *Studies in the Literary Imagination* 23 (1990): 145–63. Reprinted by permission of *Studies in the Literary Imagination*.

as it is postulated and actual women. The discontinuity shows that no single, essential notion of woman exists. With the third strategy, " 'I'-lying," women autobiographers employ the autobiographical "I" in an intentionally duplicitous way to emphasize the fictiveness of any self-representation. By showing the difficulties in truthfully depicting identity, these three strategies reflect the constructed nature of any truths that autobiography might finally convey.

Sidonie Smith is a professor of English and a professor and director of Women's Studies. Her most recent publications include Women, Autobiography, Theory: A Reader *(co-edited with Julia Watson) (1998);* Indigenous Australian Voices: A Reader *(co-edited with Jennifer Sabbioni and Kay Schaffer) (1998); and* Writing New Identities: Gender, Nation, and Immigration in Contemporary Europe *(co-edited with Gisela Brinker-Gabler) (1997). She has just completed a book on women's travel narratives called* Women on the Move: Twentieth Century Travel Narratives and Technologies of Motion *for the University of Minnesota Press.*

I begin: the first memory.
—Virginia Woolf, "A Sketch of the Past"

But, in reality, as soon as there is a locutor in discourse, as soon as there is an "I," gender manifests itself. For each time I say "I," I reorganize the world from my point of view and through abstraction I lay claim to universality. This fact holds true for every locutor.

—Monique Wittig, "The Mark of Gender"

I am a white girl gone brown to the blood color of my mother speaking for her though the unnamed part of the mouth the wide-arched muzzle of brown women
—Cherrié Moraga, "For the Color of My Mother"

IT HAS BEEN THE CRITICAL FASHION to speak knowingly of autobiography's fictiveness for at least a decade now. When Hayden White neatly conjoined the two realms of the factual and the fictive in his description of historical narrative as a "fiction of factual representation," he argued that since "facts do not speak for themselves," the historian "speaks on their behalf, and fashions the fragments of the past into a whole whose integrity is—in its *re*presentation—a purely discursive one."[1] The autobiographer is the self-historian, autobiography representation. Purporting to reflect upon or re-create the past through the processes of memory, autobiography is always, multiply, storytelling: memory leaves only a trace of an earlier experience that we adjust into story; experience itself is mediated by the ways we describe and interpret it to others and ourselves; cultural tropes and metaphors which structure autobiographical narrative are themselves fictive; and narrative is driven by its own fictive conventions about beginnings, middles, and ends. Even more fundamentally, the language we use to "capture" memory and experience can never "fix" the "real" experience but only approximate it, yielding up its own surplus of meaning or revealing its own artificial closures.

Looking historically, we recall that autobiographical and novelistic forms evolved around one another in the West and assume certain coincidences of their narrative conventions. And perhaps, following M. M. Bakhtin, we consider the ways in which autobiographers gradually incorporated the techniques of realistic fiction—dialogue, characterization, plotting—within the structures of autobiographical narrative. Our clumsiness at creating effective typologies of autobiographical forms, our current confusion at setting generic boundaries that distinguish between the autobiographical and the fictive, have much to do with the increasing novelization of the genre, a process analyzed by Bakhtin. According to Bakhtin, as genres introduce novelistic techniques "they become more free and flexible, their language renews itself by incorporating extraliterary heteroglossia and the 'novelistic' layers of literary language, they become dialogized, permeated with laughter, irony, humor, elements of self-parody and finally—this is the most important thing—the novel inserts into these other genres an indeterminacy, a certain semantic openendedness, a living contact with unfinished, still-evolving, contemporary reality (the openended present)."[2] Eventually we enter into the quagmire of generic differentiation, especially as we consider twentieth-century texts.

And then we confront the increasing destabilization of the notion of any legitimate kind of "self" in the metaphysical sense. The Marxian analysis of material conditions and their relationship to consciousness, the Freudian introduction of an unconscious that bites at the edges of the rational, the Einsteinian challenges to the certainties of chronological or developmental time, the Saussurean empowerment of language over consciousness, and the recent postmodern incursions on authority, legitimacy, origin, and meaning have all colluded in rendering the old essential self and its myth of uniqueness, coherence, and imperial power, a fictive construct. With the self under question autobiography struggles toward its object and with its subject. As certain theorists of autobiography suggest, every kind of writing partakes of the autobiographical or rather all autobiographical writing passes sometimes noisily, sometimes noiselessly into the realm of the fictive.[3]

The simplicity with which readers of autobiography can adjudicate the degree of "truthtelling" by differentiating fact from fiction in any narrative purporting to be about actual lived experience becomes ever more problematic. In the late twentieth century, we have been forced to leave behind simplistic notions of "truthtelling" founded upon what William L. Andrews describes as the "positivistic epistemology, dualistic morality, and diachronic framework[s]" prevalent in the eighteenth and nineteenth centuries.[4] We are even further removed from the juridical and ecclesiastical trials of "truthtelling" in autobiography's earliest manifestation. In "confession," the truth value of the autobiographer's account was, as Leigh Gilmore notes, subjected to specific tests, with either God and "His" priests or the court as arbiters since the one who confessed was expected "to tell the truth, the whole truth, and nothing but the truth."[5] The pressure of ideologies, the unconscious, the opaque mechanisms of language and desire, the powers of discursive determinations, the destabilized temporalities of history and memory, among others, have colluded in contaminating "the whole truth and nothing but the truth."

Yet "truth" cannot be jetissoned quite so quickly and efficiently. For the expectation of some kind of "truthtelling" still characterizes what Elizabeth Bruss calls the "autobiographical act." Since Bruss found it more reasonable to consider the bases of this "speech act" rather than to struggle to define the generic limits of a writing so amorphous and protean, she established three characteristics of the act: the identity of historical author, narrator, and protagonist; the claim for "the truth-value of what the autobiography reports—no matter how difficult that truth-value might be to ascertain"; and the claim for the autobiographer's belief "in what he asserts."[6] Rita Felski, arguing after Bruss, asserts that "autobiography . . . makes claims to historical veracity as the account of part or all of the life of a real individual written by that individual. That this claim can be undermined by exposing the distortions inherent in the writing process or problematizing the very notion of what constitutes 'truth' does not negate the fact that the intention of honest self-depiction is a determining feature of the 'autobiographical contract' which is familiar to every reader."[7] But even amidst such hedgings and wedgings of "truthtelling," another question clamors to be heard.

"Truth" to what? To facticity? To experience? To self? To history? To community? Truth to the said, to the unsaid, to other fictions (of man, or woman, of American, of black, etc.), to the genre? And truth for what and for whom? For the autobiographer? The reader? Society? At a time in the West when the autobiographical seems to surround us and yet when the autobiographical and novelistic seem to have merged inextricably with one another, what does it mean to ask about the perplexed relationship of the autobiographical to "truthtelling"? As a beginning at answering some of these questions and posing others in their wake I want to circulate "truth" through this essay, sending it in and out and around the autobiographical practice of women. In doing so I want to consider the relationship of specific women and "woman" to this "truth" and its telling.

At its simplest perhaps the question of truthtelling asks us to ponder the relationship of the autobiographer's text to her experience. Analyses of this relationship proceed along different paths depending upon the reader's theoretical orientation. Some argue for the specificity of a woman's experience outside the text, that "real" experience to which the textual narrative refers. This experience is of two kinds, the specific lived experience of the actual woman, the autobiographer whose name appears on the title page, as well as the shared experience of a commonality termed "women." Since that experience has been culturally silenced in patriarchal culture the task of the autobiographer is to give voice to the "truth" of that great unspoken through the text. "Experience" is the "truth." And sexual "difference" itself is the core of that "experience." "This experientially based position," suggests Felski, "presupposes a distinctive female consciousness which manifests itself both as a psychological constant within women and as an identifiable recurring characteristic of women's writing."[8] Adrienne Rich, for instance, posits such a generalized constant in her autobiographical consideration of motherhood, *Of Woman Born*, when she asks "whether women cannot begin, at last, to *think through the body*, to connect what has been so cruelly disorganized—our great mental capacities, hardly used; our highly developed tactile sense; our genius for close observation; our complicated, pain-enduring, multipleasured physicality."[9]

From this point of view autobiographical texts manifest a specific female consciousness, a mode of knowing, perceiving, and of being in the world. Moreover, since the original "experience" is accessible in an unmediated way to the autobiographer, she "translates" that "experience," and her text accurately "reflects" it. The call to "truthtelling" thus invokes the expectation that the autobiographer will reveal the specificities of her different body, her different consciousness. It might also require elaboration of her experience as a woman in a male-dominated culture, an uncovering of the sites both of her oppression and her empowerment. According to this theoretical framing, then, autobiographical practice for twentieth-century women would engage the autobiographers in the act of sedulous recovery and celebration of an experience erased from history, an experience wrongly hierarchized as subordinate, suspect, and specular.

In salvaging the "truth" of her "experience," the autobiographer might seek to unearth or unmask her "true" self, that unique "self" uncontaminated by the falsehoods, "half-truths," the "untruths," that her culture would foist off as the universalized "truth" of "female experience" and "female identity." Through this process of shedding layers of false selves and identities, she would struggle toward an authentic, or "truthful" reflection of her emotional life, toward a legitimate articulation of what she "really" feels and thinks.[10] The degree of "truthtelling" in the text is thus produced by various structural and linguistic strategies and effects. Felski notes that structurally the text may unfold in an episodic, disrupted, apparently spontaneous manner and resist the patently constructed, since, "through this kind of structure, the confession seeks to emphasize its status as reflecting and contingent on lived experience, rather than as a self-contained literary artifact."[11] The less obviously literary the text the more the autobiographer can claim authenticity and "truthfulness." In addition, the more the autobiographer piles up personal, specific, and compelling details, the more secrets and unknown experiences she confesses about herself, the more she seems to be speaking the "truth." As she voices the hidden story in a cultural context in which woman's voices have been suppressed and repressed, she positions herself as a "truthtelling" narrator. Even the label "autobiography" functions as an "authenticating" sign, insuring or underwriting the "truthtelling" value of the text. The "personal" is not just the political but "the truthful."

Yet "truth" to and of "self" and "experience" is a problematic phenomenon, as critics of cultural feminism argue again and again. "Given contemporary developments in linguistic, philosophical and social theory," suggests Felski, "it is increasingly difficult to hold onto any notion of the female subject as a privileged and autonomous source of truth," whether truth to the unique or the universal.[12] For one, there is little access to a "true self" to be found textually. Splittings of all kinds intervene in direct access to the "self": splittings between author and narrator; between narrator and narrated; between "I" now and the "I" then; between "I" and "me"; between the ideological "I" and the "I." Since, as Edward W. Said argues, "in any instance of at least written language, there is no such thing as a delivered presence, but a *re-presence*, or representation," there can be no simple identification between the autobiographer and that "I" that floats across the page of her text. The autobiographical text is, after all, a self-representational artifact, not the self itself. In fact, to continue with Said's argument, "the written statement is a presence to the reader by virtue of its having excluded, displaced, made supererogatory any such *real things* as [its ostensible object]."[13] And if "representations" circulate inside the text, even the representational sign "I," where can "truth" and "truthtelling" be found?

Second, the unproblematic celebration of the "experience" and "self" of the woman outside the text too easily homogenizes that "truth" into an essentialist theory of sexual difference, too easily erases the traces of social, cultural, linguistic, psychological technologies of selfhood and gender. Third, as it promotes a literary theory of reflectionism and transparency, the celebration of a reified "experience" paradoxically obscures the influence of determining structures, including those of literature and genre.[14] "Experience" is not out there to be recovered outside the interpretive grids of culture and the structural grids of language. Moreover, "experience" is culturally legitimized since only certain "experiences" are elevated to the "truthful" at particular historical moments.

* * *

Thus, "experience" recedes before a predatory textuality. Postmodern incursions on the old "self" of humanism and its privileges of autonomy, epistemological certainty, authorial intentionality, and imperial self-presence have unloosed all the ties to a convenient and secure anchorage of "selfhood" and an unproblematized "experience." What Linda Alcoff has labeled the "nominalist" position on experience would argue that there is only textuality and therefore what is of interest is the play of language and subjectivity in the text without reference to anything outside the text, including the very author of the text, including the very fact that the author of an autobiography might be a woman.[15] The very body of woman recedes, or to use a cinematic metaphor, "the lady vanishes." Hence even the authorial signature is no matter of "truthfulness" since the author is "dead" as an uncontested source of origin and legitimation. Hence, there is no "experience" outside the text to which to be "truthful," no single meaning secured by authorial intentionality, thus no vexing allegiance to "truthtelling." The overdetermination of individual consciousness by linguistic, cultural, and psychoanalytical structures renders null and void the very notion of "truthtelling." What meaning "truth," what possibility "truthtelling" in an overdetermined system without human agency?

What pertains to something called the "truthful" might be the deployment of subjectivity in and through the text, the self-conscious elaboration of the only "truth," that is the "truth" of the ficticity of the "self" and "identity," of the very "I" that marks the page of autobiography. Or, what is "truthtelling" might circulate around the impossibility of any "truthtelling," the always deferred play of meaning, the undecidability of any coherent meaning and any unified subjectivity. From this point of view only avantgarde textual practices as they confront self-reflexively the impossibility of the closure of meaning, as they promote the undecidability of meaning, would confront the "truth" with a little "t" of all autobiographical attempts at fixing "identity" and "self."

Might a woman have any particular relationship to non/truthtelling in this nominalist theoretical frame? For certain "French feminists," among them Julia Kristeva and Luce Irigaray, woman's "truthtelling" is problematized from the beginning by her relationship to the law of the father, to the symbolic realm outside of which she has never and can never be represented or represent herself. Yet for Kristeva, particularly, "woman" has nonetheless a promising and provocative access to "truth," although perhaps not actual women. Kristeva argues that "truth" becomes metaphorically the "feminine" in the text; or rather, the "feminine" is the "truth" of/in textuality. Since the father is both "sign" and "time," "what the father doesn't say about the unconscious, what sign and time repress in the drives, appears as their *truth* (if there is no 'absolute,' what is truth, if not the unspoken of the spoken?) And that this truth can be imagined only as a *woman*." This truth is "curious" since it is "outside time, with neither a before nor an after, neither true nor false." It is rather, "subterranean" because "it neither judges nor postulates, but refuses, displaces and breaks the symbolic order before it can re-establish itself." "If a woman cannot be part of the temporal symbolic order except by identifying with the father," Kristeva suggests,

> it is clear that as soon as she shows any sign of that which, in herself, escapes such identification and acts differently, resembling the dream or the maternal body, she evolves into this "truth" in question. It is thus that female specificity defines itself in patrilinear society: woman is a specialist in the unconscious, a witch, a bacchanalian, taking her *jouissance* in an anti-Apollonian, Dionysian orgy. . . . *Jouissance*, pregnancy, marginal discourse: this is the way in which this truth, hidden and cloaked [*dérobent et enrobent*] by the truth of the symbolic order and its time, functions through women.

"Truth," having no "self," is found "in the gaps of an identity." As "negativity," this "truth" can never be represented. Once represented this "unconscious 'truth,' an unrepresentable form beyond true and false, and beyond present-past-future" is recuperated in the symbolic.[16]

While Kristeva herself says nothing about the woman autobiographer, and little about the woman writer, her theories have implications nonetheless for autobiographical practice. The autobiographer might pursue the "truth" of the symbolic or she might remain open to the disruptions of that other "truth" of the semiotic; she might identify with the father or with the mother. Pursuing the former she would repress the "truth" of the unconscious, of the unsaid; pursuing the latter she would "sullenly hold back, neither speaking nor writing, in a permanent state of expectation, occasionally punctuated by some kind of outburst: a cry, a refusal, 'hysterical symptoms.'"[17] If, in either case, "truth" is repressed, what is the autobiographer to do? Kristeva answers by promoting the necessities of negativity. The only "truthful" relationship that can develop between the autobiographer and her narrative derives from the play of negativity through her text. To paraphrase Kristeva, the autobiographer would constantly be saying "'that's not [me]' and 'that's still not [me].'"[18] Gaps, disturbances, nonsense, puns, rhymes, a thousand and one subversive points, reveal the "truth" of subjectivity, including its processural dynamics, its fictiveness, instability, temporality. Such autobiographical practice would destabilize every theory of the centered subject, every reification and mystification of the autonomous "self."

In the Kristevan model, an autobiographer may or may not be attuned to the "feminine." For Kristeva unhinges "the feminine" from "woman" in such a way as to potentially erase the woman outside the text who retains no privileged relationship to the "feminine." Thus while the Kristevan notion of negativity may promise some new orientations to "truthtelling," it also proves potentially distressing as a ground upon which to construct a theory of "truth" in women's autobiography. As a nominalist position it suffers from certain disabling characteristics. Just as we cannot leave experience unproblematized, we cannot elide the woman outside the text; nor can we leave woman in the universalized position of negativity. As Nancy K. Miller argues in her essay "Changing the Subject," it is important for feminist theorists of women's writing practices to resist this position:

> The postmodernist decision that the Author is dead, and subjective agency along with him, does not necessarily work for women and prematurely forecloses the question of identity for them. Because women have not had the same historical relation of identity to origin, institution, production, that men have had, women have not, I think, (collectively) felt burdened by too much Self, Ego, Cogito, etc. Because the female subject has juridically been excluded from the polis, and hence decentered, "disoriginated," deinstitutionalized, etc., her relation to integrity and textuality, desire and authority, is structurally different.[19]

And Christine Di Stefano warns us that "with postrationalism, *she* dissolves into a perplexing plurality of differences, none of which can be theoretically or politically privileged over others." As a result, "the figure of the shrinking woman may perhaps be best appreciated and utilized as an aporia within contemporary theory: as a recurring paradox, question, dead end, or blind spot to which we must repeatedly return, because to ignore her altogether is to risk forgetting and thereby losing what is left of her."[20]

Now on the one side we have a reflectionist framing of autobiographical practice which would put a high premium on the authentic-
ity/"truthtelling" alignment of the text. On the other we have a
nominalist framing that would respond to the negativity/"truthtelling"
alignment of the text. In the former case the "I" refers to someone outside the text while in the latter the "I" is a fiction produced by the text.
In the former "truth" derives from the mimetic specificities of the text;
in the latter it derives from the nonmimetic eruptions, the subversive tensions of the text. But let us ask once again: What is the relationship of
the autobiographer to the "truth"? What "truth"? Whose "truth"?

                                    * * *

When the "I" lands on the page, so to speak, it enters a complex web of
intertextualities. Entangled in formal and linguistic operations and practices as well as discursive contextualities that intervene in the trans-
parencies of "truthtelling," that "I" is subject to and of its specific
historical moment. At that moment, discursive regimes encode and en-
force structures, power relationships, knowledges that pass for the natural, real, common-sensical—the "truth." These regimes of truth
transform cultural myths, practices, ideologies, or "fictions" into apparent "truths." Thus they effectively establish the "location" of knowledges
and "truths." "Through location," suggests Elspeth Probyn, "knowledges
are ordered into sequences which are congruent with previously established categories of knowledge. Location, then, delineates what we may
hold as knowable, and following Foucault, renders certain experiences
'true' and 'scientific' while excluding others."[21] Those denied "truth"
value are banished to the periphery of discursive systems.[22]

Regimes of truth function to normalize the "I" by configuring it in specific ways and then pressing it into the services of "truthtelling." Governing
the cultural lineaments of "I"-ness and the historical practices of self-
narrative, regimes of "truthtelling" "police" not only what is considered
"truth" but also how that "truth" can be told. At the level of language itself
these regimes of truth flavor the very tongue of the individual speaker as
she translates experience. "Language, for the individual consciousness, lies
on the borderline between oneself and the other," suggests Bakhtin: "The
word in language is half someone else's. . . . It exists in other people's
mouths, in other people's contexts, serving other people's intentions: it is
from there that one must take the word, and make it one's own."[23]

Autobiographical writing as it elaborates symbolic fictions of identity
and selfhood is one ground upon which competing notions of truthtelling
vie. Since, as Bakhtin argues, "expropriating [language], forcing it to submit to one's own intentions and accents, is a difficult and complicated
process," on that ground the autobiographer wields words with greater and

lesser degrees of self-consciousness.[24] And that self-consciousness is heightened around certain words. Certainly for the woman writing autobiography one of the critical words circulating in other people's mouths is "woman," for, if the sexed body is a most obvious "fact" about the autobiographer, the gendered person inhabiting the "I" is no such "fact" at all. The identity of the gendered entity, "woman," is one of those fictive "truths" circulating through culture and its texts. Since " 'Woman,' " according to Felicity A. Nussbaum, "can be read as a historically and culturally produced category situated within material conditions that vary at historical moments and in regional locations," when the autobiographer enters the autobiographical scene of writing she encounters "certain regimes of truth, of discourse, and of subjectivity available to women."[25]

Such regimes both effectively and partially "police" the narrative contours of "truthtelling." The autobiographer may respond to that word "woman" and the knowledges and truths allied with it in at least two contradictory ways and do so simultaneously. Participating in a certain conservative "truthtelling," the autobiographer might constitute a "truth" consonant with the regimes of truth operating culturally and temporally by configuring experience according to established conventions and practices. Unauthorized or suspect experiences, as Probyn suggests, might not be "brought to light"; rather, positioned "outside of the 'true' and the 'scientific,'" they might "circulate as women's intuition, ritual and even, instinct."[26] Consequently, the hegemonic "truth" of the cultural construct "woman" might be effectively reproduced.

But such conservative or reproductive "truthtelling," promoting as it does normative and universalistic claims, comes into conflict with another kind of "truthtelling"; and that is the "truthtelling" that derives from an individual's recognition that the regimes are not all there is, that the specificities of an individual's experience may be nonidentical with the cultural knowledges and their formal and ideological lineaments, that the words must somehow be made her own. Thus the autobiographer might also engage in contestatory "truthtelling" since that which seems to be "truthful" to regimes of truth may in fact be false; and that which appears to be "untruthful" may in fact be another kind of "truthtelling." "Experiences" positioned askew from the template of "official" knowledges may be brought in from the periphery and aligned against the old "truth" as an alternative "truth." Writing of diarists in the eighteenth century, Nussbaum observes that "the contradictions that eighteenth-century woman may experience in attempting to shape her self-representation may leak through the fissures of existent models and assumptions to speak discontinuity and produce revision and resistance. In short, these serial texts confirm the conventions for 'woman,' while they also may allow alternative configurations of identity to emerge at the periphery of the available range of meanings."[27]

Writing of the slave narrative of Harriet Jacobs, I have elsewhere, as have others, explored the ways in which Jacobs rewrites all the conventional truths promoted in certain discourses prevalent in mid-nineteenth-century America, from the seduction novel to the male slave narrative. Her text effectively gives the lie to various regimes of narrative truthtelling at the same time that it identifies factual with fictive narratives. By the twentieth century autobiographical narratives often become absorbingly contestatory and unabashedly "fictional" as the autobiographer asks the reader to follow her in order to see something new, to see the same thing anew. "Since it is notoriously difficult for women to recognize ourselves in the traditional images that literature and society (sometimes including our own mothers) project or uphold as models," notes Françoise Lionnet, "it should not be surprising for an autobiographical narrative to proclaim itself as fiction: for the narrator's process of reflection, narration, and self-integration within language is bound to unveil patterns of self-definition (and self-dissimulation) which may seem new and strange and with which we are not always consciously familiar. The self engendered on the page allows a writer to subject a great deal of her ordinary experience to new scrutiny and to show that the polarity fact/fiction does not establish and constitute absolute categories of feeling and perceiving reality."[28]

Contestatory "truth" also arises from a recognition that the autobiographer is entangled in competing, even contradictory regimes of truth. For "woman" herself is discursively multiple. There are various "womans" in the regimes of truth, differentiated by race, class, ethnicity, sexual preference. Moreover, "woman" is only one fictive ground of location.[29] Other locations characterize the speaker's position within discursive regimes—grounds also of race, class, nationality, ethnicity, sexual preference, religious identification. Thus other reproductive and contestatory "truths" mingle around and through, even contradict, the prevailing regimes: the unsaid seeps through the said; the oppositional seeps through the identical; the revolutionary interrupts the conservative. Another way of suggesting this "fugue" of voices conglomerating in the "I" is to suggest that the autobiographer does not always linger entirely in the spatiotemporal locale of gender; she lingers also and elsewhere in multiple locales whose positioning shifts with the effect that the formerly peripheral becomes central, the central moves away toward the periphery as other locales assume precedence. Entering the autobiographical scene the autobiographer negotiates multiple locales and distresses multiple locations of "truth." Moreover, the language she uses does not linger always in the realm of the explanatory and intentional but always sallies forth in the realm of the supplementary, or the undecidable.

Regimes of truth are also temporally determined. Since regimes change over time and in response to historical and cultural contingencies, notions of "truthtelling" and of "truth" are unstable, shifting. "If the flourishing of individualism and the emergence of a clear separation between the realms of 'fact' and 'fiction' in bourgeois society are necessary preconditions for the development of modern autobiography," suggests Felski, "then the modification or reformulation of such concepts in the context of changing cultural and ideological frameworks may well affect reading practices, and the kind of generic distinctions which readers actually make."[30]

Finally, we must remember that there is no monolithic autobiographical discourse, no one totalized set of policing actions, no one regime of truth operative at particular historical moments, no one location for a reproductive or contestatory practice. There are multiple technologies of autobiographical writing—res gestae, religious confession, diary, journal, letter writing, autobiographical novel, Bildungsroman, the talking cure of psychoanalysis, job application, vita. And these self-writing practices are intermingled with other writing practices as well as other behavioral practices at any specific historical moment. Moreover, they are brought to bear on myriad personal, social, political, economic, physical contexts. As Felski argues, "the nature and degree of female exclusion within existing discursive practices is thus not invariable, resulting from abstract psychosexual antagonisms, but contingent, revealing significant differences according to cultural and historical context."[31]

* * *

The textual struggle around truthtelling can for the autobiographer be potentially liberating or imprisoning, simultaneously. Thus the autobiographical can be the ground of recontainment within existing "truths" or the ground upon which existing "truths" are exposed as fictions, or "lies," and the formerly unauthorized, illicit, heretical lodged as an alternative "truth." And so, in closing, I want to briefly consider some strategic moves possible in autobiographical practice. I do not intend to provide an exhaustive typology of such moves. I only want to ponder three such moves and suggest how they partake of the "lie" and paradoxically how such "lying" lies so close to the "truth" that it becomes another form of "truthtelling."

First, we might consider "excessive truthtelling" of the first order. Since traditional autobiography, as one of the West's master discourses, purports to tell the "truth" about "man," "self," and "self-representation," it discursively colludes in constituting the appropriate writing subject as bourgeois, white, male. "Truthtelling" is "truth to" that normative cultural fiction. "Excessive truthtelling" then would be a "truthtelling" that sticks "so close" to the "truth" of that discursive fiction that there seems to be total identification. Through what Luce Irigaray has described as a narrative and rhetorical strategy of "mimicry," the autobiographer might "mime" traditional Western autobiographical self-representation by constituting herself textually as white, bourgeois, male.[32] In miming the text of "man" in the logic of the same, the autobiographer might obscure the very cultural and historical bases of the stakes of autobiographical "truthtelling," might obscure the constructedness of "truth." But she might do something else again. In identifying so closely with the model of representation and its "truth" value, she might expose it as fraudulent, as a fiction, as a kind of "narcissistic phallocentrism."[33]

For what is here exposed is identification with a difference. Introduced in this scene of mimicry is the role of the inauthentic speaker. The "truth" is in the wrong mouth, so to speak. And what happens when someone from the wrong locale locates herself in the privileged structures of the "true" and the "scientific"? Linda Kintz suggests that "mimicry" turns to "menace":

> The reproduction of the symbolic by those it has disavowed and abjected—men of color and all women—contaminates and displaces the words reserved for the appropriate speaking subject. The reproduction of that symbolic may begin to founder when inappropriate subjects learn its language because they can only repeat it partially. As incomplete mirrors, as the waste of the system that produced the identity of the white male, they can only reflect back to the male subject a partial representation of himself, a reflection that is askew, flawed, not specular. The more the inappropriate subjects learn his language, the less dependable is his mirror. Rather than reacting, they may re-*act* to change both the language and the world.[34]

In the wrong mouth "truth" can be transformed into the "lie." As "inappropriate" subjects, women (or people of color, or working-class people, all those marginalized in the dominant culture) become agents for autobiographical change in a double sense. They change their own lives and they change the discursive regime of autobiographical "truth" itself.

Or there is "masquerade" or "mimicry" of another kind. This strategy would put into textual play an overidentification with the "feminine." Mary Russo argues that "deliberately assumed and foregrounded, femininity as mask, for a man, is a take-it-or-leave-it proposition; for a woman, a similar flaunting of the feminine is a take-it-*and*-leave-it *possibility*. To put on femininity with a vengeance suggests the power of taking it off."[35] Since in this instance "womanliness is a mask which can be worn or removed," the "feminine" text would distress operative regimes of truth by exposing the constructedness of gender, by exposing the "lie" of it through purposeful excesses.[36] The woman masquerading as woman would, to draw upon Luce Irigaray's theory of mimesis, *"also remain elsewhere,"* an excess/ory to the crime/text in which the speaking position of the autobiographer would be that of the too-appropriate subject, the one totally subjected to "ideas about herself."[37] Self-consciously adopted, the staging of masquerade in women's autobiographical practice, might effectively undermine the stability of any essentialist "truth" of sexual difference by opening gaps between form and identity. Such gaps would reveal what Judith Butler argues is the discontinuity between gender and the sexed body; for, identity is performative rather than essential, "a *fabrication* manufactured and sustained through corporeal signs and other discursive means. That the gendered body is performative suggests that it has no ontological status apart from the various acts which constitute its reality, and if that reality is fabricated as an interior essence, that very interiority is a function of a decidedly public and social discourse, the public regulation of fantasy through the surface politics of the body."[38] The excesses of masquerade in autobiographical practice could effectively expose the falsity of any regime of truth that functions to essentialize identity, to create a fiction of an ontological core of "selfhood." The surface/body of the text "lies" in service to the "truth."

A third strategy moves in the direction of "lying." While there are various thematics of lying within autobiographical texts, I want to consider here a particular form of lying: "I"-lying, the autobiographical gesture of calling to the surface of attention the ficticity of the "I." Here, for instance, are some of the "I"-lies in the autobiographical texts of twentieth century women. "I am a Hottentot," Isak Dinesen reports saying to a young boy on a ship returning to Africa.[39] And the name "Isak Dinesen" itself on the title page is a gesture of duplicity: the "I" of the text is and is not "Isak." "I" am "Alice B. Toklas," teases Gertrude Stein.[40] "It would be interesting," muses Virginia Woolf at the beginning of "A Sketch of the Past," "to make the two people, I now, I then, come out in contrast." Pondering such interests, Woolf introduces multiple structures of "I"-lying.[41] When Zora Neale Hurston reflects on the disjunction between "I" and "me"—"I did not know then, as I know now, that people are prone to build a statue of the kind of person that it pleases them to be. And few people want to be forced to ask themselves, 'What if there is no me like my statue?'"—she introduces the ficticity of identity into a text throughout which the protagonist seems to keep disappearing on the reader.[42] In one of her five encounters with the powers of storytelling, Maxine Hong Kingston's "I" becomes Fa Mu Lan, the mythical woman warrior of traditional Chinese culture.[43] In *Nothing to Declare*, Mary Morris's "I" becomes at one time a bird, at another time a kitten.[44] Audre Lord in *Zami: A New Spelling of My Name* suggests toward the conclusion that "my life had become increasingly a bridge and field of women. *Zami.*[45] Gloria Anzaldúa, in *Borderlands/La Frontera*, proclaims that she "write[s] the myths in me, the myths I am, the myths I want to become"; but she figures herself most particularly as the serpent.[46] "I am spacious, singing flesh," writes Hélène Cixous in her utopian manifesto, "on which is grafted no one knows which I, more or less human, but alive because of transformation."[47] In *Loving in the War Years,* Cherrié Moraga writes "I was 'la guerra'—fair-skinned." But being "fair-skinned" or "white" becomes the "lie" of identity for her as she negotiates the dialogical and the polylogical implications of her position as a lesbian Chicana feminist in Anglo culture.[48]

These autobiographical gestures range from the patently duplicitous to the figuratively contentious and structurally troubling. They all invite careful and critical analysis in their specificity. But despite their context-specific differences, they all invite us to consider the relationship of "I"-lying to the contractual expectation of woman's "truthtelling." Discursive regimes encode certain "truths" about both the "I" and the "lie," about who "I's" and who lies. Leigh Gilmore argues that a woman's relationship to the regimes, "installed" throughout the text as the "readers" who "police the limits of truth," is especially troubled when she enters the space of autobiographical confession because of her errant position as a truthteller. Her guilt "lies precisely in transgressing codes that mark the production of truth as a masculine activity, such that when women do presume to write autobiography, the discursive form that confers subjectivity, and, in effect, constructs it, they are challenged as 'liars.'" Thus women's relationship to "truthtelling" is complicated by their position within discourse as "those who 'lie' so near the truth."[49] From one point of view, then, "lying" can provoke, as it evokes, the identification of women with duplicity, certain regulatory practices of patriarchal technologies of gender that situate women as the "I" already likely to lie. As a result, "I"-lying would become one more of those manifestations of duplicity expected of "woman"; and its disruptive potential would be recontained in the coherent organization of operative fictions of "gender" and "truthtelling."

From another point of view, however, each of these "lying" sessions provokes the serenities of such coherent organizations of self-knowledge and "truth." For each of these instances of "I"-lying gestures toward the fictiveness of the "I" that seems to speak in autobiography. Thus they disrupt, consciously or unconsciously, the surface of the unified, authoritative, essential "self," a fiction of a regime of truth that would specify identity, contain it, capture it, universalize it, essentialize it. As a contestatory gesture, lies provoke an unsettling of boundaries, of locationing, and of locales. Thus lies disrupt the superficial placidity of an autobiographical contract that assumes identity between narrator and narratee as one basis of its truthtelling claims, that assumes the comfortable "home," the secure anchorage in location. "I"-lying introduces the issue of nonidentity into autobiographical text and practice as well as the uncertainties of homelessness, what Biddy Martin and Chandra Talpade Mohanty call "not being home," which is "a matter of realizing that home was an illusion of coherence and safety based on the exclusion of specific histories of oppression and resistance, the repression of differences even within oneself."[50]

"I"-lying thus intervenes in the contractual obligation of truthtelling. With what effect? The very "I" of the autobiographer, the apparent sign of a unified "self" or "individual," is always already a phallogocentric fiction of the "real" and "true." Since gender itself is, to recall but wrench to a different context White's phrase, a fiction of factual representation and since the "I" signs for the sex of the autobiographer, "I"-lying effectively foregrounds the constructedness of not only the "I" but of gender (and race and ethnicity and sexuality) as well. "If the inner truth of gender is a fabrication and if a true gender is a fantasy instituted and inscribed on the surface of bodies," suggests Butler, "then it seems that genders can be neither true nor false but are only produced as the truth effects of a discourse of primary and stable identity."[51] Distressing the stability and primacy of an uncontested identity by lying about the "I" challenges, as does mimicry and masquerade, the politics of identity and the aesthetics of autobiographical "truth" as a gesture toward a "self-knowledge" always policed by operative regimes of truth. If we do not know who the "I" is, how do we know where the "truth" lies since the "I" is the very guarantor of truthtelling?

"Structures," argues Felski, "are only constituted through the practices of social agents, who produce these structures anew in the process of reproducing them."[52] Locating itself within each text in the nexus of identity and its politics, "truth" and its telling are constituted anew out of the text of each autobiographer. At the current autobiographical moment, "truthtelling" and "lying" lie close to one another, affectionately and contentiously intermingling with and intervening in one another.

Notes

1. Hayden White, *Tropics of Discourse: Essays in Cultural Criticism* (Baltimore: Johns Hopkins University Press, 1978), 25.

2. M. M. Bakhtin, *The Dialogic Imagination*, trans. Caryl Emerson and Michael Holquist, ed. Michael Holquist (Austin: University of Texas Press, 1981), 7.

3. See James Olney, "Autobiography and the Cultural Moment," in *Autobiography: Essays Theoretical and Critical*, ed. James Olney (Princeton:

Princeton University Press, 1980), 23; Domna C. Stanton, "Autogynography: Is the Subject Different?" in *The Female Autograph*, ed. Domna C. Stanton (New York: New York Literary Forum, 1984), 11.

4. William L. Andrews, *To Tell a Free Story: The First Century of Afro-American Autobiography 1760–1865* (Urbana: University of Illinois Press, 1986), 6.

5. Leigh Gilmore, "Autobiographics as Agency: Technologies of Women's Autobiography," paper presented at the Conference on Autobiography, University of Maine-Portland, September 29–October 1, 1989.

6. Elizabeth W. Bruss, *Autobiographical Acts: The Changing Situation of a Literary Genre* (Baltimore: Johns Hopkins University Press, 1976), 10–11.

7. Rita Felski, *Beyond Feminist Aesthetics: Feminist Literature and Social Change* (Cambridge: Harvard University Press, 1989), 90.

8. Ibid., 26.

9. Adrienne Rich, *Of Woman Born: Motherhood as Experience and Institution* (New York: W. W. Norton, 1986), 284. My reference here to Rich oversimplifies her theoretical vision. While particular pieces of her earlier work tended to universalism and essentialism, later work and the work taken as a whole manifest a much more complicated and self-reflexive theoretical position on women's experience.

10. See Felski, *Beyond Feminist Aesthetics*, 103. Felski offers a provocative and extensive critique of the feminist "confession" in chapter three.

11. Ibid., 98.

12. Ibid., 52.

13. Edward W. Said, *Orientalism* (New York: Random House, 1979), 21.

14. Felski has summarized its shortcomings thus: "Its limitations are those of all biographically based literary criticism: a tendency to reduce the complex meanings of literary texts to the single authenticating source of authorial consciousness, an inability to analyze intersubjective, intertextual conventions of signification which cannot be explained in terms of the gender of the writing subject, and a theory of literary meaning which is unable to account for literature as form and to acknowledge the aesthetic significance of self-reflexive, consciously experimental examples of modern literature and art that cannot be dealt with in experiential terms" (30).

15. Linda Alcoff, "Cultural Feminism versus Post-Structuralism: The Identity Crisis in Feminist Theory," *Signs* 13 (Spring 1988): 405–36. See also Nancy Fraser and Linda J. Nicholson, "Social Criticism without Philosophy: An Encounter between Feminism and Postmodernism," in *Feminism/Postmodernism*, ed. Linda J. Nicholson (New York: Routledge, 1990), 19–38; Jane Flax, "Postmodernism and Gender Relations in Feminist Theory," in Nicholson, "Social Criticism," 39–62; Chris Weedon, *Feminist Practice and Poststructuralist Theory* (London: Basil Blackwell, 1987).

16. Julia Kristeva, "About Chinese Women," in *The Kristeva Reader*, ed. Toril Moi (New York: Columbia University Press, 1986), 153–55.

17. Ibid., 155.

18. Julia Kristeva, "Woman Can Never Be Defined," in *New French Feminisms: An Anthology*, ed. Elaine Marks and Isabelle de Courtivron (New York: Schocken Books, 1981), 137.

19. Nancy K. Miller, "Changing the Subject: Authorship, Writing, and the Reader," in *Feminist Studies/Critical Studies*, ed. Teresa de Lauretis (Bloomington: Indiana University Press, 1986), 106. See also Felski, *Beyond Feminist Aesthetics*, 78.

20. Christine Di Stefano, "Dilemmas of Difference: Feminism, Modernity, and Postmodernism," in Nicholson, *Feminism/Postmodernism*, 78.

21. Elspeth Probyn, "Travels in the Postmodern: Making Sense of the Local," in Nicholson, *Feminism/Postmodernism*, 178.

22. Ibid., 186. From its early origins in the confessions of medieval mystics, autobiography has been driven by various regimes of truth that have, as Leigh Gilmore argues, "marked the limits of the confession by establishing what truth could be told and by installing a confessor, specifically a theologian, who would police those limits." Gilmore, "Autobiographics as Agency," conference paper.

23. Bakhtin, *Dialogic Imagination*, 293–94.

24. Ibid., 294.

25. Felicity A. Nussbaum, "Eighteenth-Century Women's Autobiographical Commonplaces," in *The Private Self: Theory and Practice of Women's Autobiographical Writings*, ed. Shari Benstock (Chapel Hill: University of North Carolina Press, 1988), 148. See also Denise Riley, *"Am I That Name?": Feminism and the Category of 'Women' in History* (Minneapolis: University of Minnesota Press, 1988).

26. Probyn, "Travels in the Postmodern," 185.

27. Nussbaum, "Eighteenth-Century Women's Autobiographical Commonplaces," 156.

28. Françoise Lionnet, *Autobiographical Voices: Race, Gender, and Self-Portraiture* (Ithaca, N.Y.: Cornell University Press, 1989), 92.

29. Probyn, "Travels in the Postmodern," 176–89. Probyn differentiates between locale, location, and local as a way of distinguishing and exploring "a central problematic within feminist theory: Whether the subaltern can speak."

30. Felski, *Beyond Feminist Aesthetics*, 91.

31. Ibid., 62.

32. Toril Moi, *Sexual/Textual Politics: Feminist Literary Theory* (London: Methuen, 1985), 131. Moi is here exploring Luce Irigaray's mimicry of Plotinus in her *Speculum of the Other Woman*. Irigaray distinguishes between a mimicry of the masculine position in the logic of the same and a mimicry of the feminine as it is constituted in phallocentric discourses. See "The Power of Discourse and the Subordination of the Feminine," in *This Sex Which Is Not One*, trans. Catherine Porter (Ithaca, N.Y.: Cornell University Press, 1985), 76.

33. Moi, *Sexual/Textual Politics*, 131.

34. Linda Kintz, "In-Different Criticism: The Deconstructive 'Parole,'" in *The Thinking Muse: Feminism and Modern French Philosophy*, ed. Jeffner Allen and Iris Marion Young (Bloomington: Indiana University Press, 1989), 131.

35. Mary Russo, "Female Grotesques: Carnival and Theory," in De Lauretis, *Feminist Studies/Critical Studies*, 224.

36. Mary Ann Doane, "Film and the Masquerade: Theorising the Female Spectator," *Screen* 23, nos. 3/4 (September–October 1982): 81.

37. Irigaray, *Speculum of the Other Woman*, 76.

38. Judith Butler, "Gender Trouble, Feminist Theory, and Psychoanalytic Theory," in Nicholson, *Feminism/Postmodernism*, 336–37.

39. Isak Dinesen, *Out of Africa* (New York: Random House, 1965), 296.

40. Gertrude Stein, *The Autobiography of Alice B. Toklas* (New York: Random House, 1960).

41. Virginia Woolf, *Moments of Being: Unpublished Autobiographical Writings* (New York: Harcourt Brace Jovanovich, 1976).

42. Zora Neale Hurston, *Dust Tracks on a Road: An Autobiography* (Urbana: University of Illinois Press, 1984), 34.

43. Maxine Hong Kingston, *The Woman Warrior: Memoirs of a Girlhood among Ghosts* (New York: Random House, 1977).

44. Mary Morris, *Nothing to Declare: Memoirs of a Woman Traveling Alone* (New York: Penguin Books, 1988).

45. Audre Lorde, *Zami: A New Spelling of My Name* (Trumansburg, N.Y.: Crossing Press, 1982).

46. Gloria Anzaldúa, *Borderlands/La Frontera: The New Mestiza* (San Francisco: Spinsters/aunt lute, 1987).

47. Hélène Cixous, "The Laugh of the Medusa," in Marks and Courtivron, *New French Feminisms*, 260.

48. Cherrié Moraga, *Loving in the War Years* (Boston: South End Press, 1983).

49. Leigh Gilmore, "Autobiographics as Agency," conference paper.

50. Biddy Martin and Chandra Talpade Mohanty, "Feminist Politics: What's Home Got to Do With It?" in De Lauretis, *Feminist Studies/Critical Studies*, 196.

51. Butler, "Gender Trouble, Feminist Theory, and Psychoanalytic Theory," 337.

52. Felski, *Beyond Feminist Aesthetics*, 56.

4

Feminine Authorship and Spiritual Authority in Victorian Women Writers' Autobiographies*

~

Mary Jean Corbett

The spiritual autobiographies of Victorian women writing from con-servative Christian perspectives challenge three prevailing assump-tions often made about women's self-representations. Critics usually claim that women's cultural and literary authority is marginal, that women oppose the conditions that oppress them, and that self-representations by women under patriarchy are always acts of trans-gression. In contrast, Mary Martha Sherwood, Charlotte Tonna, and Mary Anne Schimmelpenninck, three Victorian writers who were very popular in their own time although little known today, show how cer-tain women, mainly from the middle class, assumed cultural authority by supporting and propagating dominant values.

Religion consigned women to the domestic sphere, but the ex-amination of the self that was the duty of all Christians also offered women a way to assume authority. The writings of the three Victor-ian spiritual autobiographers capitalized on women's traditional task of developing individual character and instructing others in private virtues. Emphasizing domestic values, they presented their works as private undertakings to convey private values, in effect moving literature and reading from the public sphere to the private. Ostensibly limiting themselves to women's subordinate position, they used that position to elide the differences between lives and texts, reproducing in their works the same prevailing ideologies that oppressed them.

*From Mary Jean Corbett, "Feminine Authorship and Spiritual Authority in Victorian Women Writers' Autobiographies," *Women's Studies* 18 (1990): 13–29. Reprinted by permission of *Women's Studies*.

Mary Jean Corbett is an associate professor of English and affiliate of the Women's Studies program at Miami University, Oxford, Ohio. She has a book forthcoming from Cambridge University Press entitled History, Politics, and the Family in Irish and English Writing, 1790–1870.

IN A RECENT BOOK on women's autobiography, Sidonie Smith has argued that "the woman who writes autobiography is doubly estranged when she enters the autobiographical contract," with her estrangement founded on woman's historical subordination to male discourse and on her problematic relation to a reading audience always already configured as male. By usurping the male power of speech and writing, the female self-representing subject "unmasks her transgressive desire for cultural and literary authority" when she takes up the pen to author herself.[1] Feminist Victorianists will find this scenario familiar, for in its basic elements, it replicates the argument elaborated by Sandra M. Gilbert and Susan Gubar in *The Madwoman in the Attic* (1979) and extends it to the genre of self-representation, positing a "repressed desire" for literary—and thus masculine—authority as the subtext of every woman's life. In making this case, however, Smith's work also invites us to reconsider this interpretive model in relation to autobiography and to feminine authorship, and, as I will demonstrate below, to modify its totalizing claims about women's writing.

Smith locates "the repressed desire of a life like a man's" as the motivating principle in the Victorian text she examines, Harriet Martineau's *Autobiography* (1877). Reading Martineau's text as a paradigmatic example of how the feminine subject who "transgresses" the gendered boundary between the public and private spheres inscribes and is inscribed by the splits that structure gender itself. Smith exposes the contradictions that inhere in being a "public woman" in the Victorian period and thus in a woman's representing herself publicly as well. But her analysis is skewed because her basic and, until recently, quite orthodox feminist assumption—that only men possess authority and that women can only rebel against it—does not adequately account for the ways in which Victorian women *were* invested with authority, literary and otherwise.

I would adduce a very different reading of woman's role in relation to literary authority and cultural production from Martineau's history, the contours of which I can only suggest here, a reading I base on my understanding of Martineau as occupying a privileged position within Victorian culture. As the popularizer of a major hegemonic discourse, Martineau reproduced the lessons of high male theory for myriad private readers, male and female alike; her *Illustrations of Political Economy* (1832–34) were the fictional works primarily responsible for disseminating Utilitarian doctrine among the newly literate classes. Only when what she advocated—Malthusian principles of population control, for example— was perceived as inappropriate to "feminine" discourse did contemporary conservatives launch their scurrilous attacks against her; more sympa- thetic readers hailed her as a valuable spokesperson and propagandist for the new political economy, which legitimated the oppression of women and the working class.[2] Martineau thus textually participates in perpetuat- ing patriarchal discourse even though her life as a public woman chal- lenges some of its assumptions about women's "proper sphere"; she is, then, not marginal but central to her culture, for her literary work sup- ports the capitalist values on which that culture depends. And her *Autobiography* reenacts her ideological positioning as a woman empow- ered to speak and to represent herself publicly so long as her speech and writing do not threaten the basic socioeconomic principles that structure the culture, including the separation of the domestic world from the pub- lic one. To constitute Martineau as "transgressive," then, in the way that Smith does, is to downplay the ways in which her work upholds the cate- gories her life is presumed to undercut.

In short, Smith's paradigm contains three assumptions contested by recent socialist-feminist analyses of Victorian women's writing: first, that all writing women have a marginal relation to structures of "cultural and literary authority"; second, that women have played little or no part in reproducing the ideological and material conditions that underwrite their own oppression; and third, that for women to represent the self under patriarchy is always an act of transgression.[3] Without denying the heuristic power of her model, I would like to offer an alternative to it, for I believe that scripting a scenario in which women are always at the margins, and indeed are shown to derive their power from that outsider's perspective, occludes the ways in which certain women, primarily middle-class ones, have been empowered under patriarchy—and in its interests—by being positioned at the center, as cultural producers and reproducers of bourgeois values.

I would agree that in authoring their lives under patriarchal ideol- ogy, Victorian women writers confront the difficulty of representing fe- male literary identity within a culture that, by and large, denies them the authority to do so in the public, secular realm; to say that, however, is not to say that women's different relation to that realm necessarily bars them from representing the self according to cultural criteria for femi- ninity. Autobiography is, of course, one of the literary forms that most clearly displays its indebtedness to social conventions for representing personal identity, however that elusive concept is defined at any given historical moment; canonical nineteenth-century British autobiographies by male writers, for example, generally legitimate the individualist liberal values of capitalist culture by narrating the development of the self as a vocational history. Martineau's adaptation of this "masculine" form is, as Smith points out, clearly atypical in its time, for not until the end of the century do most middle-class women have access to the liberal rights and opportunities that allow them to map their self-representations onto a developmental model. Yet even though gender difference always continues to be constitutive of other differences, women's autobiographies throughout the century often wind up reinscribing—not challenging—cultural fictions such as fixed norms of gender and class.

In order to demonstrate how some women's autobiographical texts are produced not by transgressing but by conforming to bourgeois norms, I will look here at how one nineteenth-century discourse of the self, a religious discourse that extends interpretive authority to all believing Christians, enables and encourages writing women to represent themselves; within certain patriarchal constraints on what she can represent, the Evangelical emphasis on individual authority enables the woman writer to invoke a system of values that sanctifies her work as useful and important and designates her self-representation as exemplary.[4] Acting in conjunction with the economic logic that assigns women to the private realm, Christian discourse gives the autobiographer authority over that domestic space, which is redefined as the new locus for cultural and even literary authority. Far from being marginal, then, the woman who writes herself in relation to God and the home is at the center of the private sphere, newly invested with the power of producing and reproducing the ideologies that structure Victorian culture.

I

Today, neither the names of these women autobiographers—Mary Martha Sherwood (1775–1851), Charlotte Tonna (1790–1846), and Mary Anne Schimmelpenninck (1778–1856)—nor their works are familiar, while in their own day, the first two at least were amazingly prolific and popular writers.[5] Sherwood's *The Fairchild Family* (1817) and Henry Milner tales were among the most popular children's stories of the period, while Tonna's tracts and novels of the thirties and forties, of the strictest Evangelical tenor, were also widely read. By the time the two came to write their autobiographies, they were well known as "authors," even if they lacked the public profile of their more illustrious male and female contemporaries. And in their autobiographies, the literary space in which we might expect them to represent themselves as authors, they do not establish claims to authorial status, but rather delineate the boundaries within which feminine authorship can be constituted.

Their different rationales for working in this genre, as they explain them, do not overtly involve a wish to capitalize on their popularity: publicity, as we ordinarily think of it, is the last thing the spiritual woman writer would seek. Moreover, their explicit intention in representing themselves is to control the way in which their readers, contemporary and future, will read them. In her *Personal Recollections* (1842), Tonna attempts to seal off what she has constituted as her private self from public view; asserting the sanctity of "private domestic history" and "the sacredness of home" (15), and defending the absence of any remarks on that aspect of her life, she yet acknowledges "that when it has pleased God to bring any one before the public in the capacity of an author, that person becomes in some sense public property; having abandoned the privacy from which no one ought to be forced" (1). Writing about ten years later, and commenting on "the propensity of the age for writing and recording the lives of every individual who has had the smallest claim to celebrity," Sherwood presents *The Life of Mrs. Sherwood* (1857) as a necessary defense against what others might write if she were to leave it unwritten: "Could I be quite sure, that when I am gone, nobody would say anything about me, I should, I think, spare myself the trouble which I am now about to take" (1). She, too, assumes that the text of her life is vulnerable to all sorts of appropriation, and makes her move to autobiography a defense against that possibility of being appropriated.

Both choose to represent the self out of a desire not to be misinterpreted and misused by others; since as "public" figures they cannot count on the silence Sherwood seems to find preferable to speech, they assert a control over how they will be represented by putting their own versions of themselves into discourse. And in explaining their motives, they also signal a particular conception of the relation between the private and the public spheres not as separate realms, but as concentric circles, a conception that allows them to represent themselves without disturbing the line that demarcates their sphere from the public world. While Tonna suggests, for example, that her rhetorical representation of her "person" will become "public property," she posits some familial, interpersonal experience as prior to and privileged over public discourse; the "sacredness" of the private realm, its integrity as a space theoretically sealed off from the public world, must be preserved inviolate for, as we will see, it is precisely the sanctity of the interior that enables the spiritual woman who writes to represent herself publicly. What remains innermost and goes unrepresented—the intricacy of family life—is condensed in the figure of the woman herself.

Tonna's anxiety about making the familial public is linked to women's cultural positioning on the inside, at the center of the domestic circle, which is itself circumscribed by the larger circle of the public world.

Because nineteenth-century middle-class women derived their primary social and cultural self-definition from their identification with the private realm, for the writer to maintain her placement in that realm even as she symbolically moves outside it through writing is a difficult, though not impossible, task. A woman's "public" work in representation threatens to undercut her gendered, class-based identity by figuratively connecting her act of self-exposure with acts performed by other public women, who sell not just an ordinary commodity, but their very bodies, in a male-dominated market-place: as Catherine Gallagher asserts, Victorian writing and Victorian prostitution are metaphorically "linked . . . through their joint habitation of the realm of exchange."[6] But by enabling her to represent her work and her life as part of her ordinary course of duties, the discourse of Christian piety invests the middle-class Christian woman with authority even as it minimizes the risks of her engagement in autobiographical discourse; she negotiates the crossing from the inner circle to the outer one by always representing herself through the signifiers of domesticity and by refusing to locate herself permanently in the public realm of exchange.

If she is thus retroactively to establish her claim to the authority that enabled her to begin writing, and also to legitimate the act of self-representation she engages in at the time of writing, the spiritual autobiographer must not upset the distinction between the norms that constitute appropriate feminine behavior and the eccentricities displayed by those who exceed the prescribed bounds of middle-class femininity. Asserting her own claim to be considered representative of the norm, Sherwood expresses her desire not to be thought exceptional—and thus unwomanly—mainly in terms of her distaste for the stereotypical literary woman, the bluestocking who, forfeiting femininity in her quest for publicity, comes to represent the extraordinary and unnatural woman rather than the conventional and unexceptionable one. Recalling her father's repeated claim that she "was to grow up a genius," Sherwood recollects that back then, as at the time of writing, to be "a celebrated authoress" was not her wish: "even then I felt, if it were necessary to be very singular, I would rather not be a genius" (51–52); while "it was a matter of course to me that I was to write, and also a matter of instinct . . . I had a horror of being thought a literary lady; for it was, I fancied, ungraceful" (118). When "forced into public" (her father suggested that she should help an impoverished family friend by publishing her first work and donating the proceeds to him), "my heart sunk at the proposition": "to be set down so soon in that character which I had always dreaded," to feel "the mortification which I felt at being thus dragged into public" made her wish "that I had never known the use of a pen" (119). Her choice of the term "mortification," a word Burney and Austen also use to describe what Evelina and

Elizabeth Bennet experience when publicly exposed, either physically or psychologically, suggests that for the woman writer to enter the public world, even through the impersonal medium of print, is to incur the risk of social or moral death; Sherwood constructs the passage from the home to the world as symbolically representing the loss of the feminine self.

At this border, where the public and the private meet in self-representation, we see how competing tensions—the woman writer's need to remain situated within the domestic realm and her simultaneous engagement in the public process of writing, in which her name (if not her body) circulates at large within public discourse merely by the fact of publication—produce an anxiety about literature and literary production itself, about how texts function in the world and how their circulation affects their producers. As Mary Poovey notes, while an "objective text" like a novel "serves as a more general mediator between self and public," the avowedly "subjective" text the autobiographer composes, which formally and thematically negotiates the line between private feminine experience and the public masculine world, presents itself as neither mediated nor mediating, as a window that opens directly onto the soul.[7] For some women writers, opening that window onto the private is so fraught with danger than only fiction, or a masculine pseudonym, can provide them with the curtain necessary to shield them from public view. But by invoking a higher power than the self as the legitimating Author of their lives and their texts, by writing from the position of the Christian subject, whose life and work are always oriented toward an eternal goal, the outer circle which circumscribes all human life, women writers find a viable way of representing female experience. The combination of religious and domestic authority sanctions female authorship.

Although most feminists have, with good reason, tended to see religion as enforcing the patriarchal values that consign women to silence, recent revisionist work has begun to establish the counterpoint to the monolithic view that casts all religious discourse as inherently oppressive: as Gail Malmgreen puts it, "it is surely neither possible nor necessary to weigh up, once and for all, the gains and losses for women of religious commitment . . . the dealings of organized religion with women have been richly laced with ironies and contradictions.[8] If religion helped produce the ideology that assigned women to the domestic sphere, it also enabled them, within that realm, to write and act in ways that women who sought access to literary authority on purely secular grounds could not.

As Elisabeth Jay writes in her study of Evangelicalism and the Victorian novel, "the religion of the heart" invested its believers with "the onus of interpreting God's Word": "no appeal to any authoritative body of dogmatic pronouncements" could relieve the individual of her responsibility to establish her relation to the Bible and to God, for the eternal welfare of her soul ultimately depended on that relationship.[9] And gender, here as everywhere else in the nineteenth century, plays its role as a determining factor in prescribing the possible limits and acceptable range of feminine discourse. For example, the cultural prohibition against women engaging in public activity, in conjunction with the spiritual imperative to meekness and humility, while dictating style and content does not absolutely prevent writing. Adhering to those unwritten laws, in fact, keeps the writing woman from the spiritual and moral death Sherwood fears, as in Tonna's invocation of the religious bent of her works as a safeguard against the ever-present temptation of taking too much satisfaction in her own literary abilities:

> [T]he literary labour that I pursued for my own sustenance was perfect luxury, so long as my humble productions were made available for the spiritual good of the people so dear to me. My little books and tracts became popular; because, after some struggle against a plan so humbling to literary pride, I was able to adopt the suggestion of a wise Christian brother, and form a style of such homely simplicity that if, on reading a manuscript to a child of five years old, I found there was a single or word above his comprehension, it was instantly corrected to suit that lowly standard. (145)

In a move that oddly recalls Wordsworth's transvaluation of work in the opening lines of *The Prelude*, Tonna's "labour" becomes "luxury"; "literary pride" is transformed into the "homely simplicity" of her style and her very self once she orients her writing toward a spiritual end. The "wise Christian brother," figure of patriarchal authority, is to Tonna not an oppressor but a benefactor, for it is his warning that keeps her on the appropriate path for the righteous Christian woman.

In these terms, the religious woman's writing entails not public "mortification," but the private mortification of the self before God, which leads to eternal life, for the writer herself and for her readers as well, to whom Tonna can relate through a shared system of values and beliefs. By erasing all traces of art and artfulness, she shows herself willing and able to mortify her "literary pride" before those readers in order to establish a reading community of comprehending converts. While writing demands that she present herself to an unfamiliar audience, the religious woman writer reduces the risk of entering discourse by appealing to values, specifically religious ones, that require her self-effacement even as they invest her with a voice to which other Evangelical Christians will listen.

II

For a reader of other nineteenth-century autobiographies, the lack of information provided in these women's texts about the actual activity of writing can be quite maddening, or, at the very least, startling: when juxtaposed with Mill's *Autobiography* (1877), that classic case of the life that, without Harriet Taylor, would have almost solely consisted of readings and writings, or with Trollope's *Autobiography* (1883), with its detailed description of all aspects of his literary work, including the ledger that sums up the total of his emoluments, these texts hardly seem to be by writers at all, so thoroughly do they repress the signs of literary production. But this silence, too, supports the exemplary status of the author-autobiographer: the publicity that writing entails, even the most minimal engagement with publishers, editors, and printers, is banished, thus enabling the writer to root her identity in the private sphere, where the middle-class woman neither calls attention to whatever undomestic talents and ambitions she may possess nor trespasses on male territory by commenting directly on political events. Keeping both her discourse and her body within the limits of the feminine sphere insures that the religious woman writer will not be subjected to the kind of criticism the autobiographer Mary Sewell leveled at a mid-Victorian woman evangelist who delivered her message directly to a public audience: a public proselytizer, unlike a private didact, is cut off from the legitimating power and protection of the family, for " 'a lone woman who speaks in public,' " Sewell intones, " 'is *a very lone creature* indeed.' "[10]

Remaining private empowers the religious woman writer; keeping silent on certain subjects is a definite necessity for maintaining that power, and politics is thus a topic these texts do not speak of. Tonna, for instance, does not refer at all to her political beliefs, even though they deeply informed the rhetoric of her industrial novels; while she claims that she has been "often charged with the offense of being too political in my writings" (20), her autobiography reveals nothing to substantiate that charge.[11] While Schimmelpenninck was an adolescent at the time of the French Revolution, contemporary politics never enter her self-representation: she writes not of "public events, with which I have nothing to do," but promises to trace "the effects which they produced on the domestic sphere with which I had experience" (I.217), a promise she does not fulfill. The possibility of writing an account that would draw on the happenings of the public world is held out and then withheld; the actuality of public history is invoked only to be dismissed according to the implicit dictum that confines the woman autobiographer to writing solely about what is proper to her sphere. She cannot construct herself as "author," nor will she textually engage with public events.

What the female Christian autobiographer, like her counterpart, the female novelist at mid-century, is presumed to know best and encouraged to confine her attention to is, of course, character, and, specifically, female character. And everyone's character appears to best advantage in the private sphere, for it is "in the private lives of the children of God," as Sherwood puts it, "that we are enabled best to discern the wonderful beauty of the Divine influence . . . in the most private intercourse with the humblest and feeblest persons . . . we find the best and most lovely exhibitions of the Christian graces" (427). Like Sarah Ellis, who conceived the influence of a woman's "individual character" as "operating upon those more immediately around her, but by no means ceasing there; for each of her domestics, each of her relatives, and each of her familiar friends, will in their turn become the centre of another circle," Sherwood sees developing and shaping individual character as woman's special province.[12]

Her school for doing so is the home, the realm of affective ties which is counterposed to the heartless world; the Christian household, in Nancy Armstrong's words, "[detaches] itself from the political world and [provides] the complement and antidote to it," as the place where private virtue arms the family against public vice.[13] Ideologically endowed with the responsibility for molding moral character, and particularly in relation to girls, the private-sphere writer must protect herself from "the danger of celebrity" (Sherwood, 509) and avoid all traffic with the public world; her sphere is located on the inside, in the home and the heart, and her place is at the center. By eliminating everything external to the domestic, everything in the public world, from her texts, she both accedes to and reinforces the limits on the range of possible discourse, and so maintains her right to instruct her audience within her own realm, in the formation of everyday private-sphere virtues.

That writing itself, rightly conceived, does not conflict with women's prescribed role but, on the contrary, amplifies and extends it, proves to be a point to which all three autobiographies attest in their affirmation of the writing religious woman. Womanhood is itself valorized in these texts, in part for its disinterestedness: "'Remember, it is a privilege to be a woman instead of a man,'" writes Schimmelpenninck, recording her mother's words; "'men, heroes, and others, do things partly to do good and partly to gain a great name; but a woman's self-denial and generosity may be as great, and often greater, while it is unknown to others, and fully manifest only to her own conscience and to God: to work for this, and for this alone, is the highest of all callings'" (I.204). But invoking the language and concept of calling to define and deify womanhood, as conservative writers on femininity from Hannah More to Sarah Ellis repeatedly do in their writings, does not strictly predicate the ways in which that vocation may be practiced; it rules out only the love of fame as an end while presenting as the paramount object the necessity of making one's conscience fit for God's sight.

The way to keep that conscience clear is, paradoxically, to make its workings readable, not only to God, but to other readers: the Christian woman's self-examination, conducted through and throughout her life, externally expresses what would otherwise remain hidden from all eyes but God's, the subject's heart and mind. While the interpersonal and the political fall outside the circumscribed area of what the religious woman writer can represent, the most personal experience—the writer's relation to God—must be made legible in her text: reversing the logic of inside and outside, private and public, spiritual autobiography makes what is ostensibly most private, the inner self, the substance of the public representation.

As Carol Edkins's work on eighteenth-century American women's spiritual autobiographies establishes, the religious woman can publicly represent this individual (but not unique) experience because her readers understand the conventions of religious discourse: the shared values held by autobiographer and reader "[create] a symbolic bonding with the group" such that her exemplary spiritual progress can be read and imitated by others.[14] Spiritual autobiography, then, not only permits but demands of its writers an excruciatingly thorough self-inquisition, and particularly on the issue of writing itself, for those who produce literature and self-representations are responsible not only to God, but to other Christian readers as well, as a crisis of authorship reported in Tonna's text illustrates. Caught between the need to make a living and the demands of her husband, who apparently tried to annex her earnings as his own even after they separated, Tonna must decide between continuing to write her religious works under her own name, thereby forfeiting the income garnered by her pen, and beginning to write secular fiction under a pseudonym, which would disguise her identity and protect her income. She submits her case not to a court of law, as Caroline Norton did when entrapped in a similar situation, but to God's will:

> The idea of hiring myself out to another master—to engage in the service of that world the friendship of which is enmity with God—to cause the Holy One of Israel to cease from before those whom by the pen I addressed—to refrain from setting forth Jesus Christ and Him crucified to a perishing world, and give the reins to an imagination ever prone to wander after folly and romance, but now subdued to a better rule—all this was so contrary to my views of Christian principle that, after much earnest prayer to God, I decided rather to work gratuitously in the good cause, trusting to him who knew all my necessity, than to entangle myself with things on which I could not ask a blessing. (190)

To serve "another master"—the world or Mammon—is an option she will not choose, since it is only her dissemination of God's word that authorizes her writing in the first place; by prayerful, conscientious self-examination, she arrives at the correct spiritual and moral decision.

Moreover, to write for the secular world would entail a personal fall as well: by losing the audience of converts and believers already consti- tuted for her, by "[giving] the reins to an imagination ever prone to wan- der after folly and romance," and thus undoing the labor to submit all human desires "to a better rule" which the autobiography records in painstaking detail, she would feed her body while starving her soul and the souls of others who live and labor in "a perishing world."

Again we see that writing must come under God's rule, but we see as well the way in which Tonna conceptualizes her self, God-given but marred by "indwelling sin" (29), as a battleground between opposing forces of good and evil. Her duty, then, is to overrule the depravity of the self, including the innate tendency of the imagination to focus on vain and worldly things, by opening it to the intense scrutiny of God's light, and her readers' eyes, and by keeping careful watch over herself; in Schimmelpenninck's metaphor, which nicely illustrates the spatial re- lation between inside and outside and the permeable barrier that sepa- rates them, the self is a tabernacle and "an efficient company of porters and doorkeepers should guard every gate of access into the temple" (I.65). Only a constant self-surveillance can insure that one's soul and one's writing will not be invaded by God's enemies, but that policing of the temple only restricts access: it does not prevent the autobiographer from representing the inner sanctuary.

For middle-class women, invested as they are with the responsibility for the moral life of children and, to a great extent, of adult men, interro- gating the self is particularly crucial; for the woman writer, however, it is even more so. By writing and publishing, and thereby extending her influ- ence to include not only like-minded middle-class Christians, but often the working class as well, she could as easily become a force for evil as for good, particularly since her position makes her so much more susceptible to the "temptations" and "mortification" of the public sphere. In order to mold the character of others, her own character must be scrutinized, con- tinually searched for signs of moral and doctrinal failure. Thus the impera- tive to examine the self in writing throughout one's life, through letters and journals, and as one's earthly life draws to its close, in autobiography, is necessary for maintaining the fiction of authority that enables her to begin writing in the first place. God's sanction allows her to write, and to write the self is to test and retest the validity of that sanction.

III

Writing for the marketplace is not, of course, the most decorous way for the middle-class woman to carry out her civilizing function, nor can the writer ever fulfill the true womanly ideal as it is configured by patri- archy: as George Henry Lewes comments sardonically in 1850, "*My* idea of a perfect woman is of one who can write but won't; who knows all the authors know and a great deal more; who can appreciate my genius and not spoil my market."[15] Sarah Ellis's far less ironic view, as quoted above, which imagines the exemplary domestic woman's influence as inspiring others to create perfect circles of their own, is shared, surprisingly, by Mary Russell Mitford, who portrays her ideal woman in much the same terms:

> the very happiest position that a woman of great talent can occupy in our high civilisation, is that of living a beloved and distinguished member of the best literary society . . . repaying all that she receives by a keen and willing sympathy; cultivating to perfection the social faculty; but abstaining from the wider field of authorship, even while she throws out here and there such choice and chosen bits as prove that nothing but disinclination to enter the arena debars her from winning the prize.[16]

The ideal woman Lewes and Mitford construct is the amateur par excellence; like Ellis's woman, she rests at the still center of the domestic sphere, defined not so much by what she produces as by what she reproduces, the cultured, leisured middle-class existence that approximates an earlier, but still operative, aristocratic ideal of unproductive gentility. As a later formulation of this model suggests, the true work of women, "a mission quite as grand as literary authorship," is not to write, but to "[keep] alive for men certain ideas, and ideals too, which would soon pass out of the world in the rush and hurry of material existence if they were not fed and replenished by those who are able to stand aloof from the worry and vexations of active life."[17] Women's role in literary production, then, should be to protect and transmit culture, virtue, and private values; "feeding" and "replenishing" reproducing the material conditions of existence as well as the spiritual "ideas, and ideals" that have no home in the "arena" of the public world, domestic women also insure that art will continue to be produced.

The secular model for professional authorship suggests that male artistry requires female subordination; the ideal woman is confined to the home, where she carries out the unpaid labor of biological and cultural reproduction. Yet the religious woman who writes, whether or not she does so, as Mitford did, from financial necessity, makes up for what she might appear to lack in perfect womanhood by using literature itself as her medium for reproducing and exchanging domestic values. She sends her book out into the world only so that it will enter homes other than her own, where its influence will operate on other readers.

The autobiographers considered here definitely see literature's role in forming and disseminating the private-sphere virtues as central: that "the spiritual good of the people" of which Tonna speaks is actively advanced by their writing is not an assumption she and Sherwood ever question, and each also assumes that secular literature, which Schimmelpenninck calls "pestilential" and of "evil influence" (I.124), does the devil's work in the world. These women can thus construct their writing as one of their womanly duties, a Christian duty to push back the powers of darkness by spreading the light of truth and salvation, a duty which the middle-class woman may carry out in print along the same lines as she does in her home and in her personal relations with others. Putting the values of the domestic into a public form for public circulation, the spiritual woman writer projects what she represents (which is equivalent to who she is) into a book, a tract, or a self-representing text, which passes through the public world en route to other middle-class homes; there it will be consumed in the service of the continuing reproduction of the values her life and her text embody.

In Ellis's terms, the exemplary woman's text spawns other domestic circles, other moral centers: that task, however, is not accomplished by women's "[entering] the arena," or "the wider field of authorship," but rather through reconstituting literature, and the scene of reading, as a private-sphere activity—women do not go outside, but literature comes in. Redefined as a private agent of private values, the religious woman's work exemplifies the powerful moralizing force of private femininity, a force which in its textual form actively combats the influence of secular novels, those "gin-palaces of the mind," in Schimmelpenninck's words, and "all that stimulates unproductive sensibilities" (I.131).

Schimmelpenninck argues, in appropriately circular fashion, that women have both acted upon and been acted upon by literature, and that the mutual interchange has altered both in the process. Casting the history of literature from her youth at the time of writing as the history of its feminization, she asserts an identity between women's role and literature's purpose:

> The great increase of literary taste amongst women has wrought a wonderful change, not only in collections of books, but in their composition. Books were then written only for men; now they are written so that women can participate in them: and no man would think of forming a library in his house, without a thought that its volumes must be the companions of his wife and daughters in many a lonely hour, when their influence must sink into the heart, and tend to modify the taste and character. Thus, in literature, as in other things, and especially in domestic life, has the mercy of God bestowed on women the especial and distinguishing blessing of upholding the moral and religious influence, that spirit of truth and love by which man can alone be redeemed from the fall she brought upon him. (I.125).

Women's education in the principles of "literary taste" makes for a change in how the domestic library, the physical locus for reading, is structured as well as in how each individual constituent part, each book, is composed: the fact that more women read requires the production of books that invite and allow "feminine participation" in them as readers. While the patriarch still determines the shape of the collection, he must choose more judiciously now than he did at some earlier point in time when books were "written only for men," for books are, anthropomorphically, "companions" for women, capable, as women in particular are, of molding human lives: "their influence must sink into the heart," the innermost center of the reading subject, "and tend to modify the taste and character."

Books become, in short, like women: they are moral agents whose influence shapes the interior life of their readers, and in doing so, they also prepare women to become writers who will send back into the world the lessons they have learned from reading the primers of the heart. Schimmelpenninck projects feminine moral force into a material object that can save all readers—and the woman writer herself—from the consequences of the first woman's sin, the desire for knowledge, for if the world fell through Eve's weakness, then it can only be "redeemed" through her stronger daughters' labor as readers and writers: Adam's curse is women's "especial and distinguishing blessing." And literature shapes the character of its readers within the confines of the gentleman's private library (rather than the eighteenth-century public coffeehouse, accessible only to men) as women themselves do in their private roles as wives and mothers; it acts as an agent of that private "moral and religious influence" which, implicitly because of their role as public beings, few men can supply.[18] Thus the religious woman writer need never even leave the home to do her work, which is spatially, spiritually, and socially centered in her father's house.

In the moral economy of the Christian Victorian household, domestic women produce and reproduce the spiritual food necessary for the whole family's consumption: in its self-sufficiency and autonomy from what lies outside it, woman's sphere appears to constitute itself as the realm that saves the fallen public world from its own sins. What we see in looking at these autobiographies is that within a conservative ideological framework, writing need not be constructed as a threat to the feminine self, for writing itself is privatized and feminized by women's influence, transposed from the public world to the private one. Nor does their writing threaten to undermine the naturalness of the public-private split, for the confluence of the norms of femininity and those of Christianity produces a powerful ideology of the private sphere that simultaneously legitimates women's writing and puts it in the service of the continuing reproduction of bourgeois hegemony, since the goal of the exemplary self-representing text is to elide the differences between lives and texts, realities and representations. In the religious woman writer's self-representation, then, writing one's life as an exemplary text testifies to the ideological importance of the woman writer's leading an exemplary life.

Notes

1. Sidonie Smith, *A Poetics of Woman's Autobiography: Marginality and the Fictions of Self-Representation* (Bloomington: Indiana University Press, 1987), 49, 50. The first third of the book is devoted to developing a critical feminist theory of autobiography and puncturing the androcentric assumptions of masculinist theorists: in the remainder, Smith does readings of women autobiographers who have, by virtue of the extensive feminist critical attention their texts have received, been elevated into a feminist canon of our own—Margery Kempe, Margaret Cavendish, Charlotte Charke, Martineau, and Maxine Hong Kingston. One objection to Smith's methodology, which I do not have space to pursue here but would like to raise, is that her canon of autobiography is problematic because it does not interrogate the principle of canonicity itself: the strategy of arguing against the exclusivity of the masculinist literary standard while proceeding to inscribe another standard, one that makes certain texts "representative," unintentionally reaffirms the patriarchal logic that has relegated women's experience and women's texts to the margins.

2. For a recent reading of Martineau's life and work with which I find myself in substantial agreement, see Deirdre David, *Intellectual Women and Victorian Patriarch* (London: Macmillan Press, 1987).

3. I'm thinking in particular of Mary Poovey's *The Proper Lady and the Woman Writer* (Chicago: University of Chicago Press, 1984); and Nancy Armstrong, *Desire and Domestic Fiction* (New York: Oxford University Press, 1987).

4. My use of the term "spiritual autobiography" throughout this essay is quite different from Linda Peterson's recent definition of it in *Victorian Autobiography* (New Haven: Yale University Press, 1986). Peterson asserts that "the spiritual autobiography demands an introspective and retrospective view of personal experience and a consistent hermeneutic system with which to interpret that experience" (125), and posits that, for cultural and generic reasons, women were unable to adopt it as a mode of interpretive self-representation since "women possessed neither experience nor authority" (130). While I do not contest Peterson's use of the hermeneutic model as a cultural standard for masculine self-representation, what I propose here is a concept of women's spiritual autobiography as an exemplary mode designed to inspire imitation, not self-analysis, in female readers, a mode in which the range and the limits of women's experience and their cultural authority could be both expressed and reinscribed.

5. I here include the bibliographical information for the autobiographies to be considered: Mary Martha Sherwood, *The Life of Mrs. Sherwood*, ed. Sophia Kelly (London, 1957); Charlotte Elizabeth [Tonna], *Personal Recollections* (New York, 1842); Mary Anne Schimmelpenninck, *Life of Mary Anne Schimmelpenninck*, 2 vols., ed. Christiana C. Hankin (London, 1858). All page references will be included in the text. For bibliographical information on Tonna and Sherwood and some discussion of their fiction, see Vineta Colby, *Yesterday's Woman: Domestic Realism in the English Novel* (Princeton: Princeton University Press, 1974), ch. 4.

6. Catherine Gallagher, "George Eliot and *Daniel Deronda*: The Prostitute and the Jewish Question," in *Sex, Politics, and Science in the Nineteenth-Century Novel*, ed. Ruth Bernard Yeazell (Baltimore: Johns Hopkins University Press, 1986), 41.

7. Mary Poovey, *Proper Lady*, 41.

8. Gail Malmgreen, "Introduction," *Religion in the Lives of English Women, 1760–1930*, ed. Gail Malmgreen (London: Croom Helm, 1986), 7.

9. Elisabeth Jay, *The Religion of the Heart: Anglican Evangelicalism and the Nineteenth-Century Novel* (Oxford: Oxford University Press, 1979), 51.

10. Mary Bayly, *The Life and Letters of Mrs. Sewell*, 5th ed. (London, 1890), vi, vii; further references will be included in the text. Sewell's disapproval notwithstanding, there was a tradition of women preaching publicly dating back at least to the eighteenth century. For late-eighteenth-century evidence documenting the historical record on women preachers in the Methodist revival, see D. Colin Dew, "Ann Carr and the Female Revivalists of Leeds," in *Religion in the Lives of English Women, 1760–1930*, 68–87; for Sewell's own period, see Olive Anderson, "Women Preachers in Mid-Victorian Britain: Some Reflexions on Feminism, Popular Religion and Social Change," *Historical Journal* 12, no. 3 (1969): 467–84.

11. For introductions to and readings of Tonna's politicized industrial fiction, see Ivanka Kovacevic and S. Barbara Kanner, "Blue Book into Novel: The Forgotten Industrial Fiction of Charlotte Elizabeth Tonna," *Nineteenth-Century Fiction* 25, no. 2 (September 1970): 152–73; Joseph Kestner, "Charlotte Elizabeth Tonna's *The Wrongs of Woman*: Female Industrial Protest," *Tulsa Studies in Women's Literature* 2, no. 2 (Fall 1983): 193–214; and Deborah Kaplan, "The Woman Worker in Charlotte Elizabeth Tonna's Fiction," *Mosaic* 18, no. 2 (Spring 1985): 51–63.

12. Sarah Ellis, *The Wives of England* (London, 1843), 344–45.

13. Armstrong, *Desire and Domestic Fiction*, 48. For another recent formulation of the relationship between nineteenth-century women's writing and woman's role as the creator of character which resonates with my analysis, see Margaret Homans, *Bearing the World* (Chicago: University of Chicago Press, 1986), esp. ch. 7.

14. Carol Edkins, "Quest for Community: Spiritual Autobiographies of Eighteenth-Century Quaker and Puritan Women in America," in *Women's Autobiographies: Essays in Criticism*, ed. Estelle C. Jelinek (Bloomington: Indiana University Press, 1980), 41.

15. Vivian [George Henry Lewes], "A Gentle Hint to Writing-Women," *Leader* 1 (May 18, 1850): 189.

16. Mary Russell Mitford, *Recollections of a Literary Life*, 3 vols, (London, 1852), I: 249.

17. "Literary Women," *London Review* 8 (March 26, 1864): 329.

18. The middle-class woman's "natural" role as civilizer and moral agent was earlier argued for on the same grounds Schimmelpenninck puts forward: as Hannah More writes in *Strictures on the Modern System of Female Education* (1799), "the general state of civilized society depends, more than those are aware who are not accustomed to scrutinize into the springs of human action, on the prevailing sentiments and habits of women, and on the nature and degree of the estimation in which they are held. . . . I would call [women] to the best and most appropriate exertion of their power, to raise the depressed tone of public morals, and to awaken the drowsy spirit of religious principles" (in *The Complete Works of Hannah More* [New York, 1843], 313). Literature, as More's own career demonstrates, provides an obvious means for carrying out the feminine moral mission she recommends.

5

Gender-Related Difference in the Slave Narratives of Harriet Jacobs and Frederick Douglass[*]

~

Winifred Morgan

The slave narrative is a central American autobiographical genre. Important in their own right, these narratives also have been continuing influences over other forms of writing, particularly the novel. Frederick Douglass's Narrative of the Life of Frederick Douglass *(1845), the best known of the slave narratives, has often been viewed as representative of the genre as whole. However, recent critics have pointed out that Douglass's generic preeminence has resulted in part from the reflection in his work of the masculine and European viewpoints that have dominated American culture.*

Winifred Morgan joins these critics by juxtaposing Douglass's text with Harriet Jacobs's Incidents in the Life of a Slave Girl *(1861) to show how gender differences shaped both the lives of American slaves and their written accounts of their experiences. In his autobiographical writing, Douglass focuses on himself as an individual, and language is crucial in his account of how he achieved freedom. In contrast, Jacobs, like many women novelists and religious writers of the period, writes about her life and her quest for freedom in terms of her various relationships with other people. The emphasis on human ties and community by Jacobs and other women writers of slave narratives offers important perspectives on slave culture unavailable from male autobiographers. The women's explorations of the self in community widen the critique of slavery that male slave narratives produce at the level of the individual.*

*From Winifred Morgan, "Gender-Related Difference in the Slave Narratives of Harriet Jacobs and Frederick Douglass," *American Studies* 35 (1994): 73–94. Reprinted by permission of *American Studies* and the author.

Winifred Morgan is a professor of English at Edgewood College, Madison, Wisconsin. She is the author of An American Icon: Brother Jonathan and American Identity *(1988) as well as articles on nineteenth-century American and Southern literature. Her current research focuses on tricksters and trickster humor in contemporary American fiction.*

SINCE THE LATE 1960s, antebellum slave narratives have experienced a renaissance as dozens of the thousands still extant have been reprinted and as scholars have published major works on the sources, art, and development of the narratives; the people who produced them; and their ongoing influence on later work. Drawing upon slave narratives as well as other sources, John Blassingame's *The Slave Community* (1972), for example, drew attention to the complex social interactions developed in antebellum slave culture. Examining the milieu that spawned the narratives and their development, and providing insights into what the narratives can tell about slavery as well as what they omit, Frances Smith Foster's *Witnessing Slavery* (1979) gave readers a book-length analysis of the genre. Robert B. Stepto's *From Behind the Veil* (1979) situated slave narratives at the center of African-American written narrative. John Sekora and Darwin Turner's collection of essays, *The Art of the Slave Narrative* (1982), focused closer attention on how the narratives achieved their rhetorical effects. In *The Slave's Narrative* (1985), Charles T. Davis and Henry Louis Gates, Jr., gathered excerpts from some of the best-known narratives and essays about the narratives as history and autobiographical literature. William L. Andrews's *To Tell a Free Story* (1987) examined the narratives as public autobiographies, at once exploring and demanding freedom. Today, hardly a book is published on American autobiography without a chapter on slave narratives. Not only do scholars writing about African-American literature often refer to the slave narratives' ongoing influence on fiction and autobiography, some of the novelists themselves mention their debt to the narratives. Toni Morrison, for instance, has often referred to the fact that previous to writing *Beloved*, she read hundreds of the narratives.

Studies of the slave narrative have explored numerous themes. Much of the work concentrates on the subtext beneath the stories. In the narratives, fugitives and ex-slaves appealed to the humanity they shared with their readers. The genre's themes flow from its assertion of the slaves' humanity. Slave narratives show that slaves suffered physically, emotionally, and spiritually under slavery; that slaves yearned for freedom and resisted slavery in every way possible: that slavery was a pernicious system ultimately destroying masters as well as slaves; that the narrators were telling the truth about their own experiences; and that each narrator was a "reliable transcriber of the experience and character of black folk."[1] In addition to showing how these themes recur in the narratives, scholars have demonstrated that while early slave narratives written during the eighteenth century drew their themes from earlier narrative forms,[2] in the last three decades before the American Civil War the slave narrative moved beyond the captivity narrative's emphasis on physical enslavement and the spiritual autobiography's focus on introspection to confront the moral bankruptcy of slavery itself. Unfortunately, few scholars have systematically examined the role of gender-related differences in these themes. However, given the pervasive impact of the "social organization of the relationship between sexes,"[3] gender influenced even the way in which bondage was experienced; men and women experienced it in different ways.

Deborah Gray White outlines a series of ways in which slave women's lives differed from those of men. White discusses the networks women slaves developed among themselves. She details, for example, the ways that being a woman added burdens to a slave's life but also furthered the "cooperation and interdependence" necessary for a woman's survival.[4] For example, women and children were not shackled below decks during the middle passage to America; however, being above deck also left them "more easily accessible to the criminal whims and sexual desires of seamen"(63). Women had less mobility, and thus fewer opportunities to flee, than men (75). When they joined the men in fieldwork, they still had to finish their own domestic work at home while the men rested (122). The women's shared work, however, often offered them opportunities for camaraderie. Laundry work, for example, gave them an opportunity to talk among themselves, to share joys and sorrows; so did prayer meetings (123). Slave women passed work skills on to one another (129). Even more crucially, slave women depended on one another in all that had to do with childbirth and child-rearing. For health care they depended on midwives and "doctor women" (124); for child care they depended on elderly slave women; and sometimes they used the services of a conjure woman (135). As a consequence of these different experiences, men and women slave narrators tell different stories of resistance to their enforced servitude.

As noted above, twentieth-century scholars of the slave narrative genre have often neglected apparently gender-related distinctions between the narratives of men and women. For example, critics have almost invariably cited the hunger for literacy as one of the most prominent themes found in slave narratives; scholars repeat as a truism that the narratives stress the importance of learning to read and write. In their introduction to *The Slave's Narrative*, for example, Charles Davis and Henry Louis Gates base their explanation for several common strategies encountered in the narratives on a preoccupation with literacy presumably found in all slave narratives. Gates and Davis generalize that in their concern about their writing, narrators depict vivid scenes describing their learning to read and write, underscore the dominant culture's strictures against African-American literacy, and intertwine an "ironic apologia" for their literary limitations with denunciations of the system that has refused the slave "development of *his* capacities" (emphasis added).[5] Their characterization accurately describes male narratives. In another essay in the same book, James Olney lists among seven characteristics that a reader typically encounters in any slave narrative a "record of the barriers raise[d] against slave literacy and the overwhelming difficulties encountered in learning to read and write" (153).[6]

Discussing the autobiographies of Douglass, Lucinda MacKethan also assumes the centrality of the quest for literacy in slave narratives. MacKethan explores connections between the strategies of earlier conversion/captivity narratives and Douglass's *Narrative* and then Douglass's use of these strategies to validate his role as a "fugitive American Slave narrator . . . seeking in a written document to prove that he has successfully appropriated through language the free territory he claims."[7] MacKethan notes as well the close connection for Douglass between the acquisition of literacy and personal autonomy (57). MacKethan probes both the role literacy played for Douglass, establishing him as a man worthy of freedom, and—by implication—its significance to other slave narrators. However, such a generalization does not extend to slave narratives written by women.

Male narrators do stress the importance of reading and writing. Thus, for example, Olaudah Equiano, James Pennington, and William Craft (the actual narrative voice of *Running a Thousand Miles*) stress how illiteracy disabled them while they were slaves and how they felt the need, once they slipped their bonds as slaves, to satisfy as soon as possible their hunger for education.[8] However, the drive to become literate appears to be gender-based; unlike the narratives written by men, women's narratives do not emphasize this factor. While male narrators accentuate the role of literacy, females stress the importance of relationships. Given the importance of relationships in the lives of most women, this is hardly surprising. Through their narratives, both male and female fugitives and ex-slaves strove to counter the racial stereotypes that bound them even in "free" societies. Black men and women, however, faced different stereotypes. Black men combated the stereotype that they were "boys" while black women contested the idea that they were either helpless victims or whores. For a male fugitive, public discourse served to claim his place among men; for a female her relationships—as a daughter, sister, wife, mother, and friend—demonstrated her womanliness and her shared roles with women readers.

Two of the most widely read American slave narratives, Frederick Douglass's *Narrative of the Life of Frederick Douglass* (1845) and Harriet Jacobs's *Incidents in the Life of a Slave Girl* (1861) provide useful representative texts with which to examine gender-specific differences in both the narratives and the lives of slaves. The slave narratives of Jacobs and Douglass suggest that, while they were responding to their place and period's significant themes—among them, individualism, community, resisting oppression, and striving for freedom—strategies of coping and resistance differed by gender. In common with most male narrators, Douglass emphasizes his ability to speak in public as well as to read and write. Through their use of language, male narrators strove to demonstrate their place as men among men, that they had a *right* to autonomy in a political democracy based on a voter's ability to understand and debate the issues. On the other hand, in common with other women narrators, Jacobs emphasizes her womanliness. Women narrators related to feminine culture of their time, and that involved telling their stories in terms of relationships.

Douglass's Autobiographies

Aside from gender-related differences such as their distinct emphases on the importance of literacy and relationships, narratives written by men and women share many common characteristics. In all slave narratives, the fugitive or former slaves relate their trials as slaves, their flight to freedom, and, finally, their dedication to helping others flee slavery.[9] As in other slave narratives, Douglass's *Narrative* makes this pattern explicit; but in addition, Douglass further organizes his narrative around the theme of increasing control over his life as a path toward personal independence. A major instrument in his quest is language, and in particular, literacy. Perhaps the paramount virtue in his *Narrative* is the individual's courage, and the crucial weapon—in a struggle where armed conflict would be suicidal—is the word.

Throughout his career, Douglass was preoccupied with language, and the preeminence he gives language and especially literacy in the *Narrative* reflects this preoccupation. Douglass first gained a reputation in the North as an orator. William Lloyd Garrison's and Wendell Phillips's prefatory letters to the *Narrative* establish Douglass as someone who has witnessed effectively at abolitionist meetings. In fact, according to one editor of his works, contemporary reports noted that Douglass "charmed his audiences with his style."[10] Nonetheless, Douglass seems to have understood even during his early days as a public speaker that until he recorded his experiences and crafted them in his own literary style, they would remain ephemera, and under the control

of others. Douglass's recollections closely identify slavery with ignorance and lack of access to the written word. Thus, for example, the first
paragraph of his *Narrative* notes that he had never seen "any authentic
record" (47) of his birth. Had he not grabbed at freedom and gained the
skill to write his *Narrative*, we might never have learned of his existence. Literacy gave Douglass the power to assert his existence as well
as his freedom from those who would keep him ignorant and a slave.

When Sophia Auld first taught him to read and then when Hugh
Auld showed him—by objecting to his lessons—the importance of literacy, Douglass began on his road to freedom. Even as a young child,
Douglass realized that knowledge represented power. Words provide access to the power of communication, and the route to long-term control
of the message is through literacy. As an adult, Douglass, writing his
Narrative, had literate and articulate language at his command. He used
his command of language to reflect on the presumably inchoate insights
of the barely lettered child he once was. Douglass's musings make his
readers aware of the contrast between his polished adult abilities and his
preliterate juvenile state when he listened to Hugh Auld's comments to
his wife, Sophia:

> It was a new and special revelation, explaining dark and mysterious
> things, with which my youthful understanding had struggled, but
> struggled in vain. I now understood what had been to me a most per-
> plexing difficulty—to wit, the white man's power to enslave the black
> man. It was a grand achievement, and I prized it highly. From that mo-
> ment, I understood *the pathway from slavery to freedom*. . . . Though
> conscious of the difficulty of learning without a teacher, I set out with
> high hope, and a fixed purpose, at whatever cost of trouble, *to learn
> how to read* (78) (emphasis added).

Throughout his life Douglass demonstrated his belief in the connection between access to the written record and power. Not only did
Douglass write two further autobiographies (published in 1855 and
1881) but he also edited and published a series of weekly and monthly
newspapers,[11] and in later life toured as a lecturer and wrote for national
periodicals such as the *North American Review* and *Harper's Weekly.*
Douglass never forgot Hugh Auld's inadvertent lesson: "If you teach that
nigger . . . how to read, there would be no keeping him. It would forever
unfit him to be a slave. He would at once become unmanageable, and of
no value to his master" (78). Nor did Douglass forget Auld's insistence
that Douglass cultivate "complete thoughtlessness . . . and setting aside
[his] intellectual nature, in order to [achieve] contentment in slavery"
(139–40). In fact, by contravening Auld's insistence that he live out his
existence as a thoughtlessly contented slave, by making every effort to

achieve literacy, and finally by becoming quite unmanageable, Douglass showed how well he understood Auld's dictates.

Power and personal autonomy have special significance to the former slave who has endured utter impotency and lack of control. Lucinda MacKethan even speaks of male slave narrators crafting "master narratives" in order to explore "what it means to be a master, not what it means to be a fugitive slave."[12] In the *Narrative*, Douglass structures his story to show how he has used literacy to achieve power and control in his life. As Eric J. Sunquist notes, "Both the contents and the serial development of his autobiographical writings make evident the subversive lesson young Frederick first learned in reading the alphabet—that literacy is power."[13] The *Narrative* demonstrates in 1845 how someone has gained control of his life by gaining control over the means of communication.

Drawing on Harold Bloom's *A Map of Misreading*, William L. Andrews finds that African-American autobiographies such as Douglass's prod readers to review and sometimes revise "the myths and ideals of America's culture-defining scriptures."[14] Throughout the *Narrative*, Douglass appeals to two major legitimizing sources in American culture: the Bible and "documents" (84) of political tradition in the United States. As the youthful Douglass realizes when he reads, rereads, and mulls over his copy of *The Columbian Orator*, the American rhetorical tradition speaks in terms of universal freedom and the rights of all men. This rhetorical tradition prevailed even after laws further restricted African Americans following Nat Turner's Rebellion (1831) and in the Fugitive Slave Law (1850), enacted a few years after his *Narrative*'s publication. Yet slave owners and their sympathizers attempted to cut off Douglass and other slaves from both the scriptural and revolutionary rhetorical sources that championed human freedom.

One of Douglass's most vehement arguments against Christianity as practiced in the South was that it perverted the Scriptures—the Word of God. Thus early in the *Narrative*, an overseer, Mr. Severe, is known for his swearing as well as for his sadism, "his fiendish barbarity" (55) as Douglass calls it. And later in the *Narrative*, Thomas Auld, who "after his conversion . . . found religious sanction and support for his cruelty" (99), quotes Scripture ("He that knoweth his master's will, and doeth it not, shall be beaten with many stripes") to justify his sadism when he ties up a young lame woman and whips her until blood drips off her naked shoulders (98–99). In these and other passages where white Christians break up black Sabbath schools, Douglass clearly associates access to the written word (and sometimes to the Word of God) with control of one's situation.

Despite the "generic conventions" that mold into types all the characters and even the protagonist's voice in most slave narratives,[15]

Douglass does, in fact, manage to stamp his individuality onto his *Narrative*. In this, his *Narrative* stands apart from most of the other extant narratives. In the *Narrative*, Douglass presents himself as someone who has learned to read and write almost solely by his own efforts, who fought with Covey, the slave breaker, for his human dignity, and who finally seized his own freedom, all pretty much on his own. Douglass actually sets up two contrasting frames: he presents himself as someone who is "one of a kind" and at the same time "representative." Douglass presents himself as someone who, in order to break free from slavery, found sources of strength within himself rather than from his community. Yet at the same time, he puts himself forward as someone whom other slaves, freedmen, and fugitives can emulate. Thus he also becomes an Emersonian "representative" man, an exemplar. His story, in one sense, is every slave's; in another sense, his story is that of *the extraordinary man*. Part of the appeal of the *Narrative* is Douglass's invocation of the twin but opposing American themes of individualism and community. Douglass's challenge in the *Narrative* is to combine them.

* * *

Douglass and the other slaves in the *Narrative* live isolated and mistrustful lives. As a child, for example, Douglass uses guile to learn and practice his letters—first tricking or bribing white boys into teaching him letters he does not know and then practicing these letters in the discarded copybooks of his master's son. The youthful Douglass does not dare accept the offered help of Irish workmen because they might be trying to entrap him. In the *Narrative,* Douglass appears single-handedly to have beaten Covey to a standstill. (Douglass's second autobiography, *My Bondage and My Freedom*, reveals that Caroline, a strong slave woman, could have tipped the balance in his opponent's favor; however, she chose to stay out of the fight and was later punished for not helping Covey.) Douglass's first attempt to flee North with two other slaves by using the passes he has written almost ends in disaster because someone, presumably another slave, has warned the owners. The *Narrative* thus gives the impression that neither slaves nor whites can be trusted. Douglass primarily emphasizes his uniqueness, and the other black characters in his *Narrative* interact only warily, both among themselves and with whites; the theme of individuality, depending on oneself alone, predominates over the theme of community.

How does an individual conscious of himself, his singularity, his sense of being "self-made," come to know and understand himself without appropriating a community and a means of communication? Writing the *Narrative*, reflecting on his experience in words, helped Douglass to understand his passage from the isolation he perceived in being a slave to the community possible as a freeman. It may be that his lack of peers made the language Douglass used all the more critical. He needed to put his insights into words so that he could understand them. Telling one's own story is a particularly human way of organizing and coming to understand one's experience.

Telling his story in his three autobiographies became Douglass's means of understanding his experience and that of other African Americans. This is why, as his understanding evolved, he had to keep rewriting his story. With his "story" to communicate, Douglass could begin to connect with those who could become his community at large. Language and control of that language became both his opportunity and his vehicle. As an adolescent slave, he had written passes that he had hoped would help him and his friends on their way to freedom. As an adult writer of autobiographies, he was still attempting to use language to further his own and his people's freedom. Douglass used language to break out of the isolation he perceived in slavery; finally, through his later autobiographies, he attempted to build a relationship with the rest of the African-American population.

As the single most widely read slave narrative, Douglass's *Narrative* has often come to represent the entire genre. Despite its impressive craft, however, it presents problems as a representative text. First of all, its implicit assumption that literacy provides the power leading to individual freedom does not characterize women's narratives. In addition, its advocacy of literacy as a major route to personal autonomy might prove misguided. Valerie Smith critiques the utility of making literacy central in a struggle for equality because literacy has often served not only as a means of access for the underprivileged but also a means by which dominant groups have controlled access to society's rewards and thus preserved their hegemony.[16] Smith even credits Douglass's "story of his own success" as "provid[ing] counter evidence of his platform of radical change; for by demonstrating that a slave can be a man in terms of all the qualities valued by his Northern middle-class reader—physical power, perseverance, literacy—he lends credence to the patriarchal structure largely responsible for his oppression" (27). This does not necessarily mean that Douglass was wrong in his choice of language as his most important weapon for his struggle, merely that he had not examined or critiqued that choice.

In part because of what she perceives as Douglass's limitations, Deborah E. McDowell also has challenged the *Narrative*'s preeminence among slave narratives and suggests that a presumably inadvertent male bias has insisted on its primacy as an Emersonian "representative" text. McDowell contends that "the literary and interpretative history of the *Narrative* has, with few exceptions, repeated with approval its salient assumptions and structural paradigms. This repetition has, in turn, created a potent and persistent critical language that positions and repositions Douglass on top, that puts him in a position of priority."[17] Indeed, Douglass's *Narrative* has enjoyed a preeminent place among North American slave narratives. Yet Davis and Gates maintain that among Douglass's contemporaries, Douglass's account may have been considered most "'representative'" because it was most "presentable." "He was most presentable because of his unqualified abilities as a rhetorical artist. Douglass achieved a form of *presence* through the manipulation of rhetorical structures within a modern language."[18]

A number of critics, among them Elizabeth Fox-Genovese, have explored the process whereby Americans judge the significance and value of a piece of literature according to dominant male and European-derived cultural values. Reactions to Douglass's *Narrative* seem to illustrate this process because it affirms what his nineteenth-century white male audience valued. Although Douglass labels his confrontation with the slave-breaker Edward Covey *the* "turning point" in his life, most of the language and imagery of the *Narrative* emphasize Douglass's increasing fluency with and control over written language and how literacy gave him the means to make himself free and to live as a free man. With its emphasis on gaining control of language, the structure of Douglass's *Narrative* reflects accepted hierarchical values common to nineteenth-century Western culture: education leads to social uplift, and progress is good. The *Narrative* also accepts the assumptions that men are the natural heads of the family and society and that children "belong" to their father. When they found the *Narrative* "representative," Douglass's "fellows" may have responded to what felt comfortably familiar to them as male readers and writers educated in a cultural milieu that taught them to respond positively to specific paradigms.

The dominant culture values in Douglass's narrative, in turn, often reflect male values. The black women in Douglass's narrative are by nature subordinate to the men. They serve as examples of victimization, such as his aunt, or as shadowy helpmates, such as the free woman he marries. Sophia Auld may think independently as a young bride but quickly accommodates herself to her husband's preferences. The narrative assumes a hierarchy that places male prerogatives (such as the right of Hugh Auld to countermand Sophia's attempt to teach Douglass, of Douglass's father to impregnate and abandon Douglass's mother, of Douglass himself to use and ignore his wife) at the apex. If Valerie Smith and others are correct in their argument that traditionally, literacy and a literary canon have been used to support patriarchy and other powerful groups to suppress the right of oppressed people, then women slave narrators were right to doubt the value of learning to read and write as a major strategy in achieving their freedom. Patriarchy limited their worth both before and after slavery.[19] Women who had been slaves had reason to seek "their own independent definition of womanhood."[20]

Douglass's use of printed language to connect with others differs considerably from the relationship-building found in the work of women writers like Jacobs. Female, as well as male, slave narrators desired and strove for literacy. Nonetheless, being literate never saved women fugitives from the burdens of slavery, racism, or sexism; and they knew it. Whether they found literacy at best a weak reed on which to lean—whether they were ultimately more cynical or perhaps more realistic in confronting the economic realities of the racist and sexist societies in which they lived—women narrators do not give central significance to the acquisition of literacy. Instead, the most significant realities in these women's lives usually derived from their personal relationships. While many nineteenth-century white women also developed significant ties among themselves,[21] African-American women had little choice but to depend on one another in order to endure. Nineteenth-century social definitions of femininity marginalized white women but entirely excluded black women. The relationships that enabled women to survive slavery remain in their narratives like the framing timbers of a ship's hull, outlining how slave women used connections with others in their efforts to keep out the seas of oppression that threatened to overwhelm them.

Jacobs's Narrative

Feminists writing in a variety of fields offer contemporary readers insight into the preference of Jacobs and other women narrators of slave experience for organizing their narratives around their relationships with meaningful people in their lives rather than around how they "proved themselves." Far more so than today, asserting "rugged individualism" would have been a foreign, perhaps repellent, notion for most nineteenth-century American women of any racial heritage. Even today, as psychologists such as Carol Gilligan and Jean Baker Miller have noted, women, more than men, tend to come to make choices based on their understanding and experiences of relationships.[22]

Not only does contemporary psychological research emphasize the importance of relationships in women's lives, a look at literary forms popular during Jacobs's lifetime demonstrates that her female contemporaries also relied on sustaining relationships. For example, relationships play a central role in women's religious conversion narratives. Susan Juster notes the centrality of relationships in the published conversion narratives of women during the late eighteenth and early nineteenth century: "Authority for women is experienced as personal rather than abstract power. Embodied in personal relations, authority is exercised through the emotional and social channels which connect human beings. The exercise of authority thus requires the establishment of a relationship which is in some way significant for both partners."[23] Juster's analysis of religious conversion narratives suggests contrasting values in the slave narratives of men and women. She points out that the men and women who wrote conversion narratives during the early nineteenth century needed to suppress and assert different dimensions of themselves in religious conversion: men needed to suppress their egos and to link with others, while women needed to assert their egos and cease submerging themselves in others if they were to achieve the human wholeness demanded by religious conversion. In fact, Juster's study of religious conversion narratives seems to show men and women writers of conversion narratives following separate paths to ultimately the same goal.

Relationships also play a central role in women's novels of the period. According to Beth Maclay Doriani, Jacobs and her contemporary novelist Harriet Wilson both reshaped the slave narrative as it had been written by men,[24] in order to show "the world of the black woman—as a person *inextricably bound up with others* yet responsible for her own survival, emotionally, economically, and politically" (207) (emphasis added). While male fugitives stressed their individuality, their ability to stand alone and assume adult male responsibility for themselves, women fugitives generally saw themselves as part of their communities. So women like Jacobs and Wilson, according to Doriani, stress connections among members of their communities rather than their isolation. Female narrators envision themselves as striving with and for others. They do not think of themselves or other fugitives as alone.[25]

* * *

Harriet Jacobs's narrative differs significantly from Douglass's autobiography. While Douglass's narrative emphasizes his acquisition and development of written language, Jacobs depicts a network of relationships on which she depends and to which she contributes; her most important relationships devolve from bonds of love. She respects and fears but, above all, she loves her grandmother. She loves her children, her brother, her uncles and aunt. Her feelings for her employers, both the first and second Mrs. Bruce, and later, as revealed in her letters, for abolitionist Amy Post, derive far more from affection, acceptance, and a sense of worth than from patronage. There is nothing legalistic about these relationships. In *Incidents*, bonds of affection support and nourish the individual and contrast with the contrived and unreasonable bonds of slavery. Unlike Douglass, who tries to connect with and control his relations with both white and black communities through his manipulation of language, Jacobs already feels closely connected with family and friends. She makes sense of her responsibility to larger communities in terms of the ties that bind her to her family and friends. The support she receives from family and friends nourishes her; it assures her of her own worth; it impels her to take a role in the larger world. Not only did Jacobs write *Incidents* after her years as a nanny, she also worked with her brother, running an abolitionist library. During and after the Civil War, she joined in relief work and the education of freed slaves.

In contrast with Douglass, Jacobs does not find language much of a weapon. Although literate, Jacobs makes only limited use of reading and writing to distract her enemy, Dr. Flint. Eventually Jacobs does write letters from Edenton and has them mailed from Northern states, and later she peruses the "Arrivals" section of Northern newspapers for warnings about the presence of her enemies. Nonetheless, at an earlier point in the story, Flint actually turns Jacobs's literacy against her and uses her ability to read as a further avenue of sexual solicitation. For the most part, Jacobs feels she has no other resource than her relationships with family members and close friends and no other weapon than low cunning. Recognizing the hopelessness of overt opposition, Jacobs's narrative glories in her ability and that of other oppressed slaves to subvert the will of their oppressors.[26]

The people in Jacobs's narrative engender respect as a result of the moral authority they wield. They earn respect. Jacobs serves her first mistress because she loves her and views her as a "second mother." Her grandmother also dominates Jacobs not because of any parental "right" but because they share a bond of love. In contrast, her "ownership" by the Flints becomes an abstract and irrational legal fiction. The events of her story show that not only "ownership" of human beings is unjust; more important, the institution of slavery is evil because it perverts all relationships between men and women, children and parents, slaves and free people. The institution of slavery encourages a relatively good man such as Mr. Sands to keep his and Harriet's children in bondage. In addition, it destroys society's basic unit, the family. It poisons the Flints' marriage and condones Dr. Flint's attempted seduction of the adolescent Jacobs. It leaves a slave child unsure whether he "belongs" to his parents or his owners. Thus, for example, Jacobs's young brother Willie does not know whether his first responsibility is to answer his father's or his mistress's call (9). As women narrators like Jacobs show their readers, slavery works to weaken familial relationships: those between husbands and wives, children and parents, brothers and sisters.

Relationships in *Incidents* demand responsibility by other individuals and the larger community. Drawing out the implications of Jacobs's narrative, one might even judge individuals by how they respond to that responsibility. By this criterion, one would have to say that some characters, such as

Mr. Sands, fail as human beings. The men and women of Jacobs's family, however, invariably respond wholeheartedly to their responsibility for one another. Jacobs remains for years in Edenton for the sake of her children; later, after fleeing to the North, she works from dawn to past dark to support her children. As much as she can, she also tries to contribute to her larger community. For instance, even though the Anti-Slavery Society offers to pay Jacobs's fare and her friend Fanny's to New York through the Durhams in Philadelphia, Jacobs refuses (161). She is motivated in part by pride in her ability to pay her own way; but in addition she recognizes that if she accepts more than she needs, funds may not be available for other fugitives. Later, after the first Mrs. Bruce dies, Jacobs accompanies her "little motherless" (183) child to the girl's grandparents in England. She values the salary the child's father offers, but in part she makes the overseas trip to acknowledge the kindness she received from the child's dead mother.

The structural core for *Incidents* emerges from a series of encounters through which Jacobs learns to rely on some relationships and painfully discovers how unreliable others can prove. *Incidents* details Jacobs's testing of relationships. One of these is her relationship with God; another relationship involves the dealings of Jacobs and of all slaves with those who purport to own them. And, finally, there are all of the personal relationships of individuals with one another based on blood, sex, friendship, or employment. Examining the relationships she has experienced, Jacobs gradually comes to decide on the validity of various social and religious claims. The very length of *Incidents* seems to suggest Jacobs's evolving apprehension as to which relationships to trust and what moral and ethical principles flow from those relationships.

But personal relationships come first. What Jacobs's experience seems to teach is that few relationships, especially few relationships with whites, can be trusted because overlying all Southern and many Northern relationships is that initial and overwhelming fact noted in her first line, "I was born a slave" (1). Jacobs's narrative contrasts the unreliability of relationships with white people with the warmth and steadfastness of those with her own family. Her grandmother functions as a good angel whose virtue opposes Dr. Flint's vice. Thus Jacobs's angelic grandmother is "*always* kind, *always* ready to sympathize" (83) (emphasis added) and confronts in different ways both the "the demon Slavery" (83) and the demonic Dr. Flint, whom Jacobs's toddler son calls "that bad man" (80). Jacobs's grandmother might even be a figure of the angel of death when she warns Flint, "You ain't got many more years to live, and you'd better be saying your prayers. It will take 'em all, and more too, to wash the dirt off your soul" (82).

While Jacobs's grandmother is portrayed as a woman of universally recognized piety, perhaps her most impressive quality is her ability to forgive her enemies. Thus, after Dr. Flint's death, her grandmother actually writes to Jacobs, "'Dr. Flint is dead. He has left a distressed family. Poor old man! I hope he made his peace with God'" (195–96). In response to her grandmother's words, Jacobs comments with a summary of his sins: "I remembered how he had defrauded my grandmother of the hard earnings she had loaned; how he had tried to cheat her out of the freedom her mistress had promised her, and how he had persecuted her children; and I thought to myself that she was a better Christian than I was, if she could entirely forgive him" (196). When Jacobs finally flees to the North, her grandmother gives her "a small bag of money"— literally the biblical widow's mite that Jesus commends—and enjoins Jacobs and Jacobs's son to prayer (155). Jacobs tells readers that her grandmother had "a beautiful faith" (17). Yet she is human and reacts with consternation to the news of the teenaged Harriet's first pregnancy.[27] In contrast to her grandmother's usual forbearance, Dr. Flint "chuckle[s]" to hear of what he considers another's adversity (136), works to the death Jacobs's faithful aunt Nancy (195), and almost to his dying day is still lying to Jacobs and trying to cheat her (171–72).

While they live, Jacobs's parents and grandmother are the most important people in her life. She reveres their memories after their deaths. While she and they live, Jacobs depends on her parents, her grandmother, her uncles, her aunt, and her brother. In addition, her fugitive uncle and brother are models to emulate. And for the most part, other blacks are also almost as supportive as "family." For example, while she does not marry the "young colored carpenter" identified as "a young girl's first love" (37), he might be the "Peter" who more than ten years later risks his life to spirit her away to the North.

Jacobs's most important relationship, of course, is with her children, and this keeps her in place when she might otherwise have fled or even committed suicide. Jacobs speaks of her infant son as a "little vine . . . taking root in my existence" (62). From the time her son Benjamin is born, he and, later, his sister Ellen become the primary influences on Jacobs's decisions.[28] Jacobs fears that if she runs away, the Flints, as retribution, would sell her children; yet she takes a chance on breaking the cycle of slavery because she fears even more having Ellen grow up and repeat her humiliation. Even as her children's welfare undermines any desire she might have had to run away, her children also strengthen her resolve "that out of the darkness of this hour a brighter dawn should rise for them" (85). For them, Jacobs stays alive even during her seven years hiding in "a dismal hole" (113), the nine by seven by three foot crawl space over her grandmother's storage shed. Jacobs's physical separation from her children, despite her knowledge of their proximity and occasional glimpses of them, proves almost as difficult for her as the physical rigors of life in her "bolt hole." For years after their escape to the North, Jacobs struggles to follow her grandmother's example by caring for and educating her children. A poignant touch at the end of the narrative involves Jacobs's acknowledgment that she has not yet been able to provide a home for her children.

* * *

Jacobs's relationship with her Northern, white, middle-class women readers, her primary audience, is perhaps best thought of as analogous to her relationships with the white women in her narrative. Both were problematic. She found some of these women trustworthy, some untrustworthy, but few capable of genuine empathy. Jacobs feared that publishing her story might scandalize some of her new Northern friends. They had no way of knowing the reality of her life and might misinterpret her experience and condemn her unwed motherhood. Her relationship with her Northern reading audience lacked the trust and support she enjoyed from friends and relatives. Although her support for the abolitionist cause impelled Jacobs to make her story public, she worried about public acknowledgment of her teenage pregnancies. To communicate with this audience, she used her ability to write her own story; to do that she used a mode, a variation of the domestic novel, suited to their expectations and appealing to their sympathies. Her reliance on narrative strategies usually encountered in sentimental domestic fiction certainly shows that she assumed that this audience would have difficulty accepting, much less understanding her experience.[29] In addition to the experiences Jacobs details in the text, Yellin's research has shown that Jacobs's encounters with such antislavery advocates as Harriet Beecher Stowe had taught her not to depend much on the help or the understanding of her Northern audience.[30]

Yet given her avowed purpose—to persuade Northern readers to the abolitionist cause—Jacobs sought to engage and thus to place some reliance on her white audience. Indeed, both Jacobs and Douglass encountered overt as well as covert opposition from a part of that audience, white fellow writers who wanted to "help," perhaps, at least unconsciously, to control their narratives. Jacobs wrote only after she had finished her long day's work as a child's nurse and glorified domestic. She guarded her manuscript from the view of her de facto employer, Nathaniel Willis. A noted, presumably liberal, white writer, Willis could have helped Jacobs; but she distrusted his commitment to the abolitionist cause. Living in his home for years, she probably had cause. Jacobs did ask for Harriet Beecher Stowe's help, but Jacobs's dealings with Stowe convinced her that Stowe would co-opt her story and "use" her but never allow her to tell her own story. So Jacobs refused entirely Stowe's "help." Eventually, despite her self-doubts, Jacobs learned to trust her own work. The editor Jacobs finally chose to trust, Lydia Child, insists in the original introduction to *Incidents* that the changes she made were minor.[31]

Jacobs needed her white audience and she knew it. Valerie Smith makes the interesting points that while Jacobs flees from "one small space to another" (31) in her slow progression toward freedom, she leaves each "only with the aid of someone else" (31–32). Jacobs's white female audience provided her with one of her only partially reliable relationships. She feared their judgmental reactions. Nonetheless, she needed this audience as much as her grandmother once had needed the white women of Edenton who bought her bakery goods. Smith further notes that by underscoring a reliance on other people, Jacobs reveals an alternate way in which the story of slavery and escape might be written (34). While male narrators, including Douglass, emphasized their own derring-do, a woman like Jacobs remains aware of the role of her compatriots in her escape. She relates her own subterfuge and courage, but she also includes illustrations of the considerable courage her escape demanded of her grandmother, her uncle, and, in time, her children, as well as the white friends of her family. Jacobs's emphasis on relationships also serves as a further defense of slaves who have not even attempted to flee bondage. As her story implies, the same bonds of love that hold Jacobs, her grandmother, and her uncle in Edenton just as surely keep other slaves from dashing to freedom.

Throughout her account Jacobs values relationships because they have sustained her. Her loving relationships with African Americans in the South are based on ties of kinship, affection, and mutual interdependence. In contrast, the legal relationship of owner-slave constitutes a perversity. By the time Mrs. Bruce pays off the Flints, who now have legal title to Jacobs, Jacobs is a middle-aged working woman living in the North and longing for the healthy adult independence of a mother able to care for herself and to educate her children. Jacobs believes that she and her ancestors have fully paid for her free status. They have paid for her freedom through her grandmother's, her mother's, and her own years of service. She defines freedom as independence, as the right and ability to maintain herself and her loved ones within a network of mutual care and service to and from others. Her experience has convinced her that she already has *earned* her freedom. Thus, she comments, "I regarded such laws [as those that declared me still a slave] as the regulations of robbers, who had no rights that I was bound to respect" (187).

Although the second "Mrs. Bruce"—whom Jean Yellin has established was Mrs. Nathaniel P. Willis[32]—finally did pay the Flints' son-in-law three hundred dollars, she did so against Jacobs's will. Mrs. Bruce's payment made Jacobs feel unreasonably indebted. Valuing as she did the independence of freedom, Jacobs felt *bound* in a new way. Much of Jacobs's anger and resentment (200) at finally being *bought* and set free by Mrs. Bruce may come from Jacobs's sense that their relationship had been altered. All of her adult life, Jacobs tried to deny the validity of the slave's bond. In effect, Mrs. Bruce's action implicitly acknowledged chattel slavery. That altered their relationship from that of peers and free women, even friends, to one—at best—of patron and client. Having been redeemed, rather than acknowledged a free peer, can also prove a burden.

Incidents concentrates on slavery—and to a lesser degree, racism—which Jacobs depicts as a poison infecting relationships. (Jacobs often uses images of poisonous snakes and the devil in referring to the South and slavery.) As it poisoned most close personal relationships, slavery also distorted social relationships. Only a few exceptional people, such as the first and second Mrs. Bruce and Amy Post, seem immune to the racism that infected even the Northern states. Finally, Jacobs shows how slavery has perverted the relationship between human beings and God. As does Douglass, Jacobs shows in *Incidents* not only how slavery has perverted Christianity but also suggests her own spiritual doubts and possibly the evolution of an adult faith.[33] Jacobs admires her grandmother's adherence to a radical Christian forgiveness. But the incessant demands of the Flints make it impossible for Jacobs to follow her grandmother's example of forgiveness. The destruction of the African-American church in the woods (67) symbolizes the impossible situation of African-American slaves enjoined to live as Christians but denied the opportunity. In addition, Jacobs includes in *Incidents* many tales about ministers who do not see any conflict between their professions of "Christianity" and the "rules" of Southern slavery.

In contrast with Douglass's *Narrative*, which is the story of an individual's finding and using language as the key to effecting his freedom, Jacobs structures her narrative with incidents that illustrate her place within personal and communal relationships. Their different emphases grow out of gender differences. Most male narratives reflect the nineteenth-century popular admiration for "rugged individualists." The proportionately few women slave narrators, on the other hand, were hostages to nineteenth-century America's "cult of domesticity,"[34] which demanded a standard of feminine "purity" that slavery denied them. Unlike men, women were excluded from the public recital of their stories in a culture that at least publicly insisted on the cult of pure womanhood. Readers who insisted that women should choose "death before dishonor" would not accept mothers of fatherless children. The recital of their abuse gained female narrators neither money, power, nor social advantage. Since women narrators could not show that they had been the "perfect wives" that the cult of domesticity demanded, they emphasized instead the ways in which their relationships with their families allied them with their white reading audience.

Alternate Strategies

Male and female slave narrators had basically the same goal: to show that they deserved to live as free people in a free society. Nonetheless, in their need to contest different stereotypes, male and female fugitives and former slaves seized on different strategies. Men and women fugitives may well have had different models of freedom. The slave narratives written by men emphasize their desire to be "men" in their society, to take a "man's" role. In the words of Niemtzow, "Male slave narratives, indeed male autobiographies, are frequently stories of triumph in a public sphere."[35] In a blatantly patriarchal society, the public sphere would, of course, entail a position of power. Attaining literary and writing literature advanced those goals. Male slave narrators stress the importance of achieving literacy and their independence as men; they need to demonstrate that they are men among men.

Female slave narrators, on the other hand, have to convince their readers that they were neither the victims nor the fallen women that stereotypes have labeled them. With Sojourner Truth, they cry, "Ar'n't I a Woman?"[36] These women, therefore, stress their kinship with their white and black sisters: they remind their readers that they were someone's children, sisters, wives, mothers, and friends. For instance, throughout her memoir, Elizabeth H. Keckley emphasizes her ties with "kind, true-hearted friends in the South as well as in the North."[37] Keckley's memoir emphasizes her business accomplishments, but she considers her role as Mary Todd Lincoln's seamstress and sometimes confidante far more significant than her ability to read and write, because the former, after all, allows her to achieve the modicum of independence that she cherishes. Mary Prince, another woman narrator, tells a story of physical labor, abuse, and misery after her early years with her mother. Although Moravian ladies teach Prince to read,[38] this does not alter her situation. At the end of the narrative, living in England, she still pines for reunion with her husband (22). Male narrators relate little about their families; women always describe their close relatives. A pattern emerges in these narratives as well as those of Douglass and Jacobs: most male fugitives seem to define freedom as autonomy, whereas most female fugitives seem to define freedom as interdependence within relationships.

Women narrators are more apt than men to stress, as Jacobs does, a desire for a home of one's own. Yet to maintain their own homes, women need a degree of economic power. Male slave fugitives might earn a living lecturing on the abolitionist lecture circuit and writing slave narratives, but for women fugitives, publishing narratives frequently meant a certain amount of infamy. Even in freedom, most fugitive slave women still worked as domestics, cooks, laundresses, and seam- stresses.[39] Although most male former slaves worked as laborers, some used literacy to open up broader employment opportunities; for women, it offered little advantage. For women narrators, literacy was useful, but it only marginally advanced their "independence."[40] Even in freedom, racism and sexism combined to keep ex-slave women's status—to alter Orlando Patterson's definition of slavery—that of people suffering per- manent, violent domination, generally dishonored, as they had been from birth.[41]

Written slave narratives flourished with the abolition movement. At abolition meetings, male ex-slaves were known to bare their scarred backs as testaments to slavery's cruelty. Written slave narratives ex- tended that oral testimony by relating both the physical and psychologi- cal cruelty experienced by slaves. Readers encountered the individual, a fellow human being wounded by the system. Women fugitives, like men, told their stories because they believed that publication furthered the abolitionist cause. But for women, abolishing slavery meant more than achieving atomized, personal goals. Ultimately, in telling their stories, women were motivated by the need to build communities and—by extension—the commonwealth. Ironically, the nineteenth-century American admiration for rugged individualism actually militated against building communities that could enrich and vivify public life. Working with others seemed less valued a trait.

Further significant differences may well exist between male and fe- male narratives. Identifying them might also provide further strategies that women used in dealing with slavery. Women's narratives, as sug- gested by Jacobs's *Incidents*, offer a demanding, but humane path to public life. Their narratives stress the bonds that tie people together but also support them. Their narratives widen the critique of the slave cul- ture encountered in men's narratives. The slave narratives of male and female writers together, given the emphasis on literacy and control in the former and on relationships and interdependence in the latter, offer in- sight on balancing individualism and community. Women narrators em- phasized implicitly that sexual abuse and the breakup of their families violated the community. Women slaves regarded this as more destructive than the withholding of education.

Notes

1. William L. Andrews, *To Tell a Free Story: The First Century of Afro-American Autobiography, 1760–1865* (Urbana, 1988), 1.

2. John Sekora, for example, "Red, White, and Black: Indian Captivities, Colonial Printers, and the Early African-American Narratives," in *A Mixed Race: Ethnicity in Early America*, ed. Frank Shuffleton (New York, 1993), shows significant connections between early slave narratives and contemporary Indian captivity narratives; and in *To Tell*, William Andrews discusses the influence of black spiritual autobiography on later slave narratives.

3. Joan Scott, "Gender: A Useful Category of Historical Analysis," *American Historical Review* 91 (1986): 1053.

4. Deborah Gray White, *Ar'n't I A Woman? Female Slaves in the Plantation South* (New York, 1985), 124.

5. Charles T. Davis and Henry Louis Gates, Jr., eds., *The Slave's Narrative* (Oxford, 1985), xxviii.

6. As still another illustration of how common the assertion has been—in an endnote reminding readers that "most students of the slave narrative have commented on how central the moment of literacy is to the individual narrator," Annette Niemtzow in "The Problematic of Self in Autobiography," ed. John Sekora and Darwin Turner (Macomb, IN, 1982), 108, lists four further scholars (H. Baker, S. Butterfield, R. Rosenblatt, G. Taylor) who have characterized the acquisition of literacy and writing as an essential mark of the slave narrative.

7. "From Fugitive Slave to Man of Letters: The Conversion of Frederick Douglass," *Journal of Narrative Technique* 16 (1986): 55.

8. Equiano in *Great Slave Narratives*, ed. Arna Bontemps (Boston, 1969), weaves into his narrative his progressive steps toward a more complete education. At one point—right before he is sold by Pascal—he makes an explicit identification between his desire for freedom and education (62). Pennington, though trying to demonstrate Christian forbearance in his narrative, makes clear that his greatest resentment comes from having been "robbed of my education" (246). Having gone to great lengths of disguise in order to mask their illiteracy as they fled, the first thing William and Ellen Craft attend to during their first three weeks of relative freedom in Philadelphia is learning how to spell and write their own names (317). All three narratives are reprinted in Bontemps's collection.

9. See Houston A. Baker, Jr.'s introduction to the *Narrative of the Life of Frederick Douglass: An American Slave* (New York, 1982). All page numbers refer to this edition of the *Narrative*. In her introduction to an excerpt from *Incidents* in *Invented Lives: Narratives of Black Women, 1860–1960* (New York, 1987), Mary Helen Washington also notes specific parallels between the rhetorical arguments of Jacobs and Douglass.

10. Michael Meyer, ed., *The Narrative and Selected Writings of Frederick Douglass* (New York, 1984), xv.

11. John Sekora takes for the title of an essay, "Mr. Editor, If You Please," in *Callaloo* 17 (1994): 614, Douglass's reply when asked what title of address he preferred.

12. Niemtzow, "Problematic of Self in Autobiography," in *The Art of Slave Narrative: Original Essays in Criticism and Theory*, ed. John Sekora and Darwin Turner (Macomb, IL: Western Illinois University, 1982), 56.

13. "Frederick Douglass: Literacy and Paternalism," *Raritan* (6:2): 109.

14. Andrews, *To Tell*, 14.

15. Frances Smith Foster, " 'In Respect to Females . . .': Differences in the Portrayals of Women by Male and Female Narrators," *Black American Literature Forum* 15 (1981): 66.

16. *Self-Discovery and Authority in Afro-American Literature* (Cambridge, Mass., 1987), 4.

17. "In the First Place: Making Frederick Douglass and the Afro-American Narrative Tradition," in *Critical Essays on Frederick Douglass*, ed. William L. Andrews (New York, 1991), 207.

18. Davis and Gates, *The Slave's Narrative*, xxiii.

19. As Kari Winter succinctly reminds her readers in *Subject of Slavery, Agents of Change: Women and Power in Gothic Novels and Slave Narratives, 1790–1865* (Athens, Ga., 1992), 3, the exploitation of slave labor that developed in the Southern United States "was based primarily on race [but] secondarily on gender."

20. White, *Ar'n't I A Woman?* 141.

21. See, for example, Carol Smith-Rosenberg's "The Female World of Love and Ritual: Relations between Women in Nineteenth-Century America," *Signs* 1 (1975): 1–29.

22. Many contemporary researchers conclude that most women value relationships over, for example, abstract notions of right and wrong. Women's decisions often flow from what they have come to understand through their relationships. As May Field Belenky et al. demonstrate in *Women's Ways of Knowing: The Development of Self, Voice, and Mind* (New York, 1986), this proves true in women's understanding of themselves and their world view. Carol Gilligan argues in *In a Different Voice* (Cambridge, Mass., 1982) that women develop moral choices in terms of relationships, and the work of Nancy Chodorow, "Family Structure and Feminine Personality," *Woman, Culture and Society*, ed. M. Z. Rosaldo and L. Lamphere (Stanford, 1974), as well as those of Jean Baker Miller, *Toward a New Psychology of Women* (Boston, 1976), supports Gilligan's argument. Deborah Tannen's findings about the ways women handle language also points to the importance of relationships in women's lives. As Nancy Chodorow notes, "The Feminine personality [often] comes to define itself in relation and connection to other people more than masculine personality does" (43–44). Mary Belenky and her collaborators further argue that women develop their understanding of themselves, their worlds, and even their ethical sense through what they learn "in relationships with friends and teachers, life crises, and community involvements" (4). In her books on sociolinguistics focusing on the centrality of spoken language and relationships in the lives of women, Deborah Tannen too posits that each woman tends to come to grips with her environment "as an individual in a network of connections" (25).

23. "'In a Different Voice': Male and Female Narratives of Religious Conversion in Post Revolutionary America," *American Quarterly* 41 (1989): 39.

24. "Black Womanhood in Nineteenth-Century America: Subversion and Self-Construction in Two Women's Autobiographies," *American Quarterly* 43 (1991): 203.

25. In "Race, Gender, and Cultural Context in Zora Neale Hurston's *Dust Tracks on a Road*," in *Life Lines: Theorizing Women's Autobiography*, ed. Bella Brodzki and Celeste Schenck (Ithaca, 1988), Ellie Y. McKay emphasizes that "in constructing their personal narratives, black women negotiate the dangerous shoals of white male and female role and class oppression and white and black male sexism. Connected to black men by the history of class and race, to white women by sex and the configuration of gender roles, and to both by the politics of writing from the outside, they have, from the beginning, created unique selves-in-writing to document their individual and collective experiences" (177). Female fugitives and former slave women respond to the common pressures they share with former male slaves to strive for full freedom and with other women to perceive themselves as connected to community.

26. Luke, for instance, the brutalized slave of a dying but depraved psychopath, tricks the man's heirs into giving him a pair of the dead man's old pants

into which Luke has secreted a goodly cache of money (192–93). Jacobs explicitly praises Luke's having acted with the "wisdom of serpents." All page numbers for Jacobs's text refer to Jean Fagan Vellin's edition of *Incidents in the Life of a Slave Girl* (Cambridge, Mass., 1967).

27. Yet the reader may wonder at this point in the narrative whether Jacobs's grandmother's anger might not be directed in part at herself as well as toward Harriet. Despite Jacobs's care to name her father as well as her mother, Jacobs never names her maternal grandfather. Her grandmother's distress may stem, in part, from seeing Jacobs repeating her own mistakes.

28. Jacobs's plight reminds one of Frances Kemble's story found in *Journal of a Residence on a Georgian Plantation in 1838–1839*, ed. John A. Scott (New York, 1975), about an overseer on her husband's plantation who explained that he never worried about his wife's slave running away once she got to free territory. He noted that "I take care when my wife goes North with the children, to send Lucy with her; her children are down here and I defy all the abolitionists in creation to get her to stay North" (344).

29. While much of the current discussion of what Frances Smith Foster, *Witnessing Slavery: The Development of Ante-bellum Slave Narratives* (Westport, Conn., 1979), 55, calls Jacobs's "literary embellishments" focuses on Jacobs's use of and limitation by sentimental fiction, some of the most useful are Hazel Carby's exploration in *Reconstructing Womanhood: The Emergence of the Afro-American Woman Novelist* (New York, 1989) of the "variety of narrative forms" (61) Jacobs and other black women writers utilized to break out of the procrustean bed of either the black male-dominated slave narrative form or the white female tradition of "true womanhood" found in sentimental fiction; and Valeria Smith's parallel exploration with perhaps more emphasis on "class, race, and gender analysis" (43). Smith also emphasizes the limits for Jacobs's purposes of both the sentimental novel (41–42) and the male slave narrative (34).

30. Elizabeth Fox-Genovese outlines her belief in "My Statue, My Self: Autobiographical Writings of Afro-American Women," in *The Private Self: Theory and Practice of Women's Autobiographical Writings*, ed. Shari Benstock (Chapel Hill, 1988), that Jacobs and her contemporary Harriet Wilson "harbored deep bitterness toward northern society in general and northern women in particular" (71). A reading of Jacobs's letters found at the back of the Yellin edition of *Incidents*, including those letters describing to Amy Post Jacobs's unhappy encounters with Stowe, certainly appear to give Jacobs reason for bitterness.

31. Douglass ran into similar trouble with his white sponsors. William Lloyd Garrison had helped Douglass to a career as a public speaker, an effective orator at abolitionist meetings. Yet as Douglass changed from an object of concern, a live illustration at abolition meetings, to an independent thinker and writer who crafted his own language and focused his own message's point for his own rather than Garrison's ends, the two became estranged.

32. Jean Yellin has identified Mrs. Bruce (480) and most of the other significant players in *Incidents* for modern readers of the narrative.

33. Ann Taves in "Spiritual Purity and Sexual Shame: Religious Themes in the Writing of Harriet Jacobs," *Church History* 56 (1987), has explored the interconnections between Jacobs's "intense, female-oriented family relationships" (60) and her religious sense. Taves believes Jacobs accepted the association women whom she admired made between sexual purity with spirituality. Taves sees *Incidents* as a healthy adult "movement toward autonomy" (720) because in the narrative, Jacobs publicly acknowledges the choices she has made as a slave.

34. Barbara Welter, "The Cult of True Womanhood: 1800–1860," in *Dimity Convictions: The American Woman in the Nineteenth Century*, ed. Barbara Welter (Athens, Ohio, 1976), 21.

35. In Sekora and Turner, *The Art of Slave Narrative*, 104.

36. *Narrative of Sojourner Truth, a Bondswoman of Olden Time*, comp. Olive Gilbert (Battle Creek, Mich., 1878; rpt. New York, 1991), 133–34.

37. *Behind the Scenes: or Thirty Years a Slave and Four Years in the White House* (1868; rpt. New York, 1989), xi.

38. William L. Andrews, ed., *Six Women's Slave Narratives*, [Mary Prince, Old Elizabeth, Mattie J. Jackson, Lucy Delaney, Kate Drumgoold, Annie Burton] (New York, 1988), 17.

39. William Andrews's *Six Women's Slave Narratives*, for example, has been chosen to illustrate typical stories; the occupations of the earlier accounts typify those of former slave women living in the North. Certainly before the Civil War and Emancipation, educational and professional opportunities for black women were even more restricted than the limited opportunities available to white women.

40. Dorothy Sterling, ed., *We Are Your Sisters: Black Women in the Nineteenth Century* (New York, 1984), 72, 87, 97, 119–50.

41. Orlando Patterson, *Slavery and Social Death: A Comparative Study* (Cambridge, Mass., 1982), 13.

II   Theorizing the Female Subject: Who Writes, How, and Why?

These selections demonstrate that women autobiographers face distinctive obstacles and have unique motivations for writing the stories of their lives. Language itself reflects hierarchies at work in the larger society, where men have typically had greater freedom and power than women. With that in mind, the grammatical building blocks that form an autobiography seem well suited to the male writer, especially if we think about the egocentric, singular nature of the first-person pronoun "I." Women, in contrast, have been taught that they should not call attention to their accomplishments and that their lives have meaning only in relation to others as wives or caregivers.

The woman autobiographer, then, may write with a certain amount of self-consciousness or hesitation because she feels uncomfortable with the masculinist "I," which translates into doubt about her legitimacy as a writer. Such self-consciousness may manifest itself both thematically and structurally. The autobiographer may express uncertainty about her life, ideas, or feelings. At the same time, she may write using a double voice, one that first affirms and then undermines her authority as an autobiographer. The double voice emerges because women see themselves in two dramatically different ways. They see themselves through the eyes of society as the stereotypical feminine object. On the other hand, women have visions of themselves and aspirations for their lives that conflict with the constraining stereotypes that dictate what a woman should be and do.

Though the selections reveal some similarities in women's writing styles, they also point to significant differences among the kinds of women who write autobiographies. For example, Simone de Beauvoir belongs to an intellectual community where writing is viewed with respect. Although she feels like an outsider in that male-dominated environment, she nonetheless has support for her endeavors as a writer. Ann Rayson examines autobiographies that, in contrast, are hindered by the writers' families, their Japanese-American communities, and, both actively and inadvertently, the larger American society. Logically we would expect these factors to combine and repeatedly undermine the strong sense of self that every autobiographer must possess. Invisibility and silence serve as their own incentives to write, however, because the autobiographer can make her voice heard only if she speaks out and demands to be noticed.

6

Reading for the Doubled Discourse of American Women's Autobiography*

~

Helen M. Buss

Helen M. Buss's essay suggests that American women's autobiography can best be read by combining seemingly contradictory approaches to the subject, those that see the autobiographical self as a stable, unified individual (formalist) and those that regard the subject as fragmented, decentered, and dominated by forces largely beyond her control (poststructuralist). Both approaches are useful in dealing with the "doubled discourse" of women's autobiography, which has to tell two stories at the same time. One story is that of the stable self of traditional autobiography. However, because this autobiographical self has historically been a male, a second story is simultaneously required to do justice to the female self and female experience.

Buss examines autobiographies by Maya Angelou, Maxine Hong Kingston, and Mary McCarthy to show how they alternate between the literary techniques of hyperbole (overstatement, exaggeration) and meiosis (understatement, belittling). With hyperbolic extravagance, the writers suggest an active, independent female subject; at the same time, meiotic techniques lessen the woman, suggesting her domination by other people and by both physical and psychological circumstances. The three autobiographers depict divided female selves who have to create their own identities through their experiences of constant tension between being free and being oppressed. The difficult process of constructing an identity in these autobiographies suggests the insufficiency of options currently available to American women.

*From Helen M. Buss, "Reading for the Doubled Discourse of American Women's Autobiography," *a/b: Auto/Biography Studies* 6 (1991): 95–108. Reprinted by permission of *a/b: Auto/Biography Studies* and the author.

Helen M. Buss is professor of English at the University of Calgary where she teaches Canadian Literature, women's literature and lifewriting. She is author of Mapping Our Selves: Canadian Women's Autobiography, *which won the Gabrielle Roy Prize for the best critical study on a Canadian topic. She is currently at work on a study of contemporary women's uses of the memoir form.*

A LICE JARDINE WRYLY OBSERVES early in *Gynesis* that the American feminist "proceeds from a *belief* in a world from which—even philosophers admit—*Truth* has disappeared" (31). Although the generalization (implying all American feminists are committed to this view) deserves questioning, she does refer us to serious tensions that exist between American feminist positions and other ideological and philosophical positions: especially feminists and poststructuralists, feminists and liberal humanists. Jardine's observation reminds us as well that American feminism, in contrast to French feminism, has its roots, not so much in an academic intellectual community, as in a broadly based women's movement, one which in its beginnings was strongly influenced by liberal humanist beliefs in the possibility of social change through the assumption of personal responsibility and the choice of social action. Thus, with a strong ethical agenda always implied in their theoretical explorations, American feminists have difficulty accepting poststructuralist and postmodern views on subjectivity. As Nancy Miller argues regarding women writers and subjectivity, "the postmodern decision that the Author is dead, and subjective agency along with him, does not necessarily work for women and prematurely forecloses the question of identity for them" (106).

This difference has serious implications for literary critics, dependent as we are on theorists for the discourses we use as the tools of our trade. Feminist literary critics do not wish to adopt formalist discourses that assume a coherent individualism, both in terms of the author of a literary work and the representations of human subjects in the work. Such a stance would assume a subjectivity for females that historically and culturally has not been the case. At the same time, to assume the theory and practice of textuality advocated by poststructuralists such as Barthes in "The Death of the Author" could be equally inhibiting to the exploration of women's texts.

I hope to demonstrate, within the boundaries of my own special interest, women's autobiography, that with qualifications, critical practices derived from both formalist and poststructural discourses can be usefully adapted to the reading of texts. The tension and interest involved in the collision of humanist views on individuality and of poststructuralist views on subjectivity is nowhere more obvious than in autobiography, that mode of writing that is especially concerned with subjectivity. To read with only poststructuralist theories of subjectivity in mind yields a model of the female self that is inadequate given female experience. To begin by reading from a position of literary formalism, in this case to show how these autobiographers develop rhetorical strategies that move dialectically between hyperbole and meiosis, is to prepare the "ground" for a more sufficient poststructuralist and psychoanalytic examination of female subjectivity as expressed in these works. Contrasting reading strategies derived from both theoretical positions can be helpful in locating appropriate female centered views of subjectivity, ones which resonate with the ethical concerns central to a feminist way of being in the world.

In her essay "Changing Faces of Heroism," Susanna Egan discovers a tendency for contemporary autobiographies to break the established heroic molds and describe unfinished crises which require that we reassess the familiar autobiographical patterns. That the "heroic" archetype is losing ground will be no surprise to readers of American fiction and it would seem unsurprising that American autobiographers can no longer, with any sincerity, cast their stories in the stereotypical forms that have been popular from Ben Franklin to Malcolm X. It was Egan who described these forms in her book *Patterns of Experience in Autobiography*, and they represent life writings that generally characterize childhood as Edenic, youth as a journey, maturity as a time of crises confronted and overcome, and old age as the stage when the individual shares his life through confession, formalized in the case of autobiographers through the act of writing.

What was consistent in the stages of this archetypal patterning was the concept of the "self" as an "atomized privacy," as Sidonie Smith puts it in *A Poetics of Women's Autobiography* (48). Smith, borrowing the ideas of Mikhail Bakhtin, describes the now fading ideology of individualism that supports the kind of patterning that was assumed in the past. With the greater belief in contemporary culture that the individual is not a "unified and unique core" but the product of a "variety of discourses" (Smith 48), we are bound to see some inroads into the strict adherence to the patterns described by Egan in her study of nineteenth-century autobiographers, and these inroads are most pronounced in the autobiographies of American women.

In women's autobiographies we can see what Smith describes as the "two stories" phenomenon, a doubled discourse intensely portrayed, as each female autobiographer struggles "with conflicting purposes and postures, [sliding] from one fiction of self-representation to another as she attends to two stories, those doubled figures of selfhood in the ideology of gender" (50). On the one hand, by choosing to write autobiography at all the woman autobiographer enters the "discourse of man" seeking "cultural and literary authority," for an idea of selfhood that is individualistic, oriented toward separation of self, and attuned to personal achievement as a means of self-definition (50). On the other hand, she wishes to tell of an alternate subjectivity, one characterized in male culture as "absence, silence, vulnerability, immanence, interpenetration, the nonlogocentric, the unpredictable, the childish" (40). By Lacanian definition these are the very attributes suppressed by the male child in order to enter the world of the adult, to leave the world of the "imaginary" for the world of the "symbolic," to cast off the silent world of the mother for the discourse, the language of the father. In short, female autobiographers while insisting on their "individuality" by the very fact of writing, cling to the world of the mother, to those qualities we ascribe to the feminine, which seem in direct opposition to those attributes of selfhood traditionally portrayed in the patterns of autobiography.

Smith's theoretical groundwork allows us to locate these texts in an ideological context. By reading these women's texts in a traditional literary context, that is, in terms of the formal literary devices they exhibit (and without necessarily attributing the patterns I discover to authorial authority), and then by placing these texts in the framework of critical viewpoint that derives from poststructuralist theory, I hope to indicate something more about the significance of the subjectivity they represent. These implications are not obvious in Smith's ideological study, but have great importance for American feminist thought in the wake of such works as her *Poetics*. In the three women's autobiographies I will consider, Maya Angelou's *I Know Why the Caged Bird Sings*, Maxine Hong Kingston's *The Woman Warrior: Memoirs of a Girlhood among Ghosts*, and Mary McCarthy's *Memories of a Catholic Girlhood*, the "double story" phenomenon is expressed through the coexistence of hyperbolic and meiotic devices which figure the divided selves that these women possess.

Perhaps nowhere is the use of hyperbole more dramatically present than in the opening pages of Maya Angelou's autobiography of growing up black and female in the American South prior to the civil rights movement. For her debut in a church choir the child Maya is clothed in a dress of "lavender taffeta" that rustles every time she breathes. It is the garment that will make her a "movie star," make her "look like one of the sweet little white girls who were everybody's dream of what was right with the world" (1). The dress creates a girl with "angel's dust sprinkled" over her face, a self that will have admirers begging forgiveness because they did not recognize her magic, a self that is really white, with long, blond hair. Only through the action of a "cruel fairy stepmother . . . jealous of [her] beauty" had she been "turned into a too-big Negro girl, with nappy black hair, broad feet and space between her teeth that would hold a number-two pencil" (2). Thus, in the hyperbolic diction of the fairy tale, and the self-mocking irony of exaggeration, does Angelou introduce her two selves: one self which is an imagined version of the privileged white, female movie star, and the other image of self, the degraded one actually offered to her as a black girl in society, one so lacking in positive self-definition that the incident of her appearance in the church choir in her lavender dress ends when in her fear of the attention of others she cannot control her sphincter. Her lack of physical control reflects her lack of personality integration: ". . . I knew I'd have to let it go, or it would probably run right back up to my head and my poor head would burst like a dropped watermelon, and all the brains and spit and tongue and eyes would roll all over the place" (3). These extremes—an inflated self, worshiped, separate, and a self so lacking in substance, so vulnerable that it cannot hold the parts of its being together—illustrate the two versions of subjectivity that contend with one another in these autobiographies.

Kingston begins *The Woman Warrior* with the story her mother told her at her first menstruation, a story meant to illustrate the terrifying potential as well as the ultimate powerlessness of the female condition. It is the story of "No Name Woman," which is also the title of the first chapter of Kingston's memoirs. To begin an autobiographical text with the story of an aunt who has been cursed from the family, deprived even of her name, for the crime of an illegitimate pregnancy, and to end that chapter by telling of the aunt's suicide by drowning herself in the family well, would seem to identify one's self with the extremist degree of female degradation. Alternately, Kingston offers in her book's second section, "White Tigers," a romantic, fantasy version of self she carried as a child: a heroine, a swordswoman, who is taken magically away from her family, trained in the martial arts, and returned to become the avenger of wrongs done her people. The purpose of this heroic self is to oppose the other view of female identity. Ironically, both visions of womanhood are given to the child Maxine by her mother, Brave Orchid. As Kingston observes of her mother's influence: "She said I would grow up a wife and a slave, but she taught me the song of the warrior woman, Fa Mu Lan. I would have to grow up a warrior woman" (24).

The hyperbolic technique of Mary McCarthy's *Memories of a Catholic Girlhood* adds another element to reinforce these spectacular and contrasting visions of the self. Her method is contained in the format of her book. She alternates chapters of narrative in which she describes her orphaned childhood in the language of mythic narrative with essaylike interchapters in which she questions not only her own perceptions of the past but argumentatively confronts the patriarchal worldview in which she was raised.

She goes on to describe how she and her brothers sleep in a room called the "poor relation" (29) in the house of their paternal and Catholic grandparents. This house has a "hierarchy of chambers" (29) in the care of a "grizzled Galahad" (31) of a grandfather and a grandmother who is an "ugly, severe old woman with a monstrous balcony of a bosom" (32). In such mock-heroic images, in the diction of a satiric fairy tale, McCarthy weaves her narrative chapters. In the interchapters, which begin with one entitled "To the Reader," she continues her ironic undermining of her own narrative by addressing us in a direct, discursive prose. By doing so she undercuts the sympathetic vision of the brave, romantic, orphan-girl, a Cinderella of sorts, that she builds in the narrative chapters. In fact, the McCarthy we meet in the interchapters—intellectual, abrasive, mocking, angry, anti-Catholic, and anti-American by turns—is another hyperbole that negates the first.

All three of these autobiographies engage in this practice: the building of an almost impossibly extreme and painful childhood condition (the opposite of Edenic), made believable and sympathetic by their descriptive power, in which one self-concept opposes another. The technique undermines our sureness, undermines the notion that any consistent version of the self is possible. The ironic result of the opposing stances is that one hyperbole cancels the other and we are left with a lessened vision of femaleness, one that is reinforced by each writer as she narrates various episodes that construct a meiotic version of the self.

The central event in Maya Angelou's childhood is her rape by her mother's lover when she is eight. It is not the physical injury or the man's crime that Angelou dwells on (in fact these seem extremely understated), but the way in which, perceiving herself as guilty, she reacts to the rape, the hospital stay, the court trial, and the revenge murder of her mother's lover by her mother's brothers. She offers this self-negation:

> Just my breath, carrying my words out, might poison people and they'd curl up and die like . . . black fat slugs.
>
> I had to stop talking.
>
> I discovered that to achieve perfect silence all I had to do was to attach myself leechlike to sound. . . . I walked into rooms where people were laughing, their voices hitting the walls like stones, and I simply stood still—in the midst of a riot of sound. After a minute or two silence would rush into the room from its hiding place because I had eaten up all the sounds. (73)

The effect of this reaction is (while making the child's presence a death pall in the lives of her mother and her relatives) to create a vision of self that is not a person at all, but rather a silence, an absence, a black hole.

The sense of the damaged female self as a vulnerability, which can be filled with any dangerous, hurtful substance, is one we see also in Kingston's account. Two female victims figure prominently in her childhood and act as self-surrogates in her story. The first is Moon Orchid, an aunt who is brought to America by the efforts of Brave Orchid in a plan to revitalize the marriage of the aunt whose husband, although supporting his Chinese wife over the years, has married again in the United States. The result of the effort is failure, and the personality of Moon Orchid disintegrates until she dies in an insane asylum. Throughout the telling of Moon Orchid's story, Kingston emphasizes the ways in which her aunt depended on her traditional role as Chinese wife, even without the presence of a husband. When this was taken from her by the reality of her husband's American existence and the nontraditional life she herself has to live in America, she finds there is no substance to her self, feels she is being invaded from all directions by imagined enemies, and eventually cannot function.

Closer to the child Maxine's own fears of self-negation is a young girl at her school who is shy and silent, dependent on the protection of an older sister: "I hated the younger sister, the quiet one," Kingston confesses, "I hated her when she was the last chosen for her team and I, the last chosen for my team. I hated her for her China-doll hair cut. I hated her at music time for the wheezes that came out of her plastic flute" (201–2). Kingston uses this frail child as a scapegoat for her anger at her own lack, her fear that she may not be a person at all. She persecutes the girl, pinching her, pulling her hair, threatening her in an effort to make her talk. She believes that by talking the girl may establish some personhood, when in fact she is, by bullying, trying to establish her own personhood, albeit in a negative manner. But she fails to draw anything but tears and snot from the child. And Kingston's own reaction to her attempt to establish selfhood through bullying is to become ill, an internalization of the pain she inflicted on another, in a wasting, unnamed illness that lasts a full eighteen months, during which she is completely bedridden, cared for as a small baby. This proof of her own nonexistence as a person is satisfying to her. She observes: "I could have no visitors, no other relatives, no villagers. My bed was against the west window, and I watched the seasons change the peach tree. I had a bell to ring for help. I used a bedpan. It was the best year and a half of my life. Nothing happened" (211–12). This sense of erasure of self as preferable to the painful reality of self-conscious, ego-defined self, presents a meiotic vision of the female child about to enter puberty.

McCarthy describes puberty for the female child, as illustrated by her experiences in a Catholic convent boarding school. McCarthy, at twelve, desires more than anything to be "recognized at whatever price"

(110). Despite her high academic standing, or perhaps because of it, the nuns have never awarded her the coveted "pink ribbon" that gives status to exemplary girls. She describes herself as being in a "cold, empty gambler's mood, common to politicians and adolescents" (111). She decides to pretend to lose her faith, and strikes exaggerated poses as the lost soul unable to pray or make confession. McCarthy is sent to see a Jesuit known for his ability to confound intellectual doubt. The twelve-year-old finds she enjoys the intellectual give-and-take of argument and is beginning to actually believe what she says—she is losing her faith. But instead of the pleasurable feeling of mastery the arrival of abstract reasoning should give the girl, she finds that she "seemed to have divided into two people, one slyly watching . . . the other anxious and aghast at the turn the interview was taking" (118). In the meantime, by a coincidence worthy of a black comedy, the young Mary has injured her thigh at sports and the cut bleeds into her sheets one night. The nuns assume she is "becoming a woman" (134) and no amount of explanation will persuade them otherwise. They are convinced that Mary's failure to admit menstruation is the same as her failure to admit the comfort of faith—another proof of her eccentricity.

McCarthy finds her solution to both quandaries in elaborate pretense. She pretends to have a dream that restores her faith miraculously and she cuts herself each month to bleed into the sanitary pads that the nuns keep insisting she needs. The arrival of female adolescence involves the child in hypocrisies and dissembling as the public images of correct female behavior fail to meet any resonance with what is actually happening in the personality or body.

All three of these autobiographers present exaggerated behavior stances to the world during their adolescent years as a result of the incongruities of their divided selves. Angelou becomes a delinquent, stabbing her father's lover, and a runaway, living in a makeshift adolescent drifters' camp. Kingston strikes "bad girl" poses, refusing to cook, breaking dishes, screaming rude remarks to her parents' friends, announcing she will be a lumberjack when she grows up, and aggressively bringing home straight A's from school, as if she were a boy. As the adult Kingston ironically observes: "Isn't a bad girl almost a boy?" (56). McCarthy describes herself as a comic paradox alternating between exaggerated public feats of being the best student actor and the best Latin student and a moody idiocy in which she falls in love with every sports hero and allows her grades to drop.

The resolutions which these autobiographers offer to their adolescent identity crises have all the markings of "unfinished crises," in which as adults they seek some conditional union between their split selves. Angelou seeks female wholeness in the birth of her son when she is sixteen, but the reader recognizes the new implications for self-divisiveness in the condition of motherhood given her economic situation. Kingston learns to use her mother's traditional storytelling as a basis to make her own stories, thus reading herself into an identity as a cultural mediator. Artistically speaking, she "gives 'birth' to herself as the daughter who has passed through the body and the word of the mother," thus joining the imaginary and the symbolic (Smith 173). But it needs to be said that Kingston also confesses that in her lived life outside of story-making she continues to become sick, dependent, and empty every time she returns to her mother's house. McCarthy enters an examination of her maternal grandmother's life in an attempt to understand the silent part of herself that makes a mockery of all her inflated public poses.

For me, McCarthy's ending is the most thought-provoking. She leaves us with her confession of her lifelong fascination with her maternal grandmother, a Jewish woman who lived a pampered life of female consumerism at the center of her Protestant husband's patriarchal home. McCarthy is able to face her own connection with this woman who represents all the female weaknesses she fears. She finds under the vain, selfish externals of her grandmother's clothing and secret bathroom rituals that the woman is a tragic but intensely attractive figure. In a moment late in the autobiography she describes how as a young girl she watches her grandmother eat apricots: "My grandmother's voracity, so finical, so selective, chilled me with its mature sensuality, which was just the opposite of hunger. I conceived an aversion to apricots . . . from having watched her with them, just as though I had witnessed what Freud calls the primal scene. Now I, too, am fond of them and whenever I choose one from a plate, I think of my grandmother's body, full-fleshed, bland, smooth and plump, cushioning in itself, close held—a secret, like the flat brown seed of the apricot" (225). Thus, in this understated moment of contact with the dark female interior does McCarthy tentatively offer, not an absence, a black hole, but a vast potential for female fecundity and with it the possibility of healing the divided self of her public persona which is felt to be individualistic and solid and a private self that has been so unknown and misunderstood as to have been debilitating.

The careful reader senses that only by making that other self one's own, reaching for the fruit of its fleshy darkness, will the split between the hyperbolic and meiotic division of self be healed. It is interesting to note that it is in this last portrait of McCarthy's autobiography that the split between narrative and interrogating essay ends. The style of the section, entitled "Ask Me No Questions," incorporates the questioning into its own narrative, and in doing so the questions become less abrasively aggressive. But, ironically, they offer a closure (or lack thereof) which is more profoundly and ideologically disturbing to humanist values of subjectivity.

There is a sense that there may be no language available to McCarthy to reach for that "secret" place inside femaleness. The forms of representation offered contemporary American women by society and its discourses may not be able to contain the world she is reaching for. In fact, McCarthy's own representation of herself at the end of the text is telling: She is rushing around her grandmother's room grabbing at combs, brushes, perfumes, pincushions as her grandmother screams for the "watchemacallit," the mirror she can no longer name. McCarthy and her grandmother are women trying to communicate from a position of insufficiency, in a symbol system that does not speak to them.

This traditional reading of the texts for meaning brings into question the careful optimism with which these three writers represent their lives. In fact, for me, the kind of reading I have just made becomes a way of opening texts to other kinds of inquiries, other discourses. It is at this point that poststructuralist methodologies can become useful to feminist readings.

Ihab Hassan, in *The Postmodern Turn*, observes that "autobiography is rife, running both in high and low repute: it enjoys the sublime attention of literary theory, suffers the base association with cultural narcissism. More to the point: it has become the form that the contemporary imagination seeks to recover" (147). It is in this context that I would recommend we consider works such as the ones under discussion. But in typical texts descriptive of postmodern literary production, women's autobiographies (in fact women's writing generally) are largely excluded. To read Hassan's books, or Brian McHale's *Postmodern Fiction,* is to confirm the male bias of such discussions. One contemporary critic who does include many references to women's texts, in fact to one of the three texts discussed here (i.e., Kingston's *The Woman Warrior*), is Linda Hutcheon. In *The Poetics of Postmodernism* she considers certain women writers as part of the eccentric phenomenon in postmodernism: "the off-center, ineluctably identified with the center it desires but is denied" (60–61). These "eccentrics" wish to locate their subjectivity through the writing act. Quoting Derrida, Hutcheon insists that "the subject is absolutely indispensable. I don't destroy the subject; I situate it" (159).

But much postmodern literature, in matters of subjectivity, emphasizes the de-centering of the subject, its fragmentation, its "death." From Vonnegut's *Slaughterhouse Five* to Barth's *Lost in the Funhouse*, male subjects deconstruct themselves, admit their lack of ego center, learn to live with (if not play with) their multiplicity of mirrored selves. But as Hutcheon observes in her conclusion, "Feminist theory and art . . . know they must first inscribe female subjectivity before they can contest it" (226). The three autobiographers in question perform the double and ironic inscription of both gesturing toward and contesting female subjectivity at the same time. In doing so they highlight a particular concern in postmodern thinking on the self.

Angelou's *Caged Bird*, in its use of traditional conventions of the realist novel, also exposes that tradition's inability to encompass the female condition and thus leads the reader to perform an act of deconstructive reading in order to more fully comprehend Angelou's "self." For example, the final chapters of Angelou's text, by a traditional reading for meaning, plot the young girl's growing consciousness of her body, the shedding of illusion and the entrance into heterosexual activity and maternity. The birth of the boy child marks the girl's achievement of womanhood and her reunion with her mother in the mutuality of their care for the child. In short, we are offered the happy ending of a traditional realistic novel wherein the problematics of the plot situation are resolved within the strictures of society. Lennard J. Davis observes in *Resisting Novels* that the plots of such works are a "devotion to consistency and the subsuming of events under a more totalizing structure" (202). But the penultimate chapter 35 of Angelou's text undermines the "consistency" of the "totalizing structure" of chapter 36.

In this section the young Angelou begins to discover her growing body, confuses her reading about hermaphrodites with what she has heard whispered about lesbians. Her mother, using the authority of *Webster's Dictionary*, explains to the girl that her development is normal, and that she is not a lesbian. A few weeks later Angelou is moved by the sight of another girl's breasts and all her former doubts about her "womanhood" return: "I wanted to be a woman, but that seemed to me to be a world to which I was to be eternally refused entrance." Angelou theorizes that "what I needed was a boyfriend. A boyfriend would clarify my position to the world and, even more important, to myself. A boyfriend's acceptance of me would guide me into that strange and exotic land of frills and femininity" (238). Even as she constructs this "exotic land," she mocks it by associating only "frills" with such boyfriend-defined "femininity." As her entrance into this land continues, its barrenness becomes its chief characteristic. Her act of sex with a boy she hardly knows culminates "in the knee which forced my legs . . . laborious gropings, pullings, yankings and jerkings" during which "not one word was spoken" (240). Thus, while the totalizing effects of novelistic conventions drive toward the birth of the child as "happy ending," the ironic language of the text implies that the coldness of entry into womanhood through concourse with a male offers nothing to compete with the sensual detail of her experience of womanhood through her talk with her mother about maturation and her admiration of her girlfriend's body. Thus the seemingly most "conventional" of these three autobiographical texts (in terms of form) is also radically disruptive of its own conventions.

Kingston's *Memoirs*, by ambitiously taking on American and Chinese cultures and their contrasting identity stereotypes in formal measures that range from short story, through biography to mythic narrative, creates a subjectivity that challenges the traditional divisions between history and literature and writes the postmodern "historiographic metafiction," the hybrid form that Hutcheon proposes as generically central to postmodernism (xii). In fact, in her chapter "Decentering the Postmodern," Hutcheon foregrounds Kingston's *Memoirs* as a text that "links the postmodern metafictional concerns of narration and language directly to her race and gender" (70). Nowhere is this more obvious than in the way Kingston plays with the various meanings of "voice." Brave Orchid claims she cut her daughter's frenum in order that she not be tongue-tied: "Your tongue would be able to move in any language. You'll be able to speak languages that are completely different from one another" (190). These words are at the beginning of the section of "A Song for a Barbarian Reed Pipe," in which Kingston's text self-consciously comments on its own creation. It is figuratively, if not literally, true that Brave Orchid's action as mother has made the many languages of Kingston's text both possible and necessary, as the chapters can be seen as different languages of an identity in process: formulating, disintegrating, reforming.

At the same time the act of frenum-cutting is analogous to clitoridectomy, as each affects the ways in which females mediate the world and each comes painfully to the child through the mediation of the mother (Smith 168). As images of how wounding creates femininity, they help us feel Kingston's situation. Kingston describes the conflicting demands of learning to be feminine through being silent and learning to be feminine by obediently speaking up when so ordered. Her voice becomes "a crippled animal running on broken legs. You could hear splinters in my voice, bones rubbing jagged against one another. I was loud, though. I was glad I didn't whisper" (196). Neither does her text whisper as it works its way through its various splinters to the song of the reed pipe, the voice of a woman sold into slavery who creates her songs from the initial wound. Her songs "seemed to be Chinese, but the barbarians understood their sadness and anger" (243). In tying her voice metaphor always to the investigation of actual history, the personal autobiographical detail, and actual cultural issues of gender and ethnic identity, as well as using "voices" as a comment on the formal elements of her text, Kingston creates a postmodern "historiographic metafiction." Such a text joins history, theory, and fiction in the way that Hutcheon describes, by which the text's "theoretical self-awareness of history and fiction as human constructs . . . is made the grounds for its rethinking and reworking of the forms and contents of the past" (5).

However, women's autobiography, in creating "historiographic metafiction," does not merely perform the same acts as other postmod-

ern "fictions." In its ability to focus on subjectivity as central to the concerns of postmodernism (through the use of the ground of the intimate
autobiographical account), it extends postmodern thinking on subjectivity. What Kingston is constructing is an "interpellated subject" whose
"discerning" Paul Smith proposes as the "new responsibility" of current
theoretical discourse (152–60). Smith credits recent feminist discourse
with recognizing

> the operations of subjectivity and ideology in a way at once more so-
> phisticated and more appropriate to contemporary conditions than
> most of the other discourses or oppositional movements which have
> arisen. . . . The "subject," in the widest catchment of feminist dis-
> course, has been formulated both in terms of its experience as domi-
> nated "subject" and also as an active and contestatory social agent.
> (152)

Putting aside for the purposes of this discussion Smith's tendency to
appropriate the feminist subjectivity discussion without recognizing its
necessary ties to a feminist ethical agenda, I wish to illustrate how both
subject as "dominated" and subject as "contestatory" are available in
women's autobiographical texts and how the previous close readings of
the texts' hyperbolic and meiotic characteristics aid that illustration.
While Angelou's thoroughly male-defined and male-dominated teenage
identity is contested constantly by her ironic diction and Kingston's self-
displacing "talk-stories" both accept and contest various patriarchal definitions of female selfhood, McCarthy's choice of story interpellated by
essay is perhaps the most paradigmatic illustration of Smith's description of contemporary ideas about selfhood.

In each of her "stories" McCarthy narrates one or other versions of
the "dominated" female subject. In one she is the archetypal Cinderella,
orphaned, neglected, abused. In another she is the rescued Snow White,
cushioned in the comfortable but mindless materialism of her maternal
grandfather's world. But in the intervening essays her investigations into
the hyperbole of her own memory contests, destabilizes and problema-
tizes her narrative. The purpose of this strategy is not to erase the dominated subject before a triumphantly stable and dominant self, but rather
to hold two oppositions in tension with one another, to recognize the importance of both processes in self-formation. This kind of negative capa-
bility is referred to by Paul Smith as the attempt "to locate within the
'subject' *a process*, or a tension which is the product of its having been
called upon to adopt multifarious subject-positions" (157). It is in this
"process," situated at the interface between contradictory versions of self,
that something akin to a choosing subject, something like a responsible

individual can be located, that is, as opposing structures meet, the possibilities for a consciously constructed selfhood multiply. What, in a humanist context, would need to be resolved, in a poststructural context needs to be embraced, creating an identity capable of holding oppositions in a dynamic tension.

In fact, in this regard I believe the practice of these three autobiographies exceeds Smith's view of the contestatory subject. For Smith the construction of a "singular history" remains only a possibility, a utopian concept. Kathleen Martindale contends that Smith, in not referring to feminist art as his exemplum, misses the fact that such writings are already creating counterdiscourse[s] and offer means of exploring or even enlarging the "agential elements in subjected subjects" (10). Martindale's examples of feminist writers who construct "counter histories which provide opportunities for questioning [the] received accounts" (16) of phallocentric texts are recent productions by Québécois Suzanne de Lotbiniere Harwood and black performance artist Adrian Piper. I find that the same "agential elements in subjected subjects" are present in what are now almost "traditional" texts such as Angelou's, Hong Kingston's, and McCarthy's autobiographies. McCarthy's text serves to illustrate these "agential elements." In the last section of *Memories*, in "Ask Me No Questions," narrative is continuously interpellated by the discourse of the essayist so that as she builds the tragic narrative of her imprisoned grandmother, McCarthy both celebrates that narrative and contests it with the opinions and memories of her childhood and adult selves. She takes responsibility for her version of her grandmother and thus her version of selfhood by integrating story and essay. By self-consciously revealing the ways in which she has remembered her experience of her grandmother, she allows the reader to observe the process of the creation of her palimpsest of selfhood.

McCarthy's text ends with the granddaughter realizing that the aging grandmother, still tied to the version of self given her by her mirror, a mirror that in her forgetfulness she cannot any longer name, is tragically dependent on such identity markers even in senility. Of the three autobiographies, this one offers the least disguise of its subversive ideological position, which is that no satisfactory "mirror" of self is available to McCarthy through the various figures of femaleness offered by American society: the mothers, grandmothers, teachers, nuns, friends. The tragedy below each image is revealed. Subjectivity, then, becomes the ability to negotiate between insufficient and often opposing subject positions and yet to create (construct) selfhood through the autobiographical act and by implication to challenge and change the reader's views on subjectivity. I find that all three of these texts offer this challenge to our thinking on subjectivity: both humanist views of a stable individual and poststructural views of the dominated subject.

The insufficiency of subject positions offered by American society to women, as represented in these texts, is exposed by a return to traditional readings, while adopting poststructuralist readings can foreground a feminist version of subjectivity in which the individual is, as Chris Weedon observes in *Feminist Practice and Poststructural Theory*, "an active but not sovereign protagonist" (41).

In using the discourse of poststructuralism as feminists revising our humanist literary training, we can answer Alice Jardine's question at the end of *Gynesis*. She asks: "What happens when women take over this discourse [the discourse named "Gynesis" and marked in male texts by male paranoia] in the name of women?" (263). What happens is that we relearn an old feminist lesson: to write/speak is to empower the self, to learn a new discourse is to interpellate the self with the power of that discourse. We may answer also, as literary critics, that "since an autobiographical text, like any text, will only speak to us in the critical languages in which we address it, why not learn as many critical languages as we can?" (Seibenschuh 152).

Works Cited

Angelou, Maya. *I Know Why the Caged Bird Sings*. Toronto: Bantam, 1970.

Davis, Lennard J. *Resisting Novels: Ideology and Fiction*. New York: Methuen, 1987.

Egan, Susanna. "Changing Faces of Heroism: Some Questions Raised by Contemporary Autobiography." *Biography* 10, no. 1 (Winter 1987): 20–37.

———. *Patterns of Experience in Autobiography*. Chapel Hill: North Carolina University Press, 1984.

Hassan, Ihab. *The Postmodern Turn: Essays in Postmodern Theory and Culture*. Columbus: Ohio State University Press, 1987.

Hutcheon, Linda. *The Poetics of Postmodernism: History, Theory, Fiction*. New York: Routledge, 1988.

Jardine, Alice A. *Gynesis: Configurations of Women and Modernity*. Ithaca, N.Y.: Cornell University Press, 1985.

Kingston, Maxine Hong. *The Woman Warrior: Memoirs of a Girlhood among Ghosts*. New York: Vintage, 1977.

Martindale, Kathleen. "The Ethics of Negotiating Subject Positions." Faculty of Humanities Colloquia Series, University of Calgary. Calgary, November 15, 1989.

McCarthy, Mary. *Memories of a Catholic Girlhood*. San Diego: Harcourt, 1957.

Miller, Nancy K. "Changing the Subject: Authorship, Writing, and the Reader." In *Feminist Studies/Critical Studies*, edited by Teresa de Lauretis, 102–20. Bloomington: Indiana University Press, 1986.

Siebenschuh, William R. "Cognitive Processes and Autobiographical Acts." *Biography* 12, no. 2 (1989): 142–53.

Smith, Paul. *Discerning the Subject.* Minneapolis: University of Minnesota Press, 1988.

Smith, Sidonie. *A Poetics of Women's Autobiography: Marginality and the Fictions of Self-Representation.* Bloomington: Indiana University Press, 1987.

Weedon, Chris. *Feminist Practice Poststructuralist Theory.* Oxford: Blackwell, 1987.

7

Woman as Other, Other as Author, Author as . . . Man? The Au*t*hobiographical Dimension of *The Second Sex**

~

Donna Perreault

Donna Perreault coins the term "authobiography" to describe lifewriting by authors whose works self-consciously foreground the unique emotional, economic, and professional challenges that are part of a writer's life. In this selection, she focuses specifically on Simone de Beauvoir's early autobiographical writing and argues that the texts reflect de Beauvoir's transition from viewing herself as simply a writer to regarding herself as an author. Authorship, Perreault explains, had been regarded by many as an elite, intellectual, and exclusively male institution. Thus, tensions emerge in de Beauvoir's autobiographical writings: she simultaneously describes what it means to be a woman writer and discounts the role femininity plays in shaping her life, fearing that she will undermine her credibility as a serious author. Perhaps nothing reflects that tension better, Perreault suggests, than the groundbreaking treatise she published in 1949, The Second Sex, *in which de Beauvoir reflects on women's roles in a male-dominated world.*

O NE PECULIARITY OF SIMONE DE BEAUVOIR CRITICISM is that it treats de Beauvoir as an author while throwing doubt on her authority. She has important and irrefutable signs of authorship to her credit: her 1954 Goncourt Prize, her world-renowned work on women's situation, and her more than twenty publications legitimize her attraction to growing numbers of critics. But awakening critical attention usually entails awakening critical quandaries. And arguably the most common quandary that feminist and

*From Donna Perreault, "Woman as Other, Other as Author, Author as . . . Man? The Au*t*hobiographical Dimension of *The Second Sex*," *a/b: Auto/Biography Studies* 8 (1993): 286–302. Reprinted by permission of *a/b: Auto/Biography Studies*.

other critics of de Beauvoir's work are discussing concerns the power and authority of her literary and theoretical voice. Whose ideas really authorize *The Second Sex*? What is so original about her memoirs' (seemingly) endless chronology of her life? "[D]id Simone de Beauvoir know the first thing about men and women, most particularly men-and-women, or about tradition, the rationale of sex, the requirements of the heart, or the common sense of loyalties?" (Gallant 963)[1] Even from her most eloquent supporters a certain defensiveness often persists concerning de Beauvoir's originality which eclipses assurances that this "mother" of contemporary feminism will have an enduring authorial reputation.[2] In brief, critics of de Beauvoir's writing typically become critics of de Beauvoir, and their collective judgment— from the 1950s through the 1980s—portrays her as a woman of derivative authority.

To determine whether or not this portrait is appropriate and meaningful, it helps to consider how de Beauvoir's writing may justify it. To be sure, the weighty autobiographical dimension of her entire oeuvre may be partly responsible for the slippage between work and woman in the criticism. But the most compelling invitation to make this elision— and to make it in such a way as to put de Beauvoir's authority in question—comes in the form of her multivolume aut*h*obiography, which spans her life from baby to celebrated *"femme écrivain."*[3] "Aut*h*o-biography," a neologism I invented for the purposes of a larger project, identifies those literary autobiographies which critically examine what is literary about their authors' lives.[4] In contrast to the bulk of literary autobiographies, this subset illuminates the ideologies of authorship current during their authors' lifetimes by interrogating—always from an author's specific, and so finite, subject position—psychological, socioeconomic, and professional realities which attend life as an author. Though the term lacks grace, aut*h*obiography serviceably calls attention to distinctions between "writer" and "author," on one hand, and "self" and "author," on the other. Critics and theorists of autobiography too often blur these distinctions; in so doing, they pass opportunities for reading a discourse of resistance to ideologies of authorship which hinge on masculinist, individualist notions of autonomous subjectivity. Like other twentieth-century aut*h*obiographies, de Beauvoir's monumental project generally queries the relationships between self, writer, and author rather than assuming a simple equivalence between those terms.

Not content just to be an author, de Beauvoir needed *"se mettre en question"* as a woman author in a published life-writing project begun at fifty and continued for more than two decades.[5] Her autobiographies thus demonstrate her lifelong penchant for self-dialogue. Besides keeping a diary in adolescence (and through many periods of her adult life), she wrote a dialogue at twenty between two personae, "both of whom were

[her]self" (231).[6] Also, as an adult she admitted to preferring the task of both posing and answering questions for herself to the role of interview respondent (*La Force des Choses* II, 128). Putting herself and her life as a publishing writing woman in question in her late-in-life narrative aut*ho*biographies, de Beauvoir continues this process of self-dialogue, raising it to the second power as it becomes both the impulse and substance of her autobiographical works.[7] Notably, unlike the emplotted variety of autobiographies, her project advances with increasing concessions to the waywardness and contradictions which scrupulous self-dialogue naturally begets. As a whole, it possesses an intensity, particularity, and reflectiveness that are hard to find matched in other multivolume literary autobiographies.

While recognizing these qualities, however, critical interpretation regularly turns their detail and so-called "excess" against de Beauvoir's autobiographies.[8] All of these people and places and travels accounted for—for what? So many others in de Beauvoir's life come to share and even dominate the stage of her lifewritings: Jean-Paul Sartre principally, but her mother and father, her friends and lovers, authors and artists known and unknown to her, as well. The profusion of others creates what Claude Roy insightfully saw as the centrality of relationships in the autobiographies.[9] But the metaphor of centrality logically entails the opposing concept of margins. If others are central to de Beauvoir's life, lifewritings, and philosophy, does that relegate her role as author to the margins? More importantly, does her aut*ho*biographies' ontogenetic explanation of her writings and her life as a writer, in foregrounding her relationships to others, argue for her marginalization in her own eyes?

The thesis of my study of all of de Beauvoir's aut*ho*biographies is that, on thematic and structural levels, they disrupt the antipodes of center and margin, self and other, in their critique of authorship. This is to say that the otherness that pervades them—in the innumerable "characters" included, in the wandering and proliferation of anecdotes, in the sustained criticism of bourgeois individualism, in the critical portrait of her protean self created from an equally protean because processive point of view—this otherness serves de Beauvoir as the means to question her authority as a self and an author. No criticism to date of these most favored works of de Beauvoir has remarked on what I see as their principal strength: their detailed attention to others and otherness combined with their investigation of one woman's experience as an author.

In my analysis below of de Beauvoir's *The Second Sex* (*Le Deuxième Sexe*, 1949), I show how and where de Beauvoir inaugurates her dual and sometimes duelling interests in otherness and authorship. I want to stress up front, though, that this most celebrated of de Beauvoir's works is merely the start—the preface, if you like—of an aut*ho*biographical venture which is not, in my estimation, identical to de Beauvoir's total autobiographical project. After her essay on Woman, de Beauvoir continued her then explicitly self-aware critique of authorship through her first three autobiographies—*Mémoires d'une Fille Rangée* (1958), *La Force de l'Age* (1960), and *La Force des Choses* (1963). Their inquiry into the process of de Beauvoir's author-ization—her transformation from writer into author—unites these four texts. Furthermore, the first three memoirs are set apart from the later ones—*Tout Compte Fait* (1972) and the epitaphic *Une Mort Très Douce* (1964) and *La Cérémonie des Adieux* (1981)—by their extended chronological form, by the historical proximity of their composition (1957–1963), and by their questioning preoccupation with their author's lifework as a woman author. In fact, by the time she was writing *Tout Compte Fait*, de Beauvoir admits to having lost a sense of her life's directedness, so evident in the aut*h*obiographies:

> For me life was an undertaking that had a clear direction, and in giving an account of mine I had to follow its progress [chronologically]. The circumstances are not the same today. . . . I no longer feel that I am moving in the direction of a goal, but only that I am slipping inevitably towards my grave. (Prologue, not numbered)

De Beauvoir's interest in the aging process in these final autobiographies supplants her *joie de vivre*, an optimism about living which fueled her inquiry into the why's and how's of her life as "*une femme écrivain*." In brief, limiting the definition of de Beauvoir's aut*h*obiographies to *The Second Sex* and the first three memoirs has two advantages: it recognizes the evolutionary aspect of her autobiographical critique of authorship while acknowledging that, although the autobiographies go on, the critique is after all limited. Like all aut*h*obiographies, de Beauvoir's are rooted in and conditioned by the author's history, in the history of herself she represents. They thus partake of that history's particularity and finitude.

In de Beauvoir's case, however, reference to finitude may seem mistaken. Her aut*h*obiographical questions are broad and her answers voluminous. For example, she requires 684 pages in the Gallimard edition of *La Force de l'Age* to answer (among other questions) why she writes and why she writes what she writes. In keeping with her changing relationship to her writings and her readers, no one retrospective assessment will do for de Beauvoir. Her struggle for understanding is ongoing, beyond the scope of a single emplotted and artfully rendered volume; and it is historical, conditioned by the logic of chronological growth that her narratives imitate. In a fashion not unlike Sartre's habit of thinking against himself in *Les Mots*, de Beauvoir evidences in her aut*h*obiographies the need to question ceaselessly the structures of authority and the shibboleths of authorship by putting herself into question. But in a fashion wholly unlike Sartre's, de Beauvoir puts herself into question not just by studying her particular experiences as a mid-twentieth-century bourgeois-born woman writer who aspired to and attained authorial success, but also by directing her panoptic gaze at the world, at her relationships, at her contemporaries. She does not begin with a view of a centered self as author or the reverse. Rather, as Terry Keefe notes, "Broadly speaking, her interest is in the world rather than herself, or rather in the world, with herself as one object in it" (45).[10] To revolutionary effect, de Beauvoir's self-world view ultimately advocates an experimental context wherein authority—and specifically that brand of authority inscribed in and conferred on the production of published texts—is seen as derivative, shared, cooperative.

But this perspective comes at the end of the aut*h*obiographies, after de Beauvoir has journeyed some twenty-seven hundred pages into her past and outward into authorship. In the prefatory *The Second Sex*, de Beauvoir begins by degrading derivative authority, as exemplified by women. Jacques Ehrmann has discussed how de Beauvoir's two· main topics were the situation of women and the situation of the intellectual (writer). While Ehrmann does not provide more than a general, humanist connection between these two interests, he indirectly underscores the need to explore what is gendered in de Beauvoir's critique of authority.[11] We can begin this exploration with the fact that de Beauvoir's aut*h*obiographical enterprise grew out of her research and writing on the socialization of women around the world and across time. The converse is also true: her research on women came in response to a challenge to write her autobiography. A passage in *La Force des Choses* describes the autobiographical genesis of *The Second Sex* and reveals how, from the start, self-reflection tempers de Beauvoir's thoughts about women. De Beauvoir says (my translation):

> I desired to speak about myself. I loved Leiris' *L'Age d'homme*; I had a taste for the martyr-essays where one explains oneself without pretext. I began to dream about it, to take some notes, and I spoke about it to Sartre. I saw that a primary question posed itself: what signifies for me what a woman is? I first believed I could quickly rid myself of this question. I had never had a feeling of inferiority: no one had said to me: "You think this way because you are a woman"; my femininity hadn't bothered me at all. I said to Sartre, "For me, [femininity] doesn't count, so to speak." "All the same," he replied, "you haven't been raised in the same manner as a boy: it might be necessary to look at the issue more closely." I looked and I had a revelation. This world was a masculine world, my childhood had been nourished by myths

forged by men, and I hadn't at all reacted to these myths in the same
manner as I would have as a boy. I was so interested that I abandoned
the project of a personal confession in order to occupy myself with the
feminine condition in its generality. (135)

Many critics take these remarks as an invitation to find where in her
observations about women de Beauvoir is "really" speaking of herself.
Judith Okley amongst others has written of the "hidden subjectivity" of
the narrator of *The Second Sex* to justify connections she draws between
de Beauvoir's experience and that of capital "W" Woman (72).
Identifying this subjectivity need not, however, simply support attempts
to see de Beauvoir's Woman as her mirror reflection. Indeed, the above
passage implicitly warns against making a simple equivalence. At a distance of fifteen years de Beauvoir owns up to the difference femininity
(not being "un garçon") has had on her development; but she does not
admit this difference in *The Second Sex*. What she says there is, "But if I
wish to define myself, I must first of all say: 'I am a woman'; on this
truth must be based all further discussion" (xxvii).[12]

Moreover, the passage above indicates de Beauvoir's persisting
sense that femininity entails inferiority—which she says she has never
felt—thus arguing against her sense of proximity to her subject.[13] True,
she reveals her understanding that her research would reflect the meaning of Woman for herself. But she equally emphasizes that composing
The Second Sex meant abandoning her personal writing project. In short,
the essay caused her to see herself *in relation* to Woman while at the
same time seeing herself as *other* than women: other than the Other who
by her famous definition Woman becomes (267). The shift in genre,
from autobiography to theoretical treatise, underscores this affirmation
of distance between herself and the subject she knew to be intimately
her own.

For critics exploring de Beauvoir's vexed relationship to the Woman
she authorized in *The Second Sex*, reckoning with the voice of the essay is
the preeminent challenge. This voice has generated accusations of de
Beauvoir's misogyny: it has grounded claims like Mary Lowenthal
Felstiner's that the essay "uncovers the pervasion of sexism more than the
potential of feminism" (269).[14] My general interest in de Beauvoir's voice
in *The Second Sex* is to discover what makes it such an ambiguous but important lead for other women who write as women about gender. Specifically, I examine how the voice reveals the essay's aut*h*obiographical
dimension: that dimension of the text where de Beauvoir's interest in authorship dovetails with the inscription of her subject position. How did the
writing and publishing of the text help authorize de Beauvoir's voice, and
authorize her in such a way as to make her both a feminist and a woman

henceforth committed to the autobiographical narration of her life?[15] How does this authorization of de Beauvoir's voice as a woman-advocate enact the "solution" to women's oppression which she details? How, in turn, do the ambiguities inherent in this "solution"—authorship—reflect back on the ambivalences and conflicts of this other-than-Other woman's narrative voice?

De Beauvoir recognizes that her authority to pose the question "What is a woman?" needs to be established early, so in her introduction she provides two bases. It is the tension between these two bases that accounts for the oscillations in tone and argument that feminist critics have heard. On one hand, de Beauvoir asserts: "Man is at once judge and party to the case; but so is woman" (xxxix). In an atypical jest, she speculates that an angel or a hermaphrodite would be the ideal interlocutor, but in their absence "we" must look to "certain women who are best qualified to elucidate the situation of woman" (xxxix). Of course, she means herself:

> Many of today's women, fortunate in the restoration of all the privileges pertaining to the estate of the human being, can afford the luxury of impartiality—we even recognize its necessity. . . . [A]lready some of us have never had to sense in our femininity an inconvenience or an obstacle. Many problems appear to us to be more pressing than those which concern us in particular, and this detachment even allows us to hope that our attitude will be objective. Still, we know the feminine world more intimately than do the men because we have our roots in it, we grasp more immediately than do men what it means to a human being to be feminine; and we are more concerned with such knowledge. I have said that there are more pressing problems, but this does not prevent us from seeing some importance in asking how the fact of being women will affect our lives. (xxxix–xl)

De Beauvoir's language supports her point that she is an exceptional woman, a *human* first, but nevertheless a woman with firsthand knowledge of femininity. She speaks in several registers simultaneously: the impersonal third-person plural, the collectivizing first-person plural, and even the self-implicating first-person singular. Her condition as woman authorizes her; and her insulation from this condition authorizes her. It is an argument from subject-identification as well as subject-demarcation. But the basis, source—or authority—for de Beauvoir's self-perceived difference from other, feminine females remains obscure. I will return to this point.

On the other hand, de Beauvoir argues for the authority of her analysis of women by affirming the authority of the "existentialist ethics" she deploys. She explains:

> Every subject plays his part as such specifically through exploits or projects that serve as a mode of transcendence: he achieves liberty

only through a continual reaching out toward other liberties. There is
no justification for present existence other than its expansion into an
indefinitely open future. Every time transcendence falls back into immanence, stagnation, there is a degradation of existence into the
"ensoi"—the brutish life of subjection to given conditions—and of liberty into constraint and contingence. This downfall represents a moral
fault if the subject consents to it; if it is inflicted upon him, it spells
frustration and oppression. In both cases it is an absolute evil. Every
individual concerned to justify his existence feels that his existence involves an undefined need to transcend himself, to engage in freely
chosen projects. (xl–xli)

Recent criticism has both lauded and condemned de Beauvoir's analytical
framework, a topic beyond the scope of this analysis.[16] Of vital concern
here, however, are the related biases of humanism and individualism
which mark the above explanation. In this passage, subjectivity as such is
not gendered; there are only humans. As de Beauvoir says elsewhere, "For
us woman is defined as a human being in quest of values in a world of
values" (52). The operative duality within the category of humans is not
masculine/feminine but rather transcendence/immanence, two general an-
tinomies that map onto free/enslaved, mental/physical, acting/passive, jus-
tified/unjustified, essential/inessential, growing/stagnant throughout the
essay. De Beauvoir adopts the perspective of dualities in order to break up
their historical bond with the duality of masculine/feminine (xxviii). But
in so doing she apparently throws her values in with those of a humanism
that perpetuates binary oppositions, a way of thinking heavily targeted in
recent feminist theory as doomed to perpetuate a sexist logic.

Can Woman escape from the logic of these oppositions? Judging
from the language of the passage above where de Beauvoir explains her
existentialist premise, nothing could be less certain. The individualism
marking its vision of a being (or "existent") at liberty to "reach out toward other liberties" consigns the oppressed subject to the moral iniq-
uity of a brutish life of her own making. Whether an oppressed subject
can be properly said to consent to her situation is a question de Beauvoir
here begs. As Carol Ascher has noted: "[D]e Beauvoir's requirement of
determining oppression is a demanding one: if, and only if, one has *tried*
to reach toward a goal, and that attempt has been definitively thwarted,
can one speak of being oppressed" ("Women" 178, Ascher's emphasis).
Sporadically, de Beauvoir insists that "the compulsions of a situation in
which she is the inessential" inhibit or limit the exercise of Woman's liberty (xli). But the existential ethic framing her theoretical remarks in the
essay makes no provision for these compulsions, nor apparently for their
eradication. Indeed, the framework in itself disregards gendered differences between subjects, although that is de Beauvoir's topic, because in

her conclusion the withering away of these differences is the utopian-socialist vision she entertains.[17]

The narrator's voice thus derives her authority from a gendered subject position de Beauvoir has purportedly transcended and from a humanist philosophy denying that position's pertinence. The theme scattered throughout *The Second Sex* which signals the tension between these two accounts of de Beauvoir's authority on Woman is that of Woman's complicity with her oppressors:

> When man makes of woman the *Other*, he may, then, expect her to manifest deep-seated tendencies toward complicity. Thus woman may fail to lay claim to the status of subject because she lacks definite resources, because she feels the necessary bond that ties her to man regardless of reciprocity, and because she is often very well pleased with her role as the *Other*. (xxxiii)

In *The Second Sex*, the concept of women's complicity with the values that denigrate them reflects de Beauvoir's contention that what sets women apart from other historically oppressed groups is their widespread internalization of negative myths about Woman (481). The narrator's voice audibly bristles with the double bind this internalization places women in: females become women because they are socialized and they stay socialized because they are feminine.

To offset the determinism of this internalizing process, de Beauvoir uses the language of failure and choice: "In truth, however, the nature of things is no more immutably given, once for all, than is historical reality. If woman seems to be the inessential which never becomes the essential, it is because she herself fails to bring about this change" (xxxi). A more sustained example of this language is found in the section on psychoanalysis. There de Beauvoir stresses her dissatisfaction with the lack of choice(s) psychoanalytic schemata hold out to women (46, passim). Choice undermines the fixed, transhistorical destiny that de Beauvoir—armed with her belief that "the individual defines himself by making his own choices through the world about him"—rejects (49). In general, women who internalize masculine values relegating them to Otherness suffer doubly in de Beauvoir's harshest theorizations in *The Second Sex*: they have their material "enslavement"—to their bodies, to their men, to their poverty—and they have their burden as moral transgressors, choosing against a life of liberty.

There is much to criticize in the theme of complicity as de Beauvoir elaborates it: principally, her blaming-the-victim rationale, but also her blindness to the value of women's culture as it has evolved within oppressed and variegated conditions.[18] But there is also much to appreciate:

especially de Beauvoir's unflagging attempt to address both the constructedness and the givenness of women's situation—women enter into
the Myth of Woman through a complex blend of circumstances and decision.[19] Of most crucial interest to the aut*h*obiographical import of the
essay is the way in which de Beauvoir vocalizes her position on
women's complicity only by turning her attention away from the Myth
of Woman. While, as Jane Flax notes, "none of us can speak for
'woman' because no such person exists except within a specific set of
(already gendered) relations," de Beauvoir slyly employs the referent
Woman throughout *The Second Sex* and describes her in highly contradictory if rich detail, in order to call attention to the essentializing
and mythic components of her subject (Flax 642). However, whereas
this description affords de Beauvoir the comforts of objectification and
representation—luxuries she admits have been earmarked historically by
men (143)—her discourse on women's complicity (re)turns her to contemplation of society, and contemporary society in particular, in which
she is a woman among other women.

   In other words, the issue of women's complicity closes the distance
de Beauvoir has assumed between herself and her subject. Only real,
historical women can be said to have wills, to be able to choose, to be
counted as human individuals. But oddly enough, whereas de Beauvoir
speaks with detailed concreteness in her analysis of physical and material circumstances illustrative of the Myth of Woman, she waxes poetic
and abstract in her pronouncements on complicitous real women, taking
recourse in the discourse of existential individualism. To recognize the
methodological variety in *The Second Sex* is a commonplace; to recognize those thematic junctures where methodological shifts transpire, is
not. When de Beauvoir most severely condemns women's culture, or
most vehemently proposes an alternative to it, she is least specific:

> I shall pose the problem of feminine destiny quite otherwise [than psy-
> choanalysts]: I shall place a woman in a world of values and give her
> behavior a dimension of liberty. I believe that she has the power to
> choose between the assertion of her transcendence and her alienation
> as object; she is not the plaything of contradictory drives; she devises
> solutions of diverse ranking in the ethical scale. (50)

What she notably does not specify are the kinds of choices she finds
women failing to make for themselves, the kinds of decisions in which
women do not assert themselves, with the result that they give up liberty
and stagnate.

   The "I" in the above citation—one of the rare uses of this pronoun
by the narrator—gives an important clue about the kind of assertion

de Beauvoir values. One of the aut*h*obiographically significant ironies of the essay is that while de Beauvoir chafes against the ungrounded value system that sustains women's subjugation, she herself only indirectly divulges the values she recommends for women. An exception is the equitable friendship, very near in spirit to Plato's concept of *philia*, which she valorizes with reverberative insistence as an alternative to the "religion of love" which she roundly condemns in "The Formative Years" section (140, 544, 692–95, passim). Much more covert is her valorization of literary production, and the activity/institution which sustains it: authorship.

Literature as a cultural production receives a good amount of attention in *The Second Sex* as the basis for many of de Beauvoir's examples about human life. Indeed, her section "Of Woman in Five Authors" only focalizes the value she places on literature; in other sections, it is through quoting Colette or Leiris or Aristophanes that this value manifests itself. By the time she was composing *The Second Sex*, de Beauvoir herself had newly joined the ranks of known authors with the publication and success of *L'Invitée* (*She Came To Stay*, 1943). But writing, above all else, had for twenty-five years been her life's ambition or work. Published, this writing constituted an assertion of will, a transcendence of environment, a renunciation of those aspects of the Eternal Feminine (as she thematizes it) which inculcate women's silence, and, most emphatically, an entrance into a public, male-dominated domain. When de Beauvoir inserts her "I" in the above citation, she discloses for a moment quite nakedly the choice she most heartily advocates women make: authorship. It is this choice that sets her apart from Woman, both mythic and historical. Authorship entails the authorizing process that is both response and solution to women's oppression for de Beauvoir. The concreteness of her textual "I" and of her present writing project counterbalance the abstract imperatives of existentialism and affirm implicitly, as philosophy cannot, something to choose, some means to transcend by. Asserting oneself in the public sphere through publishing a treatise like *The Second Sex* is an*other* response to women's lived otherness in this, de Beauvoir's earliest aut*h*obiography. In the above citation, de Beauvoir demonstrates the strength accruing to the "*femme écrivain*": "I will place woman. . . ." (If only, lament so many contemporary readers of the essay, she had not so often placed Woman, and in a bourgeois context so nearly mirroring her own.)

Perhaps the weightiest evidence in the text that authorship assumes this preeminent if unarticulated value is found in the book's structure. The whole essay's critique tends towards the final section before the Conclusion, Part VII, in which de Beauvoir reflects on "Liberation: The Independent Woman." It is common for contemporary readers of *The*

Second Sex to comment on the book's utopian Conclusion—that women may "unequivocally affirm their brotherhood" with men—while ignoring the socially sensitive analysis and ambiguous conclusions of the penultimate section. In keeping with the writer on women who informed her ideas on the connection between financial independence and intellectual freedom, de Beauvoir also adopts Virginia Woolf's equivalence between intellectual woman and emancipated woman in this section. It is not enough, she says, that women are employed: "working, today, is not enough" (680). Those women who work towards financial self-sufficiency through intellectual activities, especially literary endeavors, most nearly approach de Beauvoir's ideal of the "independent human individual" (682). The female intellectual in de Beauvoir's eyes "thinks about her situation" (critically, we may suppose) and so rejects the security of the feminine dependent for the risks attending the "masculine world" (684, 685). Thought, it seems, guarantees liberation as mere cash cannot. The slippage between authorship of literature, intellectual activity, and extrication from feminine bonds throughout this section causes its discussion of the means for women to seek liberation to be useful to only a narrow sector of diverse womenkind. It is possible to come away with the vexing sense that one and only one path toward liberation is open to women. More fruitfully, the section can be studied as the most aut*h*obiographically revealing section in *The Second Sex*, where de Beauvoir patently interweaves her queries about authorship with her very personal sense of the ambiguities of a bourgeois liberation of women's situation.

The liberation of women through writing—and writing publicly, to publish—was a life pattern forty-year-old de Beauvoir believed in as tried and true. It was the pattern she had reified if not minted in her own life's experience, and what optimism one reads in *The Second Sex* is owing to her deep pleasure in this experience. As Elaine Marks has pointed out, de Beauvoir supported to the end of her life women's writing and women's participation in authorship in contrast to the original position of *écriture féminine* practitioners, who "considered her activities complicitous with the reigning networks of power" (*Essays*, 4). In *La Force des Choses* de Beauvoir articulates her sense of her own complicity, of a kind wholly separate from that which she critiques in *The Second Sex*. But that is seventeen years and two thousand pages of memoirs hence. In 1947 de Beauvoir only began to question the complex set of advantages and compromises entailed in women's entrance into the institution of authorship. Specifically, she exposes the obstacles thwarting their historical and contemporary literary production. In the "Liberation" section, she abandons the abstract mandates that women choose liberty, as well as the existential framework underpinning those imperatives; and she addresses the "inner confusion" attending the woman intellectual/author's choice of a life between gender norms. Not that de Beauvoir's subject position is any more forthcoming. Simply, the urgent and plaintive tone of this section indicates her infusion of self/authorial experience and observation of others into an ostensibly general description of female independence.

Throughout the writing of this section de Beauvoir thematizes the "temptations" and acculturated insecurities that "haunt" the aspiring woman intellectual (681, 686, 698–99). Deirdre Bair's biography of de Beauvoir provides a detailed history of her conflicted relationship with Nelson Algren, developing during the time of the composition of *The Second Sex*, which may help explain the degree to which haunting self-doubts appear as the necessary legacy of the authorizing woman.[20] More to the point, Bair's research on the de Beauvoir-Algren transatlantic affair provides an autobiographical context for this thesis of "Liberation": "Thus the independent woman of today is torn between her professional interests and the problems of her sexual life; it is difficult for her to strike a balance between the two; if she does, it is at the price of concessions, sacrifices, acrobatics, which require her to be in a constant state of tension" (697). Even when the source of confusion is relationships with other women rather than with men, de Beauvoir in this section expresses a fund of sympathetic support for the woman choosing with unsteady steps to cross established gender boundaries. It is with a kind of gentleness that she laments the restless and wandering path of this aspiring woman (698–99). While this section repeats earlier sections' endorsement of a life of self-assertion, it mitigates the masculine bias of this pattern by suggesting the difficulties women have in discovering a self to assert. Indeed, she explains what she judges to be women's "modest" successes in literature and art to have stemmed from their inability to forget themselves, from their preoccupying search for themselves (702).

It may seem ironic that de Beauvoir herself would turn soon after writing *The Second Sex* to a sixteen-year life-writing project searching for herself. But more than simple irony or self-deception are worth noting here. De Beauvoir's voice in "Liberation," less hortatory than in previous sections, evinces a kind of critique of her own writing position, a position that began with Sartre's challenge to her in 1939: " 'Well! Why don't you put yourself personally into what you write?' he asked me with a sudden vehemence" (*La Force de l'Age* 360; my translation). She seems to be questioning here the thoroughness with which authorship solves women's problems when their lives as a whole are considered.[21] Through her discontent with the Brontës' novels she registers her sense as an author in 1947 that women's relationships to the act and production of successful writing have been handicapped by their historical subjugation in their relationships with men. Men, de Beauvoir reflects, have had all material, physical, and ideational freedom to become authors; thus authorship for her represents a virile human life project for which men are "naturally" only because socially groomed. Even at the epoch of writing *The Second Sex*, then, de Beauvoir would not deny the claim of proponents of *écriture feminine* that hers was both a humanist and an accommodationist authorial position. But it is instructive to recognize, as she did, that she was one woman writing among many men; one woman who was struggling to perceive the differences of her writing position without compromising the authority she had begun to shore up in the male-dominated Paris intellectual community.

Wandering and restless, the voice of the "Liberation" section reveals conflicts and opens questions which not only de Beauvoir but no living woman author could answer. The betweenness of her own hidden subject position—gendered yet resiliently humanist—has in turn created a position on female self-authorization through authorship that is similarly ambiguous. Cultivating ambiguity can be, as Jane Flax points out, a strength in feminist theory, exposing as it does "our needs for imposing order and structure no matter how arbitrary and oppressive these needs may be" (643). But de Beauvoir's ambivalence had not yet come into the service of feminism: only the writing of the essay brought her to a feminist identification (Dayan 67–68). At its most ambivalent, de Beauvoir's voice in *The Second Sex* warily positions itself between the 1947 categories of feminist and antifeminist, giving her the freedom to assert both the power and the inner confusion experienced by the authoring woman.

Or by this authoring woman? The division between her and other women having grown so indistinct, it is impossible to set the book down without a sense that even the genre of this essay grows ambiguous as it progresses. Midway between aut*h*obiography and theoretical essay, *The Second Sex* constitutes de Beauvoir's first self-searching attempt to problematize her profession at the same time that she holds it out to other women as an authorizing lifestyle (or project) essentially about choosing. Or about indecision? She begins to demonstrate—despite her existentialist frame—that indecision and waywardness caused by relationships with others modify the masculine paradigm of the self-asserting subject in the case of aspiring women authors. It will take subsequent aut*h*obiographies, beginning with *Mémoires à une Jeune Fille Rangée* and culminating in *La Force des Choses*, for de Beauvoir to explore this essential if not essentializing difference. But the subject will no longer be hidden; she will be in search of herself.

Notes

1. In her astute introductory essay to *Critical Essays on Simone de Beauvoir*, Elaine Marks foregrounds the lightness of de Beauvoir's authority with her critics: "At least half of the critical essays I have included in this volume are, whether discreetly or obtrusively, sarcastic. They present Simone de Beauvoir as a slightly ridiculous figure, naive in her passions, sloppy in her scholarship, inaccurate in her documentation, generally out of her depth and inferior as a writer. Indeed, the tone of superiority that many critics, of both sexes, adopt when writing about Simone de Beauvoir deserves special attention" (2).

2. For appraisals stressing de Beauvoir's re-visionary originality, see McCall (209–23), Simons (165–79), Le Doeuff (144–53). On the use of the term "mother" to refer to de Beauvoir, see Carol Ascher's quasi-autobiographical queries in "On 'Clearing the Air': My Letter to Simone de Beauvoir" (87).

3. De Beauvoir explicitly defines herself as *"une femme écrivain"* in the important epilogue to *La Force des Choses* (2: 495).

4. The introduction of my dissertation elaborates the concept and rationale for the neologism "aut*h*obiography." My project discovers and examines various threads of this discourse in the aut*h*obiographies of Richard Wright and Jean-Paul Sartre, de Beauvoir, Gertrude Stein, and Zora Neale Hurston.

5. De Beauvoir uses expressions of self-questioning in the prefatory section to *La Force des Choses* which apply to her autobiographical project as a whole while becoming increasingly urgent to her with time's passage: e.g., "I wanted my blood to circulate in this *récit*; I wanted to throw myself into it alive and to put myself in question before all the questions were extinguished. Maybe it is too early; but tomorrow will surely be too late" (7).

6. In *Memoirs of a Dutiful Daughter* de Beauvoir explains: "On my nineteenth birthday, I wrote in the library at the Sorbonne a long dialogue between two voices, both of which were mine; one spoke of the vanity of all things, of disgust and weariness; the other affirmed that life, even a sterile existence, was beautiful" (231). Of course, her acclaimed philosophical essay *Pyrrhus et Cinéas* likewise makes use of the dialogue format.

7. For a discussion of "the emergence into adulthood" to which de Beauvoir's published self-inquiry attests, see Francis Jeanson (101–9).

8. See, for example, Elizabeth Hardwick's mixture of complaint and bedazzlement before "the bewildering inclusiveness" of *The Second Sex* (50). The most probing and ingenious critical voice on the subject of de Beauvoir's putative excess is Elaine Marks ("Transgressing" 181–200).

9. Roy observes,

> It seems to me that in her novels and essays Simone de Beauvoir dealt with one theme only: relations between human beings. Such a statement seems trite: is there any other topic? Yet when I think of other great works, a personality comes forth, a face, silhouette, detached from all others, and one might say, sufficient unto themselves emerging out of an apparent solitude. In contrast, what I remember of Simone de Beauvoir's books are not essentially characters, types, or personalities. The world she describes is a universe of relations. (78–79).

10. Jeanson suggests why de Beauvoir wrote (of herself) in this way: "one undertakes to disclose the world by disclosing oneself within it" (105). This view, like Keefe's remark, blurs the distinction between subject and object, self and other.

11. Nancy K. Miller takes up the related question of the influence of de Beauvoir's femininity on her autobiography in "Women's Autobiography in France" (258–73).

12. Deirdre Bair, Judith Okley, and others have chronicled the errors and philosophical weaknesses of H. M. Parshley's 1953 translation, and yet, lamentably, it is the only translation of the text that we have. My purpose in using this text is to provide an English translation of de Beauvoir's remarks, not to cast my critical vote for the book.

13. In the introduction to *The Second Sex* de Beauvoir contends that "when an individual (or a group of individuals) is kept in a situation of inferiority, the fact is that he *is* inferior. . . . Yes, women on the whole *are* today inferior to men; that is, their situation affords them fewer possibilities. The question is: should that state of affairs continue?" (xxxvi; author's emphasis).

14. Deirdre Bair's introduction to the Vintage Edition of Parshley's translation of *The Second Sex* cites several examples of critics fuming about de Beauvoir's disservice to women in writing this essay (xix–xx). See also Naomi Greene. More typical, though, are assertions of the book's pessimism as a record of sexism against women, such as in Felstiner, Leighton (where the pessimism is explored with reference to de Beauvoir's autobiography), and Ascher. Many of these critical assessments employ the terms "ambivalence" and "ambiguity" which I also find useful, especially given de Beauvoir's *Ethics of Ambiguity*. But oddly, the ambiguity, too, is typically held against her, as if it were imponderable that inconsistencies would arise from being for women but against their situation(s).

15. For a discussion of the predominance of autobiographical narratives in de Beauvoir's corpus after she turns fifty, see Marks ("Transgressing" 184).

16. Le Doeuff has particularly influenced my view that de Beauvoir's existentialist framework revises Sartrean existentialism in important ways (144–53). De Beauvoir's existentialist ideology functions as a nonsystem of thought, ill equipped to deal with the systemic oppression of sexism she was studying. In this way, it betokens the derivative authority generally at issue in de Beauvoir's aut*h*obiographies. Here it is important to stress that de Beauvoir's existentialist framework disrupts simple notions of originality in favor of original uses of ideas.

17. See Young on the differences between humanist feminism and gynocentric feminism, and the relative weaknesses of these two positions (173–83). De Beauvoir's voice in *The Second Sex* epitomizes the humanist feminist in her revolt against, and concomitant denigration of, femininity and women's culture.

18. See Gerda Lerner on the masculine bias in de Beauvoir's conception of history (154–68).

19. Butler makes this argument brilliantly (35–49).

20. See chapters twenty-seven through twenty-nine of Bair. Providing contextual information of this kind is this biography's greatest use; on certain matters, as critics have long noted, de Beauvoir is silent, her pretensions to honest and total self-revelation notwithstanding. But the biography's usefulness is severely curtailed because de Beauvoir did provide so much information about herself. Bair seems to me, as she feared, to "end up simply rehashing [de Beauvoir's] own version of her life," only with fewer scruples than de Beauvoir had about the historicity of her autobiographical accounts (12). Bair frequently melds together snippets from writings and interviews separated by decades to draw her conclusions, without considering the attachments de Beauvoir's autobiographies have to their narrative contexts. This practice rendered her impressively researched biography of little value to my inquiry.

21. McCall makes nearly this same point when she says, in response to Leighton's accusation of de Beauvoir's misogyny: "Beauvoir's critique of what she calls woman's complicity with her situation is in part a critique of herself" (221). I

rather perceive that de Beauvoir's rapprochement with the women whom she distances herself from in her complicity theme, comes primarily at the essay's end in the "Liberation" section.

Works Cited

Ascher, Carol. "On 'Clearing the Air': My Letter to Simone de Beauvoir." In *Between Women*, edited by Carol Ascher, Louise DeSalvo, and Sara Ruddick, 85–103. Boston: Beacon, 1984.

———. "Women and Choice—A New Look at Simone de Beauvoir and *The Second Sex.*" In *Faith of a (Woman) Writer*, edited by Alice Kessler-Harris and William McBrien, 173–78. Westport, Conn.: Greenwood, 1988.

Bair, Deirdre. *Simone de Beauvoir.* New York: Summit, 1990.

Beauvoir, Simone de. *All Said and Done.* Translated by Patrick O'Brian. New York: G. P. Putnam's Sons, 1984.

———. *La Force de l'Age.* Paris: Editions Gallimard, 1960.

———. *La Force des Choses*, I and II. Paris: Editions Gallimard, 1963.

———. *Memoirs of a Dutiful Daughter.* Translated by James Kirkup. New York: Harper, 1959.

———. *The Second Sex.* Translated by H. M. Parshley. Introduction by Deirdre Bair. New York: Vintage, 1989.

Butler, Judith. "Sex and Gender in Simone de Beauvoir's *Second Sex.*" *Yale French Studies* 72 (1986): 35–49.

Dayan, Josée, and Malka Ribowska, eds. *Simone de Beauvoir.* A film produced by Josée Dayan. Paris: Gallimard, 1979.

Ehrmann, Jacques. "Simone de Beauvoir and the Related Destinies of Woman and Intellectual." Marks, *Essays*, 89–94.

Felstiner, Mary Lowenthal. "Seeing *The Second Sex* through the Second Wave." *Feminist Studies* 6 (1980): 247–76.

Flax, Jane. "Postmodernism and Gender Relations in Feminist Theory." *Signs* 12 (1987): 621–43.

Gallant, Mavis. "A Couple and Their Family." *Times Literary Supplement*, September 14–20, 1990, 963–64.

Greene, Naomi. "Sartre, Sexuality, and *The Second Sex.*" *Philosophy and Literature* 4 (1980): 199–211.

Hardwick, Elizabeth. "The Subjection of Women." Marks, *Essays*, 49–55.

Jeanson, Francis. "'Autobiographism,' 'Narcissism,' and Images of the Self." Marks, *Essays*, 101–9.

Keefe, Terry. *Simone de Beauvoir, A Study of Her Writings.* London: Harrap Ltd., 1983.

Le Doeuff, Michèle. "Operative Philosophy: Simone de Beauvoir and Existentialism." Translated by Colin Gordon. Marks, *Essays*, 144–53; rpt. from *Ideology and Consciousness* 6 (1979): 47–57.

Leighton, Jean. *Simone de Beauvoir on Woman.* London: Associated University Presses, 1975.

Lerner, Gerda. "Women and History." Marks, *Essays*, 154–68.

McCall, Dorothy Kaufmann. "Simone de Beauvoir, *The Second Sex*, and Jean-Paul Sartre." *Signs* 5 (1979): 209–23.

Marks, Elaine, ed. *Critical Essays on Simone de Beauvoir.* Boston: G. K. Hall, 1987.

———. Introduction. Marks, *Essays*, 1–13.

———. "Transgressing the (In)Cont(in)ent Boundaries: The Body in Decline." *Yale French Studies* 72 (1986): 181–200.

Miller, Nancy K. "Women's Autobiography in France." In *Women and Language in Literature and Society*, edited by Sally McConnell-Ginet, Ruth Barker, and Nelly Furman, 258–73. New York: Praeger, 1980.

Okley, Judith. *Simone de Beauvoir: A Re-Reading.* London: Virago, 1986.

Perreault, Donna. "Questioning Authorship in Twentieth-Century Literary Autobiography." Ph.D. diss., Louisiana State University, 1991.

Roy, Claude. "Simone de Beauvoir." Translated by Germaine Breé. Marks, *Essays*, 77–84.

Simons, Margaret A. "Beauvoir and Sartre: The Philosophical Relationship." *Yale French Studies* 72 (1986): 165–79.

Young, Iris Marion. "Humanism, Gynocentrism and Feminist Politics." *Women's Studies International Forum* 8, no. 3 (1985): 173–83.

8

Beneath the Mask: Autobiographies of Japanese-American Women*

~

Ann Rayson

In this selection, Ann Rayson builds on the insights of early feminist autobiography critics, who argued that women's autobiographies had characteristics that distinguished them from works by male writers, and applies them to a specific group of women writers. She examines texts by the Nisei (second-generation Japanese-Americans born in the United States) women writers Mine Okubo, Monica Sone, Jeanne Houston, Akemi Kikumura, and Yoshiko Uchida, which focus in part on the writers' internment during World War II. Rayson attempts to explain why so few male writers have produced narratives about the experience. She argues that while internment had many negative consequences, it also disrupted the traditional male-dominated Japanese family structure. That disruption had two key consequences. First, Japanese-American men experienced a loss of self-esteem and thus wanted to suppress their memories of internment. Second, in contrast, Japanese-American women, who had been oppressed within their families and discriminated against by the dominant American culture, had little to lose and much to gain in speaking out about their lives.

Ann Rayson is an associate professor of English at the University of Hawaii. She teaches courses in African-American and American ethnic literatures. She has published several histories of Hawaii, including Hawaii: The Pacific State *(1995). Rayson's current research focuses on female resistance in American slave narratives and novels.*

*From Ann Rayson, "Beneath the Mask: Autobiographies of Japanese-American Women," *MELUS* 14 (1987): 43–57. ©1987 MELUS, The Society for the Study of the Multi-Ethnic Literature of the United States. Reprinted by permission of *MELUS* and the author.

IN RECENT YEARS there has been a rise in the number and variety of ethnic autobiographies available to the reading public. Not surprisingly, we might ask why many of these seem to be by ethnic American women. Currently black American women writers and Asian-American women writers are dominating the literature coming from their particular ethnic groups. The increasing presence of autobiographies by ethnic American women in the twentieth century is due to several factors such as the inclusion of women in the workforce and industry, the growth of immigrant populations, and the development of a larger reading public through mass education. Over the last twenty years, the rise of the women's movement has encouraged women to speak out. Writers are drawn into expression of the ethnic dimension through autobiography as they become acculturated and realize that multiplicity is acceptable. Since ethnic writers are dealing with society and history on certain levels, as well as their place in this culture, autobiography becomes the proper form for the transmission of cultural reality and myth.

Ethnic writers and women, or ethnic writers as women, must search for a definition of self within, but as different from, the dominant culture. Elaine Showalter discusses women's writing in "Feminist Criticism in the Wilderness" (1981) as a double-voiced discourse containing a "dominant" and a "muted" story. Analyzing the existence of muted groups other than women, then combinations of muted groups, Showalter says:

> A black American woman poet, for example, would have her literary identity formed by the dominant (white male) tradition, by a muted women's culture, and by a muted black culture. She would be affected by both sexual and racial politics in a combination unique to her case; at the same time, . . . she shares an experience specific to her group. (202)

The Japanese-American woman writer, in speaking out autobiographically, is abandoning the traditional silence of her muted culture in order to become a part of the larger culture. She is emerging from beneath a mask imposed by both racial and sexual stereotypes. These writers are moving in varying degrees from "the major concern of showing a 'good face' to the *hakujin* (Caucasian)"[1] to expressing an independent voice through a genre incompatible with Japanese behavioral codes and traditions. While these writers are taking off the mask, the outside label that protects them, to face the world, they sometimes paradoxically employ masking devices in their uses of language and silence. Thus, at the same time these writers are taking off the mask of stereotype (Japanese-American and female), they are still concealing pride in themselves and their accomplishments. As Estelle Jelinek argues in *The Tradition of Women's Autobiography* (1986), this pride is "usually masked, understated, or presented modestly because of the expected negative response to their 'vanity' in writing a life study at all, in believing that their experiences are 'worthy' of an autobiography." Paradoxically, as they mask their egos, Japanese-American women autobiographers emerge as "mavericks, outcasts, or, at the least, rebels against what society expects of them" in revealing their personal lives to the public (186–87).

For Japanese-American women autobiographers there seem to be two predominant motives for writing: the historical motive and the feminist motive, which are interrelated. For example, Estelle Jelinek points out in *Women's Autobiography* (1980) that "the history of America and the history of autobiography have developed together and . . . the periods of greatest productivity in autobiography correspond to important events in American history" (5). The peak periods of autobiographical productivity for women were 1890 to World War I (the progressive era and the suffragette movement) and during the late 1960s and the 1970s, the high point of the women's movement. For Japanese-Americans the historical watershed was the Relocation of World War II. The five Japanese-American autobiographies I will discuss—*Citizen 13660* by Mine Okubo (1946), *Nisei Daughter* by Monica Sone (1953), *Farewell to Manzanar* by Jeanne Houston (1973), *Through Harsh Winters* by Akemi Kikumura (1981), and *Desert Exile* by Yoshiko Uchida (1982)— were written after World War II and basically describe the coming to terms of the author with a split cultural identity whose dichotomy was exacerbated during the camp experience. Several questions arise. What is the motivation for writing autobiographically of the camp experience? Why are all of the authors Nisei, or the second generation born in America? (The parents of these writers all spoke Japanese as their primary language and could not legally become American citizens until the Naturalization Act of 1952.) Finally, why do Japanese-American women rather than men tend to write these personal accounts? In exploring these questions, I wish to make a case for the importance of Japanese-American women's autobiographies.

The historical motive for Japanese-American autobiography is starkly compelling since this is the only American minority to be interned en masse in concentration camps solely on the basis of race. For years Japanese-Americans tried to forget this "shame" until the acclaimed photographic exhibit, "Executive Order 9066," and subsequent book on the exhibit published in 1969 opened the floodgates of memory for many who had been put in the Relocation camps. The documentary film "Guilty by Reason of Race," followed in 1972 and traced the history of the camps, focusing on Manzanar and the cultural renaissance among Japanese-Americans working for reparations. Then Jeanne and James Houston published *Farewell to Manzanar* in 1973. This act of self-revelation and exploration, the first contemporary version of the wartime Relocation experience, influenced thousands of Japanese-Americans and gave national impetus to a new dialogue over the question of reparations. Over twenty million Americans alone saw the filmed version of "Farewell to Manzanar," released in 1976, the first Hollywood movie with an all Japanese-American cast. Since *Farewell to Manzanar*, other Japanese-Americans have written of the internment, notably Michi Weglyn, whose documentary history, *Years of Infamy* (1976), has become a standard. The new accounts by Uchida and Kikumura and the 1987 Smithsonian Institution exhibition, "A More Perfect Union: Japanese Americans and the Constitution," point to a continued outpouring of personal and historical experience concerning this turning point in Japanese-American life.

Japanese-American women, rather than men, have written autobiographically of the internment because, I suggest, they were better able to accept the loss of self-esteem which, as women, they never had to the same degree as did Japanese-American men. Accepted into the larger culture as exotic, but, as women, nonthreatening, they were better able to distance themselves from the Relocation experience and then assess it. Now a part of the larger culture through conversion, they are permitted to remember the indignities of the past. Finally, since women as autobiographers may also be given more to introspection than men, as Estelle Jelinek argues, and since Asian-Americans are inescapably writing of cultural clash and conflict, this revelation of self, history, and culture is more natural and less demeaning to women than it is to Japanese-American men, who want to establish themselves as part of the mainstream and are loath to reawaken memories of World War II.

In support of the theory that Japanese-American women, being more circumscribed by a muted culture than the men, are more motivated to speak out and acculturate, Akemi Kikumura cites numerous studies in her appendix to *Through Harsh Winters*. As factors in the Japanese-American's rapid assimilation, she mentions the compatible value system of Japanese culture and the American middle class, the use of adaptive mechanisms such as "suppression of desires and real emotional feelings," and the camp experience.

> The wartime evacuation and concentration have also been pointed out as one of the most influential factors in the Japanese-American's speedy acculturation (Kitano, 1976). Their incarceration broke up the communities in which the Japanese were previously concentrated, dissolved old institutions and structures (such as business establishments, Japanese associations, churches, and Japanese language schools), divided community members into separate factions, stripped them of their land and possessions, weakened and reordered the family structure, broadened

generational differences, and separated and scattered family members into different parts of the country that formerly had no Japanese population. The push to prove themselves loyal American citizens led many in the younger generations of Japanese-Americans to deny their ancestral heritage. (Kikumura, 1981, 121)

Additionally, "Americanization" pushed by the war and internment allowed Japanese-American women to move away from the traditional family system which demanded specific behavior, obligation, duty, loyalty, and respect with observance of rank order between husband and wife. The war scattered many families and camp life led to a breakdown of traditional family roles. In camp men became as women in the hierarchy where all were in actuality treated as children. No one was forced to work; people lined up in mess halls for meals. The roles behind the traditional family unit no longer had substance. As men lost power and status, the women in a sense gained these as they became equals in the new order. Camp life also hastened the breakdown of parental authority. Jeanne Houston in *Farewell to Manzanar* describes her experience: "My own family, after three years of mess hall living, collapsed as an integrated unit. Whatever dignity or feeling of filial strength we may have known before December 1941 was lost, and we did not recover it until many years after the war."[2] Houston's mother immediately takes a job in camp as a dietician while her father, after a hard year at the Fort Lincoln camp, returns to spend his time brewing sake. "Like many of the older Issei men, he didn't take a regular job in camp. He puttered" (70). This pattern continues after the war. "The closing of the camps, in the fall of 1945, only aggravated what had begun inside. Papa had no money then and could not get work" (27). Houston's mother accepts a fish cannery job to support the family. Her father, too proud to stoop to this, begins drinking and loses his children's respect. He has become dependent on his wife and son in a complete reversal of the prewar family structure.

The historical motive leads inevitably to the feminist motive for writing autobiography as the two are intertwined. The post–World War II parent-child conflict often concerned Nisei daughters who rejected the "overtly submissive Japanese female" pattern taught by Issei parents. "Caudill (1952) discovered that among Nisei women great hostility and competition were directed toward the Nisei male." Recent studies on interracial marriages show Japanese-American women continuing to dominate statistics. An important factor here is "personal dissatisfaction and conflict" (Kikumura, 1981, 134).

Personal dissatisfaction among Japanese-American women in their expected female roles may also be the primary reason for the observation made by scholars that the females of this group appear to be acculturating more rapidly than the males (Arkoff, Meredith, and Iwahara, 1962; Caudill, 1952; DeVos, 1951; Fisher and Cleveland, 1958). (Kikumura, 1981, 134–35)

According to Jelinek (*Tradition*, 187), female autobiographers have a strong and real sense of alienation from the male world, here particularly defined by Kikumura as the Nisei male.

The feminist motive may be reflected in attempts by the authors to resolve the contradiction of opposites as Japanese women and Americans. The motive is historical, sociological, and psychological, and the writer seeks to define herself and American culture as a synthesis of opposites, but also as the congruence of similar value sets. These Japanese-American texts are not at all isolated, but rather see the self in an historical context that justifies the methodology of autobiography. From another standpoint, these autobiographies can be interpreted as tales of "conversion" in that most ethnic autobiographers are converts to America or to community. James Holte has found evidence to suggest that "ethnic and immigrant autobiographers used the autobiography as a means to impose order on an experience that was both disruptive and confusing."[3] The internment disrupted both the "assimilation" of Japanese-Americans and their family structure, to some degree overturning male and female roles and positions in society.

As a result of the camp experience which led to an outward trend, the self-esteem of the Asian-American woman writer is more secure than that of the Asian male in America, but only in terms of the white heterosexual norm, perhaps because she had been taught to have fewer expectations. Operating within a circumscribed social mobility to begin with, Japanese-American women, literally imprisoned during World War II, have less to lose psychologically than their fathers, brothers and husbands. Thus, as they move into new circles of the social structure, these writers encounter a world of acceptance. No longer is speaking out discouraged as it is in traditional Asian culture. The act of moving away from one's ethnic culture in itself can be a revolutionary act as is the act of writing, particularly writing about the self when one has been schooled in reticence. Cultural conflict brings forth a creative response to one's history, environment, and sexual role in the autobiographies by Japanese-American women.

Six major Japanese-American autobiographies were published after the Relocation. All of the post-World War II autobiographies are by women except for *The Kikuchi Diary* (1973) by Charles Kikuchi on his four months in Tanforan.[4] It is significant that Kikuchi's life was not typical of the lives of most Japanese-Americans. At the age of eight he was placed in an orphanage by his parents, an unprecedented act.

Removed from the milieu of his ethnic community, being the only Japanese in a Salvation Army orphan home, he grew up with unusual "anti-authoritarian attitudes" (19) that prompted him to various political involvements while a student at Berkeley and after, and to the keeping of a diary for years. In many ways, Kikuchi's life is almost a paradigm of Richard Wright's in *Black Boy*; Kikuchi is rejected by his parents, grows up confronting the "system," educates himself and becomes politically active. He speaks out where most Japanese-Americans prefer to be "quiet but effective."[5] I think it is important to emphasize the singularity of Charles Kikuchi, because his example serves to strengthen my thesis as to why Japanese-American women rather than men write autobiographies and also write autobiographically of the Relocation.

The first book published on the relocation, Mine Okubo's autobiography, *Citizen 13660*, is about the Japanese Relocation, but is primarily self-expression through art. Her book is a chronicle of her imprisonment at Tanforan Relocation Camp in San Bruno, California, and the Topaz Camp in Utah. Okubo gave a major showing of paintings and drawings in 1972 at the Oakland Museum; she reveals herself more in the museum catalog for this exhibition than she does in *Citizen 13660*.[6] Brought up in an artistic family, Okubo earned her M.A. in art from Berkeley in 1936. By 1938 she was in Europe until the outbreak of World War II sent her home, on the last boat out of Bordeaux after the borders were closed. In San Francisco she worked on the Federal Arts Project under the New Deal until the evacuation order came in 1942. In her catalogue, Okubo says of herself:

> I don't care where I am. I'm still the same. I adjust and adapt. I guess most Orientals are trained that way. Most of American life consists of people caught up in entertaining themselves.
>
> I never thought about marriage, don't kid yourself, you're number two. Besides, I don't want to cook three meals a day and still have to say, 'You're cute!' If you truly want to dedicate yourself to the highest, there's no other way. Somehow I do everything the hardest way—my way. (48)

The statement "I don't care where I am," is akin to what Jeanne Houston later says of the Japanese-American attitude toward the camp experience as "a kind of acquiescence on the part of the victims, some submerged belief that this treatment is deserved, or at least allowable" (114). Okubo's comments also help explain why she was the first to write of the camps. Here she reveals herself as an artist and as an individual from a family background that differs from that of the more "typical" Asian-American family of Jade Snow Wong, Monica Sone, or Maxine Hong Kingston. Okubo's family is educated and artistic, unlike the standard immigrant Asian family. She has an uncle who lives in Paris, a mother who writes poetry, and is from a cultured family tradition. Okubo's narrative of camp life is as spare and direct as her drawings are naive or primitive. She is not given to introspection in *Citizen 13660* and does not discuss herself outside of the historical context of the Relocation. Yet she is one of the very first to reveal the intimate details of daily life in the camps. Okubo gives one the sense of having established her identity prior to 1942 (she was born in 1912) and not being seriously affected, at least in terms of her self-esteem, by the relocation. As she stated in her catalogue,

> The Evacuation experience was most tragic for the isseis. The first generation mothers and fathers have suffered and sacrificed much to find a better place for their children. They have fought persecution and intolerance and struggled ceaselessly. Now they've lost everything they've worked so hard for—their homes, their businesses. And they're too old to start all over again afterwards. For them, it's all blown to the winds. (35)

Jeanne Houston similarly describes her father as completely broken by his internment at Manzanar. The young and old may have endured the most self-devaluation from this experience, but no one was exempt. Okubo's spare account in *Citizen 13660* may very well be masking the drama within as seen through the drawings that accompany every short paragraph of text. The art is bleak, depressing, and sad. Susan Langer discusses the issue of *absence* as an aspect of point of view in *The Narrative Act* (1981):

> The philosopher Merleau-Ponty has asked: "But what if language speaks as much by what is between words as by the words themselves? As much by what it does not 'say' as by what it 'says'?". . . . Particularly in the study of women's roles as authors and narrators, the question of silence sometimes becomes as crucial as the question of voice; "who does not speak?" is as revealing as "who speaks?" (42–43)

Thus, a muted account such as Okubo's can be a mask in the same way, paradoxically, as can be a very complex syntactic form. What Okubo is *not* saying becomes more important than what she does say. Here the language is a mask for the expressive artwork. Understatement and oblique reference are keys to Okubo's style and point to a tendency toward the bare style in Asian-American women's writing, notably excepting that of Maxine Hong Kingston.

Monica Sone, whose *Nisei Daughter* was considered, along with Jade Snow Wong's *Fifth Chinese Daughter* (1950), to be the best and most famous Asian-American autobiography until Houston's *Farewell to Manzanar* and Kingston's *The Woman Warrior* appeared, was also interned. Sone was a teenager during the Relocation and treats her experience at Puyallup and Minidoka, Idaho, with a combination of levity and avoidance. She centers her autobiography largely on her family life in the Seattle hotel her father owned before the evacuation. The short section on the actual internment concentrates on her brother's wedding and the anecdotal trip to "town" to find the bride's wedding gown. What Estelle Jelinek says in *Women's Autobiography* about women's self-narratives can be applied to Sone:

> Women's self-image is projected by the very means used to distance or detach themselves from intimacy in their life stories—a variety of forms of understatement. In place of glowing narratives, women tend to write in a straightforward and objective manner about both their girlhood and adult experiences. They also write obliquely, elliptically, or humorously in order to camouflage their feelings, the same techniques used to play down their professional lives. (15)

Mitsuye Yamada, who has written of her own Relocation experience in the book *Camp Notes*, said in a *MELUS* reassessment of *Nisei Daughter* in 1980 that when she first read the autobiography in 1953, "I felt that it was too familiar in content to be of much value as literature, and I promptly put it aside for the 'real' literature I was engaged in at the time." In reassessing this work, Yamada asserts that

> the denial of our own history and of the internalization of white America's standards were so thorough that we failed to recognize the experiences of our own lives as valid material for literature, and failed to support our own writers, thereby contributing to the atrophied state of Asian-American writing in those years. (19)

In her introduction to the 1979 reprint, Sone stands by her early work and does not apologize, but instead lobbies for congressional redress of the United States government's wrongs during World War II.[7] She ends her early autobiography as a postwar college student on a positive note; indeed, the tone of her book is throughout cheerful, enthusiastic, even breezy. Sone chooses the mask of humor, anecdote, and oblique reference to engage the American public of the 1950s as she tries to move verbally from her muted culture to emphasize to herself and the reader the fact of her assimilation. She summarizes, leaving camp,

> I had discovered a deeper, stronger pulse in the American scene. I was going back into its main stream, still with my Oriental eyes, but with

an entirely different outlook, for now I felt more like a whole person instead of a sadly split personality. The Japanese and the American parts of me were now blended into one. (238)

Sone here perfectly encapsulates the Japanese-American's motivation for writing autobiography, particularly after the camp experience, but makes the "blending" process sound more easily achieved than it, in fact, ever was. By contrast, Jeanne Wakatsuki Houston's more contemporary autobiography is both introspective and told through the double perspective of child and adult, whereas Okubo's was told from a mature perspective and Sone's by "a Northwest Japanese American girl," as one catalogue describes it.

Farewell to Manzanar was "told" by Jeanne Houston to her husband, James Houston, who actually wrote the book. Published in 1973, *Farewell to Manzanar* is highly readable and at the same time does not hesitate to confront the cultural conflict at the root of every Japanese-American's experience during World War II. Jeanne Wakatsuki spent her childhood years from seven to ten at the Manzanar camp in California, and later said, "It had taken me twenty-five years to reach the point where I could talk openly about Manzanar" (ix). The youngest child of a large, close family, she saw her father break and grow old while the family structure collapsed at Manzanar. We are introduced to the Wakatsukis when the father is a successful fisherman prior to the Pearl Harbor attack. Because of his occupation, (he could be sabotaging the American navy and sending signals to the Japanese fleet), he is sent to the high security men's camp at Fort Lincoln, Nebraska—and beaten. His story signals the breakdown of Japanese-American social structure and loss of self-esteem, while Jeanne states, "At seven I was too young to be insulted" (25). We are given a comprehensive narrative of life at Manzanar and the accompanying history of the internment, but also a full account of the author's life after 1946 as she grew up in the 1950s in a still racist California. Her story is archetypal as she concludes, "Suffice it to say, I was the first member of our family to finish college and the first to marry out of my race" (133). Of her return trip to Manzanar with her husband and three children, twenty-five years after the release from camp, she reveals: "I had nearly outgrown the shame and the guilt and the sense of unworthiness" (140). She has also examined her own participation in the evacuation as an acquiescence on the part of the victims, a passive acceptance that the internment was deserved or permissible. "It's an easy attitude for nonwhites to acquire in America. I had inherited it. Manzanar had confirmed it" (114). Houston's action of telling her autobiography and facing her past of imprisonment for race is representative of the impulse to reveal the self. Furthermore, she had achieved the degree of self-worth necessary in order to tell her story as, for many complex reasons, ethnic American women do.

Quite recently two new autobiographies by Nisei Japanese-American women have appeared: *Desert Exile* by Yoshiko Uchida and *Through Harsh Winters* by Akemi Kikumura. Uchida was a college graduate of twenty when sent with her family to Tanforan, then Topaz, while Kikumura, the youngest of thirteen children, was born at the Arkansas concentration camp. Kikumura, an anthropologist now at UCLA, writes her mother's oral history from five years of tape recordings and research. *Through Harsh Winters* is an unusual Japanese-American autobiography for several reasons. Kikumura is forty years younger than her mother and more than two generations of change have come between their lives. Her mother, Michiko Sato Tanaka, was raised out of the traditions of feudal Japan and came to America with her young husband, Saburo, in 1923. Her story is one of continual hardships and constant work. Because Saburo is a compulsive gambler, Michiko has to keep the family together, largely by migrant farming. After she bears thirteen children, her husband dies and she continues, actually relieved of his burden. For her, the Relocation is a rest because she doesn't have to work; there are only four pages devoted to the war years in her history. Michiko says, "My biggest worry had been money for food and shelter. In camp that burden was wiped out. The government fed us and gave us a monthly allowance of $10.50" (52). Although she briefly discusses camp conditions, this experience, we are led to believe, was a minor one in her life. Michiko's quick dismissal of the war years could be a purposeful silence, her form of masking. Perhaps the author's lack of experience concerning the camps influences what she says about this chapter in her mother's history. Michiko works indefatigably until her seventies, when she is forced to retire. She finally becomes an American citizen in 1980 after fifty-seven years of living in America, saying, "I should be entitled to citizenship, but I'm still considered a foreigner" (108). Kikumura, as an anthropologist, has documented her mother's autobiography with notes, charts, and appendices on "The Japanese American Family in Process of Acculturation" and "Methodology," making *Through Harsh Winters* both an autobiographical and a social/anthropological study of what was likely a typical experience for the majority of first generation Japanese immigrants who could only find work in the fields as migrant workers. By contrast, the family of Yoshiko Uchida was educated, cultured, and comfortably middle class. These two recent autobiographies offer a composite of the range of the Japanese-American experience in the twentieth century.

Yoshiko Uchida, an established author of some twenty-two children's books, has written of the Relocation before, but for juveniles. She finally decided to write "as well for all Americans, with the hope that through knowledge of the past, they will never allow another group of people in America to be sent into a desert exile ever again."[8] She almost echoes the moral tone of slave narratives in teaching a lesson and exhorting Caucasians to be less prejudiced. Yet Uchida's autobiography is straightforward and simply written. She gives us a realistically detailed narrative of life in both the Tanforan and Topaz camps, but begins with the standard "before" description of family life. Her father came to California in 1906 at age twenty-two, eventually becoming a manager for the San Francisco branch of Mitsui and Company. Fortunately, he had been retired at the age of fifty-five according to the Japanese custom and thus was not officially working for the enemy at the time of the Pearl Harbor attack. His marriage to Uchida's mother was arranged; she arrived from Japan in 1917. Both parents had been educated at Doshisha University in Kyoto, one of Japan's foremost Christian universities. This fact alone—that they are both college graduates and Protestants—sets the Uchidas apart from most Japanese immigrants to America. Yoshida grew up in a Caucasian neighborhood and went to Berkeley. Her father was a prominent member of the Japanese community and continued in that role while incarcerated. The family also frequently entertained Caucasians from the business world.

About growing up, Uchida expresses a strong assimilationist drive prevalent at that time:

> As I approached adolescence, I wanted more than anything to be accepted as any other white American. Imbued with the melting pot mentality, I saw integration into white American society as the only way to overcome the sense of rejection I had experienced in so many areas of my life. (40)

She learned to be careful on the "outside." " We avoided the better shops and restaurants where we knew we would not be welcome" (42). In analyzing this conflict, she explains:

> Society caused us to feel ashamed of something that should have made us feel proud. Instead of directing anger at the society that excluded and diminished us, such was the climate of the times and so low our self-esteem that many of us Nisei tried to reject our own Japaneseness and the Japanese ways of our parents. We were sometimes ashamed of the Issei in their shabby clothes, their rundown trucks and cars, their skin darkened from years of laboring in sun-parched fields, their inability to speak English, their habits, and the food they ate.
>
> I would be embarrassed when my mother behaved in what seemed to me a non-American way. I would cringe when I was with her as she

met a Japanese friend on the street and began a series of bows, speaking all the while in Japanese. . . . I felt disgraced in public. (42)

Jeanne Houston also writes of her mortification when, while she walked to the podium to receive a school award, her father commenced bowing to one and all from the audience. She relates:

> They received this with a moment of careful, indecisive silence. He was unforgivably a foreigner then, foreign to them, foreign to me, foreign to everyone but Mama, who sat next to him smiling with pleased modesty. Twelve years old at the time, I wanted to scream. I wanted to slide out of sight under the table and dissolve. (Houston 1973, 120)

As children both writers convey a strong urge to mask their ethnic identity and blend in with public society as they bridge the gap between the Issei and Sansei.

Yoshiko Uchida is twenty when interned in the spring of 1942. In her last semester at Berkeley, she is allowed to graduate on the basis of her midterm grades, as were the other Nisei. Her age and education made Uchida a useful chronicler of the camp experience. Not a child like Houston and not a mother overwhelmed by family duties, she is able to assess the internment with perspicacity; she was an elementary school teacher in the camp schools at Tanforan and Topaz. Uchida's autobiography is also a valuable social and historical narrative as she tells both her personal story and the parallel political history of the internment. Language itself is crucial. New arrivals at Topaz are given a notice on words: "Here we say Dining Hall and not Mess Hall; Safety Council, not Internal Police; Residents, not Evacuees; and last but not least, Mental Climate, not Morale" (109). In a footnote Uchida explains her use of the terms used at the time:

> "Evacuation" was the Army's official euphemism for our forced removal, just as "nonalien" was used when American citizen was meant. "Assembly center" and "relocation center," terms employed to designate the concentration camps in which we were incarcerated, were also part of the new terminology developed by the United States government and the Army to misrepresent the true nature of their acts. (52)

Language is purposely used to mask reality so that prisoners must reinvent their own experience. In another sense, Uchida's autobiography serves as a classic model of Japanese-American assimilation. On the subservience of her mother to her father in the traditional Issei pattern, she explains:

> Being a Japanese woman, . . . she behaved as a Japanese wife, and ad-
> justed even to having Papa stride several paces ahead of her, not from
> arrogance, but from impatience. For many years she sat in the back
> seat of the car, too self-conscious to take the seat up in front beside my
> father. (21)

Uchida herself would never go out with Caucasians socially in high
school or college. Today she reveals that her closest friend for the past
twenty years has been a "white" man. In her epilogue, the author tries to
answer the questions: "Why didn't you fight for your civil rights?"
"Why did you let it happen?" She answers:

> In 1942 the word "ethnic" was yet unknown and ethnic consciousness
> not yet awakened. There had been no freedom marches, and the voice
> of Martin Luther King had not been heard. . . .
> Today I would not allow my civil rights to be denied without
> strong protest. (148)

Yoshiko Uchida has become the ideal of the "American" personality,
having progressed from leaving Topaz "determined to work hard and
prove I was as loyal as any other American. I felt a tremendous sense of
responsibility to make good, not just for myself, but for all Japanese
Americans" (149). Perhaps now she does not have to "represent all
Nisei," yet *Desert Exile*, in a sense, does just that. Uchida spent two
years in Japan as a Ford Foundation Fellow in the 1950s and met all the
family relatives and friends. Apparently this introduction to her parents'
culture completed her circle of identity.

> My experience in Japan was as positive and restorative as the evacua-
> tion had been negative and depleting. I came home aware of a new di-
> mension to myself as a Japanese American and with new respect and
> admiration for the culture that had made my parents what they were.
> The circle was complete. I feel grateful today for the Japanese values
> and traditions they instilled in me and kept alive in our home, and un-
> like the days of my youth, I am proud to be a Japanese American and
> am secure in that knowledge of myself. (152)

Hers is the archetypal journey, whether real or metaphorical, of the ethnic American.

Monica Sone's final sentence in *Nisei Daughter* asserting that the
"Japanese and the American parts of me were now blended into one" re-
inforces the theme of the ethnic autobiographer's conversion to America.
In *Citizen 13660,* Mine Okubo avoids assessment as she leaves the
Topaz camp:

I entered the bus. As soon as all the passengers had been accounted for, we were on our way. I relived momentarily the sorrows and the joys of my whole evacuation experience, until the barracks faded away into the distance. There was only the desert now. My thoughts shifted from the past to the present. (209)

Later, Okubo was to reveal in her 1972 exhibit catalogue:

"The impact of evacuation is not on the material and physical. It is something far deeper. It is the effect on the spirit. What hurts most was the idea of being segregated and put away in a camp completely divorced from the national defense effort. Such action only helps to bring about greater hatred and to create further misunderstanding." (136)

Houston concludes *Farewell to Manzanar*, watching her eleven-year-old daughter walk around the ruins of Manzanar in 1972, "It was so simple, watching her, to see why everything that had happened to me since we left camp referred back to it, in one way or another" (139). Like Uchida's trip to Japan, Houston's pilgrimage to Manzanar enables her to face her past. Her brother had "found" himself in Japan after the war, while communing with Great-aunt Toyo and the ancestors in Ka-ke. "It took me another twenty years to accumulate the confidence to deal with what the equivalent experience would have been for me" (133). Of these five writers, Houston has been the only autobiographer to fully confront the effect of this experience on the postcamp life.

All of these Japanese-American writers reflect the painful process of coming to terms with a history imposed from without, despite the very private and immediate concerns of Akemi Kikumura's mother. The authors admit to a growing prejudice toward Asian-Americans on the West Coast prior to 1940, and there is even a suggestion of some inevitable watershed because of the inimical racial climate. Once World War II ended, the internees were supposed to quietly fade away or creep back home, which they did to a great extent despite the loss of some $400 million in property and other hardships. From the late 1960s on, the collective voice of protest initiated by the Sansei has garnered national recognition. These autobiographies by Japanese-American women and the anomalous Charles Kikuchi represent the formalization of a willingness to confront the self as a product of America's psyche. That women are writing these autobiographies is very revealing. They are not sitting in the back seat of the car; they do not walk a few paces behind either the Asian husband or the Caucasian. Neither do they try, anymore, to efface themselves from the dominant "American" culture. Japanese-American women have found a voice through the process of writing autobiography that was largely denied them by two conflicting cultures on the basis of both race and sex. In risking to lift the mask of silence, they have created and become themselves.

Notes

1. Akemi Kikumura, *Through Harsh Winters: The Life of a Japanese Immigrant Woman* (Novato, Calif.: Chandler and Sharp, 1981), 125. All further references to this book will be indicated by page number in the text.
2. *Farewell to Manzanar* (Boston: Houghton Mifflin, 1973), 27. All further references to this book will be indicated by page number in the text.
3. "The Representative Voice: Autobiography and the Ethnic Experience," *MELUS* 9, no. 2 (Summer 1982): 28.
4. *The Kikuchi Diary*, Introduction by John Modell (Urbana, Ill.: University of Illinois Press, 1973), 19.
5. "Quiet but Effective" was former Hawaii Governor George Arioyoshi's campaign slogan.
6. *Mine Okubo: An American Experience* (Oakland, Calif.: The Oakland Museum, 1972), 48. All further references to this book will be indicated by page number in the text.
7. *Nisei Daughter* (Boston: Little, Brown, 1953). Rpt., University of Washington Press, 1979.
8. *Desert Exile: The Uprooting of a Japanese American Family* (Seattle, Wash.: University of Washington Press, 1982), 154. All further references to this book will be indicated by page number in the text.

Works Cited

Holte, James C. "The Representative Voice: Autobiography and the Ethnic Voice." *MELUS* 9, no. 2 (Summer 1982): 25–46.

Houston, James, and Jeanne Wakatsuki. *Farewell to Manzanar.* Boston: Houghton Mifflin, 1973.

Jelinek, Estelle. *Women's Autobiography: Essays in Criticism.* Bloomington: Indiana University Press, 1980.

_____. *The Tradition of Women's Autobiography from Antiquity to the Present.* Boston: Twayne, 1986.

Kikuchi, Charles. *The Kikuchi Diary*, with an Introduction by John Modell. Urbana: University of Illinois Press, 1973.

Kikumura, Akemi. *Through Harsh Winters: The Life of a Japanese Immigrant Woman.* Novato, Calif.: Chandler and Sharp, 1981.

Langer, Susan. *The Narrative Act.* Princeton: Princeton University Press, 1981.

Mine Okubo: An American Experience. Oakland, Calif.: The Oakland Museum, 1972.

Okubo, Mine. *Citizen 13660.* New York: Columbia University Press, 1946.

Showalter, Elaine. "Feminist Criticism in the Wilderness." *Critical Inquiry* 8, no. 2 (Winter 1981): 179–205.

Sone, Monica. *Nisei Daughter.* Seattle: University of Washington Press, 1979.

Uchida, Yashiko. *Desert Exile: The Uprooting of a Japanese American Family.* Seattle: University of Washington Press, 1982.

Yamada, Mitsuye. Review of *Nisei Daughter. MELUS* 7, no. 3 (Fall 1980): 91–92.

III   Rethinking Genre: Autobiography in Other Forms

Though every autobiography tells the unique story of one individual's life, certain standards have nonetheless developed with regard to the narrative's content and form. Historically, the practice of writing autobiography grew out of the Christian confession. For example, many critics view Saint Augustine's *Confessions*, which he recorded at about the turn of the fourth century, as a classic example of the spiritual autobiography. These links with the religious confession led to texts that emphasized abstract ideas over concrete experiences. The mind, played a large role in autobiographies, while bodily matters rarely appeared.

Not surprisingly, these autobiographies' content also dictated certain typical forms. For example, the writers work their way to some particularly significant accomplishment or arrive at a deeper self-knowledge through the course of the text, and thus the autobiographies contain identifiable narrative climaxes. The intellectual nature of these texts means that they are artfully crafted documents, because writers do not tell readers about everything that happened in their lives. Instead, they choose to re-create the most compelling or powerful details. Of course, any thoughtful, well-crafted narrative can only develop when an autobiographer has been educated and has the time to write, along with adequate financial resources.

The following selections call all of these characteristics of the standard autobiography into question and reveal that such texts most often portray the lives of men from elite social classes. Women, in contrast, typically write autobiographies that focus on the material conditions of their lives. Indeed, women and working-class men are frequently associated with corporeality, while dominant cultural masculinity is associated with the mind. Clearly, such associations are not value free; the familiar phrase "mind over matter," for example, shows the extent to which we have been taught to value intellectual matters over bodily ones. Women autobiographers may not write linear texts that end with a definite narrative climax due to the demanding nature of their work or home lives along with the expectation that they will always put others' needs above their own. Thus they have found forms that allow them to record their lives more accurately than traditional autobiographies would. Diaries, for instance, enable the writer to jot ideas in brief sittings and may also contain a great deal of repetition. These selections demonstrate that expanding the definition of lifewriting to account for a variety of forms and themes will result in a rich and diverse category called "autobiography," which reflects a broad range of human experiences.

9

Expanding the Boundaries of Criticism: The Diary as Female Autobiography*

~

Judy Nolte Lensink

Autobiography critics typically defined the autobiography as a ret-rospective narrative tracing the author's journey from childhood to adulthood, or one that focused on significant events in the writer's life. However, feminist critics have recently argued that such a defi-nition typically applies to texts by male writers who have the time and resources to craft such retrospective accounts, and who have been taught to take pride in their ideas and achievements. In this se-lection, Judy Nolte Lensink represents one such feminist voice. She critiques the narrow definition of traditional autobiography and suggests that nineteenth-century diaries offer compelling accounts of women's lives. While many scholars dismiss the diary as a lesser, artless form of autobiography, Lensink's analysis of one text by Emily Hawley Gillespie, an Iowa farmer's wife, reveals that quite the opposite is true. When critics begin to examine women's diaries as autobiographies, she contends, they will not only have a new body of literature to study but also a richer understanding of women's lives.

IN RECENT YEARS, a few American women's autobiographies have en-tered the boundaries of the curricular canon, particularly in women's studies courses. The life stories of notables like Elizabeth Cady Stanton and autobiographically grounded texts like Tillie Olsen's "Silences" and Adrienne Rich's *Of Woman Born* have become classics. This acceptance of autobiography as a means for teaching about American lives began approximately a generation ago in interdisciplinary courses where such

*From Judy Nolte Lensink, "Expanding the Boundaries of Criticism: The Diary as Female Autobiography," *Women's Studies* 14 (1987): 39–53. Reprinted by permis-sion of *Women's Studies.*

diverse texts as *The Education of Henry Adams* and *Black Boy* were read as case studies in intellectual history. But along with hard-won acceptance by the academy came limitations, as autobiographical texts were subjected to traditional literary criteria.

The current study of autobiography has moved steadily away from readings of what James Olney calls "the simplest and commonest of writing propositions" to increasingly literary forms of the genre such as Vladimir Nabokov's *Speak, Memory* and Maxine Hong Kingston's pastiche of myth and memory, *The Woman Warrior.*[1] The autobiographies of ordinary people like Lucy Larcom and "plain" Anne Ellis are defined as historical/social documents rather than as literature from distinctive American voices. Autobiography scholarship has become established, complete with high-ranking theoretical scholars, classic essays, a canon of heavily studied texts—and boundaries.

The diary, that form of written personal narrative least colored by artifice, closest to the American life, truly "the story of a distinctive culture from within," that autobiography was once touted to be, is outside the interest of most scholars. The few diaries included in the canon are read for their content, rather than for their innovative literary form. For it is content writ large—significant periods in our military/political history, famous people encountered—that permits a few "important" diaries inside the boundaries. The only diary extensively studied for its form is Anaïs Nin's, which is certainly atypical of this genre. Thus the diary is acknowledged as a legitimate autobiographical text only when either the times recorded are extraordinary—William Byrd's, Mary Chesnut's—or the writer is extraordinarily established in literature—Henry Thoreau, Anaïs Nin.

Why are the estimated 100,000 American diaries, which record that dynamic interaction of the individual and society we seek in American studies and women's studies, virtually ignored as both literary and cultural texts by the very scholars who once expanded the critical boundaries of history and literature to encompass autobiography? Partially it is because we have yet to establish the critical tools that will make the unwieldy form of the diary accessible. It is also because we were trained as scholars to see the stories within ordinary peoples' diaries as inherently less interesting than those told by Henry James, Henry Thoreau, or Henry Adams. But on a deeper level, I would argue, the diary is resisted because in both form and content it comes closest to a female version of autobiography. As more about female psychology, language and historical experience is illuminated by theorists such as Carol Gilligan, Suzanne Juhasz, and Carroll Smith-Rosenberg, the diary is emerging as a female text.[2] The narrative of an American life that is both female *and* ordinary, the diary remains marginal. Mary Jane Moffat has ironically linked the terms that both women and their diaries engender: ". . . emotional, fragmentary, interrupted, modest, not to be taken seriously, private, restricted, daily, trivial, formless, concerned with self . . . endless. . . ."[3]

We can invert the critique of diaries that excludes them as too problematic for literary/historical study and find that the insistence upon an obviously literary Design in autobiography obstructs our reading of a separate "Truth" as told by female diarists.[4] By crossing many of the formalist "bindaries" of published autobiography, I would argue, diarists both tell their truth *and* create female design—a supersubtle design, similar to a quilt's, made up of incremental stitches that define a pattern. How can we as scholars, brought up on the canon, trained by the academy's fathers, learn to read these designs? First, we can look anew at the diary's characteristic language, content and narrative structure, then reassess it *sui generis*, as itself, rather than as "deficient" autobiography.

The language of ordinary people's diaries is considered tedious because it is often literal and repetitive. As Elizabeth Hampsten noted in her study of North Dakota diaries—and as I have found in the four-thousand-page diary I am studying—intensity of experience is usually signaled by quantity of language rather than by metaphor.[5] But if the public literary language of metaphor is indeed a male tongue, as Helene Cixous argues, then the private, plain-speaking voice within a woman's diary may be close to her true tongue.[6] Using a both/and strategy, we can look at diary language as both a truer rendering of "real life" via real speech, and yet as design.

If quantity of concrete language is characteristic of the prose, content analysis is one way to find out, literally, what "counted" in women's diaries. Note that I said diaries and not lives, for there is not always a correlation between what a diarist writes about and what really matters. In fact, topics upon which most diaries were virtually silent—sexuality, birth control—were probably so important that they were taboo. Therefore we need to read between the lines as well as count sentences. While content analysis such as that done by John Faragher on Overland Trail diaries is still vulnerable to a scholar's interpretation, it is one route beyond the limitations of infinite individual texts to conclusions based on a body of literature.[7]

When the language within a diary is excessively metaphoric, on the other hand, it may obscure rather than inscribe true emotion, just as it may so fetchingly in public autobiography. Ann Douglas has argued that lush metaphor in nineteenth-century women's prose about death and children, for example, is obfuscation, a camouflage of pat imagery provided by a culture that no longer values the very things it sentimentalizes in language. The sanctioned images that diarists use to cope with death, for example, perhaps employ metaphor to stop raw emotion from pouring out onto the page.[8]

Finally, a diarist's language may form a design of unconscious metaphor. For example, in almost every middle-class nineteenth-century woman's diary I have read, the image of *Home* recurs. I will return to this particular iconography later to show its function as a unifying metaphor in the diary I am studying. The deceptively simple language of the diary, then, can be denotative, consciously literary, or approach the truth "slant" through its unself-conscious choice of imagery chosen from daily life.

In the critical literature on the content of autobiography, certain criteria recur: coherence, significance, and systematic retrospection. This view of the self and life, transposed to the writing of the life, is an androcentric one, as Patricia Meyer Spacks and Suzanne Juhasz have argued.[9] Diarists write around these criteria and still create cohesive autobiographies, as I will show.

The initial sense of incoherence one gets when reading an ordinary woman's diary—comments on the weather, health, tomato canning, followed by a stanza of sentimental poetry—occurs because we are used to constructed books rather than those that "happened," as Thomas Mallon defines diaries.[10] Anaïs Nin called them organic texts, rather than the imposed texts that result from a controlling intelligence.[11] On the other hand, the diary is obviously not a literal transcription of a day. The diarist too selects what to describe and creates what I call "diary time"— giving a full page to a lover's single sentence, while describing fourteen hours of the day with the single telling phrase, "did usual work." In fact, diary-writing is one way in which women have made coherent their experiential lives. Paul Rosenblatt observes, "As one writes about what has happened and how one feels, one is defining the situation and one's reactions. The act of defining may be seen as an act of controlling, delineating, and shaping. . . ."[12] Within the text of the diary, then, a coherent world formed by the writer's perceptions exists: populated by reappearing characters, mappable, even if only the size of a household. The changes that occur across time form the natural plot of the diary. While women's life stories generally do not fit the individualistic, linear narrative form of men's, as feminist scholars have noted, they do move forward within a subtle sequence of relational cycles. Rather than playing the mannikin who arrives at multiplicity from chaos, a woman may see *herself* as multiplicity—daughter, wife, mother, teacher, widow. This lack of closure, of denouement, gives the diary a form similar to life itself and renders autobiography the more lifeless form. Anaïs Nin, a writer in several genres, described why she preferred the diary form:

> The diary made me aware of organic and perpetual motion, perpetual change in character. When you write a novel or a short story [or an auto-

biography?] you are arresting motion for a period of that story, a span of time. There is something static about that. . . . And so in many cases, reading novels, I had the feeling of still life rather than a perpetual motion.[13]

In the classic autobiography, the author attempts, as Yeats did, "to stand apart" from his life in order to "judge." The diary, by contrast, demands everyday composition, an immersion in the text which parallels the immersion in life. The significance demanded by Goethe, who avoided in his autobiography "the incoherent realia strewn about [that] must necessarily disturb the good effect" is the antithesis of the contextual diary, rich with realia, that reflects a different view of life. Reading *from* the diary, rather than disregarding it or editing it to show some applied concept of significance, we might discover a different *bios*, a life lived by women, as did psychologist Carol Gilligan when she listened to women's words rather than to men's theories:

> When one begins with the study of women and derives developmental constructs from their lives, the outline of a moral conception . . . begins to emerge and informs a different description of development. In this conception, the moral problem arises from conflicting responsibilities rather than from competing rights and requires for its resolution a mode of thinking that is contextual and narrative rather than formal and abstract.[14]

Likewise, the diary-writer, less concerned with "significance," can create a more vital version of her life, in situ, rather than pulling one out of context with some intellectualizing forceps to be examined "objectively" in the light of significance.

The critics' insistence on "the retrospective stance" is still considered essential to truth in personal history, laments Albert Stone.[15] Yet it must soon crumble, as autobiographers like Maya Angelou and Maxine Hong Kingston write perceptively about their childhoods and young adult lives with white-hot immediacy. Angelou's multivolume life story, told by a still-evolving persona, forms a serial autobiography not unlike that formed by the diary.

In reassessing our ideas of what constitutes legitimate autobiographical design, we can elicit a nearer truth from diary texts. I liken reading a diary to watching a young child at play. If you can catch her in a private moment, you come close to hearing her real voice; once she knows you are listening, however, that voice becomes adulterated, then becomes even more modified for a larger audience. It still poses as a child's, but the private voice was much better. A study of diaries may reformulate our ideas of how ordinary women spoke, thought, and perceived their worlds. Once diaries are considered texts (no longer subtexts), we can use them to read women's culture—no longer seen as a subculture.

By way of illustration, I would like to turn to my study of a long diary to show how it is both autobiography, with thematic purpose, persona and imagery, and something more—a document that traces at great length an ordinary individual's encounter with ideology. When read intertextually with other women's narratives, this type of diary will help us rewrite nineteenth-century women's history through their own autobiographies.

The diary was written faithfully by Emily Hawley Gillespie, a Midwestern woman, for thirty years—from 1858, just before she turned twenty, to 1888, the year of her death. It tells the story of an idealistic young woman who courts selectively, marries hopefully, and works ceaselessly on an Iowa farm, only to see her labor, her dreams and eventually herself disregarded.[16]

The purpose of the diary, as stated on its opening page, is to give "reminiscences of the life, from day to day, of Miss Emmie E. Hawley." The use of "reminiscences" at the start of a diary can alert us to as many meanings as Henry Adams's use of "mannikin." It could signal a conscious selectivity operative in the diary, a sign at the outset that this writer will record what she wishes to remember, rather than the whole story. We can expect and do find flattering suitors, personal triumphs, and incidents that vindicate the diarist. In a later volume opened with a poem, the autobiographer is again signaling the theme and bias of her text: "Another book is added to my journal of life/May it not be filled with sorrow and strife. Let pure & undefiled Virtue, its pages unfold/ May our hearts be as pure & bright as fine Gold."

The rather literary term "reminiscences" might also indicate Hawley's lofty plans to start a book. And, indeed, the diary graduates from loose sheets of foolscap, to tied "booklets," to account notebooks, and finally leather-bound journals. If such a youthful diarist was intending to author a bona fide book, as chapter headings like "Home" and "Virtue" show at one point, rather than an ephemeral record, then questions of audience would arise, as they do in her very first volume. In one incident she asks "dear reader" if she should not be pitied, a form of authorial address straight out of sentimental fiction. She also early shows a strong sense of privacy. While she elliptically refers to an event as a memory aid, she keeps details away from the public realm of language. She writes, "George . . . and I went to take a walk; we went perhaps forty rods from the house and sat on a log beneath a beautiful shade tree and talked,—well never mind what about."

This explicit show of the "author-ity" to omit perhaps the most important events of her life (which may have been sexual, since she was also coding her menstrual cycle in the diary's margins with exclamation marks) shows both the strength of diaries—their refreshing honesty about their own construction—and their ultimate limitation, like all autobiography, as documents about "reality." Later in her life, when the tale of romance has become instead a painful chronicle of a wronged woman, Gillespie still withholds the most unpleasant aspects of her story from the eyes of whatever audience she anticipates. After detailing her husband's cruelties, she declares, "I have written *many* things in my journal, but the worst is a secret to be buried when I shall cease to be." This reluctance shows what a powerful entity the diary has become. Rather than bury the book because it tells all, she will take her agony to her grave so that the diary itself will never "cease to be."

In Gillespie's diary, the goal to reminisce increasingly wars with the desire to have an "undefiled" book, despite her unhappiness. She insists on remembering, however, drawing small Victorian-style hands in the book's margins to point to entries for quick reference: death dates, proud moments in her children's lives. She also threads together her life by intratextual reference, noting on a certain date where she was ten years earlier, according to her diary. This leads to a type of internal closure which this diarist seems to have desired, as she links together thematically significant events far apart in time: comets observed, the history of a piece of fabric, her teaching salary of two decades ago compared to her daughter's. And while she never stands apart from herself to judge, as did many formal autobiographers of her era, she does rather ruthlessly objectify others, as does every diarist who portrays people via language.

Another, more cynical reading of the term "reminiscences" would alert the scholar to the possibility that the title was applied after the moment of the diary's origin, perhaps years later when the writer reread her journals, as Gillespie noted doing. Almost no century-old personal document remains unaltered by either an author with second thoughts, a nervous relative, or the elements. Indeed, practically every published diary I have encountered, from Mary Chesnut's to the more obscure Samuella Curd's, contains the editor's explanation of alternations detected in the manuscript. This inability to leave well enough alone suggests that an autobiographical impulse to potentially go public lurks within those who persist in keeping a diary.[17]

While the need to remember stays consistent throughout the composition of Gillespie's book, the narrative's purpose—and therefore her choice of literary form—changes across three decades. Her book, definitely not a still-life, is a meta-autobiography. It opens in a sentimental vein. Emily quotes her many suitors on the same pages in which she refers to sentimental fiction like *Tempest and Sunshine*, wishing perhaps in her diary's pages to mirror the trysts of novels. She describes the courtship methods and failings of men with drinking habits, fiery tempers and speech defects, saving herself for "*the* one" who will honor her ideal of a husband and lover. As she moves to Iowa to live and work in her uncle's inn, the diary briefly lapses into the form and language of a travel account, for which there were many published models. After her arrival in Iowa, the diary returns to the sentimental mode, with Emily playing the orphan alone in the wide, wide world of the Far West.

Early in her marriage to wealthy James Gillespie, her choice as she neared her twenty-fourth birthday, the romance drops out of the diary, as entries like this show: "do my wash,—finish shirt—my cow has a calf this morning. James chop wood & kill the calf." Or perhaps Emily Gillespie decided that as a wife she should record less frivolous memories and instead emphasize financial accounts, an element in her diary all along. The diary soon becomes the couple's book; Emily mentions several times asking her husband at day's end what she should write for him. This literal "accounting" for Gillespie's time fits her belief that those who work hard will see their wealth—and happiness—accumulate.

When the two Gillespie children become old enough to appreciate Emily's life plan for them as "young folks"—academy educations, minimal farm chores, fancy dress clothes—her diary becomes a record of their mother's deeds and beliefs. Again, the diary follows a tradition, that of the memento book. Anne Bradstreet's autobiography was dedicated "To My Dear Children" and began with her wish that the book would in some way show her children "their mother's heart." Soon Emily's and James's activities take up less diary space, the children's activities and virtues more. The egotism necessary to write a diary, at war with the altruism Gillespie feels for her children, is resolved in the act of dedicating the books (as she did her life) to her offspring.

As Emily Gillespie's heart becomes more embittered by strife with James, her late diary increasingly resembles the accounts of "injured females" like Elizabeth Ashbridge's, which were popular in England during the eighteenth century. In this genre, drama and religious messages were combined in tales wherein women played the Christians and their husbands the lion, according to Daniel Shea.[18] James, Emily now reveals in a narrative of much different tone, had never been an ideal husband; now she records his unnatural failure as a father in the diary kept to burn memories into her children's minds as well as her own. The diary becomes so vital a "confidant" and family member that when she is ill the children take dictation for it. After her death, both children wrote their own observations in the diary margins after reading it. Sixty years later, daughter Sarah devoted much time transcribing the diary's early sections into more permanent books and in essence "publishing" it by placing copies in several historical archives.

Despite the grotesque mutation that domestic dreams take in Gillespie's life and the changing form of her diary, her narrator's voice remains almost rigidly consistent, as did Franklin's in his autobiography. Thomas Mallon has described this type of older diary persona as "horizontal" in that one's personality is perceived as staying consistent across time. Like the Puritans, Gillespie asks in her diary, "How well was I myself today?" (Modern diarists of the psychoanalytic age usually envision themselves as mutable, moving vertically through time. They ask, "Who am I today, compared to myself two years ago?") Gillespie's diary, however, does not completely follow the earlier religious model of daily self-criticism. She is quite well pleased with herself, often defending her viewpoint in her book. Her diary, then, is a transitional one, as reflected in its persona.

Because Gillespie views her life through the lens of relationship, her persistent persona—the striving sufferer—is often portrayed relationally. At the diary's start, she is an underesteemed daughter who obeys her mother's warning about going to New York for art training and agrees to stay home. As a betrothed young woman, she describes a nightmare in which she finds it impossible to please her fiancé and his parents. Then she strives to be the perfect mother, castigating herself in her diary for chastizing her children, writing prayers that ask for more patience. Later she describes herself as the unappreciated wife of a farmer, the misunderstood daughter of an elderly resident father, the maligned sister of jealous siblings. Only at the very end of her diary does she begin to look beyond relationships, to criticize the social structure that has predetermined the pattern of her life and book, rather than the individual antagonists. Ironically, this insight comes via personal relationships. When a dear neighbor woman is institutionalized, Gillespie writes, "I only wonder that more women do not have to be taken to that asylum. Especially farmers' wives. No society except hired men to eat their meals. Hard work from the beginning to the end of the year." Later, she worries when her daughter is courted by an attractive man and again goes from the specific relationship to the generalization: "Ah, marriage is a lottery."

Gillespie's creation of "characters" in the diary is clearest in her evolving depiction of James. In the early years, his activities are seen as heroic, his moods as "fine temperament," his words as quite romantic. In the last years, he is described as insane; when Emily quotes him, she writes his words in the dialect of a rube. While her self-portraiture is more consistent, her persona does develop an increasingly vigorous voice. My content analysis shows that her use of evaluative commentary, both positive and negative, rises dramatically as she ages. Her ego emerges, reinforcing my earlier interpretation—that this never was intended to be a diary that recorded life. Rather, it was a book in which to frame an authorized version of life—selective, mutable as the ideology driving it, eventually vocal and judgmental.

If we accept this diary as constructed autobiography then, rather than mere recorded narrative, certain images can be traced that serve as metaphors for Gillespie. One such that I alluded to earlier, *Home*, informs her book, as it did dozens of other women's diaries and the prescriptive literature of the nineteenth century. Gillespie's book shows how difficult it was to enact an idealized image with real-life people.

For young Emily Hawley, home was called "father's" and it was clear that a dependent unmarried daughter must leave it. Never "at home" at her uncle's inn, forced then to live in a wing of her new father-in-law's house, Gillespie finally delights in a rented place of her own: "we are at home enjoying life finely." When adorable children are added to this home, she thanks the Lord for her "happy family circle." While neighbors succumb to the agricultural depression of the mid-1870s, the Gillespies build a large house and Emily receives a deed to the entire farm from her husband. (The autobiographer's interpretation of this incident changes with her marriage: at the time of the event, the present of the deed is treated as a great honor from James. Only later, in the embittered years, does Gillespie write that James deeded over the farm to protect it from creditors.) Later, as a carpenter completes an addition to the home, the entire family argues over money; when a Brussels carpet and new furniture are put in the parlor, Emily excludes James from her image of the home, noting that the finery is too nice for him. "Home" also turns upon Emily Gillespie, who complains about the social isolation of the farm which causes her to "always be at home," a phrase she wrote with such pleasure ten years earlier. When the marriage explodes and she is forced to rent her own home from James, Gillespie sees the embodiment of her life's round of "usual work" slipping away. Moved as an invalid to a rented house in town, where she had always wanted to live for the society, she is ultimately confined to a bedroom. Having achieved the ideal home for only a few years of her life, Gillespie records through its imagery the diminishment of her dreams that could find no residence. Her diary, an unrelenting descriptive document, stands as a stark counterpoint to the home so touted by writers like the Beechers, balancing our view of women as seen through prescriptive literature.[19] By first reading within diaries, and then conducting an intertextual analysis, we can begin to understand what happened to Victorian women living among icons of children, church, and home.

Another image in the Gillespie diary, that of perpetual motion, connects stunningly with Anaïs Nin's use of the same conceit 117 years later for her own diary, that "novel of the future." It seems almost inevitable that a pioneer woman immersed in the "usual work" of daily routine might arrive at the image of perpetual motion in a complaint. But for Gillespie, the image appears in an unearthly dream that shows her desire to exist on a higher plane, to somehow profit from the "perpetual motion" that was her life:

> Oh how grand it would be if one could live two hundred years, live to see the wonders wrought, to see the progress in art & science, *not* live for mere life alone, it almost enraptures us in reverie of thought to even have an idea of such a life. *There is one invention which I do believe can be made to be a perfect success*, and that is *perpetual-motion as I dreamed it about 15 or 18 years ago*, it must be done by weight and pressure by springs on an inclined plane, similar to a machine used by putting a horse into a sort of tread-mill—
>
>> The frame was silver and sparkling stones,
>> The horse was gold-tied with a golden chain,
>> Beneath his feet was an inclined plane
>> So bright, as it turned beneath his tread,
>> That it seemed too real to be only a dream.
>> Within the golden horses feet, cut in notched form
>> Were diamonds, to fit & drive the bars of gold
>> On which were notched plates of dazling brightness.
>> Standing near this wonder of art and skill
>> Was the inventor: his raiment—gold and silver thread,
>> A cloak embroidered with glistening diamonds.
>> Right proud he was, of his rare invention.
>> I too—for once—was dressed in gorgeous array
>> If *'twere* in a *dream*. Aye three times this presentiment.
>> As I stood beside him I asked "What's the name of this?"
>> With uplifted hand he answered "Perpetual Motion."

The way that Emily Gillespie made sense of real-life perpetual motion was to recount daily what her drudgery amounted to, both literally in her financial records—and emotionally in the record of her children's developing character. Gillespie's diary, then, is a self-kept tally of how she did indeed account for something. Her chosen persona of the sufferer was perfectly enacted in the autobiographical form of the diary, kept privately and relentlessly while she silently endured life's hardships. When she was ultimately silenced by death, her diary, passed through generations, would proclaim her angelic sacrifice more movingly than any words on a headstone. Emily Gillespie at last could speak and be appreciated through the accumulative narrative that paralleled the pattern of her life.

What I hope this brief introduction to my study suggests is that rich autobiographical texts reside in ordinary women's diaries. If we can see the gender-blindness of the current literary criteria that disregard diaries, and overcome our fear of new forms when faced with dusty, scribbled narratives, I predict that we will again expand the boundaries of our reading and thinking to include new literature about American lives.

Notes

1. James Olney, ed., *Autobiography: Essays Theoretical and Critical* (Princeton: Princeton University Press, 1980), 11.

2. See, for example, Carol Gilligan, *In a Different Voice: Psychological Theory and Women's Development* (Cambridge: Harvard University Press, 1982); Suzanne Juhasz, "Towards a Theory of Form in Feminist Autobiography," in *Women's Autobiography: Essays in Criticism*, ed. Estelle Jelinek (Bloomington: Indiana University Press, 1980); Carroll Smith-Rosenberg, "The Female World of Love and Ritual," *Signs* 1, no. 1 (1975): 1–29.

3. Mary Jane Moffat and Charlotte Painter, eds., *Revelations: Diaries of Women* (New York: Random House, 1974).

4. I refer here to the framework still powerful in autobiographical criticism set out by Roy Pascal in *Design and Truth in Autobiography* (Cambridge: Harvard University Press, 1960).

5. Elizabeth Hampsten, *Read This Only to Yourself: The Private Writings of Midwestern Women, 1880–1910* (Bloomington: Indiana University Press, 1982).

6. Helene Cixous, "The Laugh of the Medusa," reprinted in *The Signs Reader*, ed. Elizabeth Abel (Chicago: University of Chicago Press, 1982).

7. John Mack Faragher, *Women and Men on the Overland Trail* (New Haven: Yale University Press, 1979). For a primer on content analysis, see Gordon Allport, *The Use of Personal Documents in Psychological Science* (New York: Social Science Research Council, 1942).

8. Ann Douglas, *The Feminization of American Culture* (New York: Alfred Knopf, 1977).

9. Patricia Meyer Spacks, "Reflecting Women," *Yale Review* 63 (1973): 26–42; and Suzanne Juhasz, "'Some Deep Old Desk or Capacious Hold-All': Form and Women's Autobiography," *College English* 6 (February 1978): 663–68.

10. Thomas Mallon, *A Book of One's Own: People and Their Diaries* (New York: Ticknor and Fields, 1984).

11. Anaïs Nin, *The Novel of the Future* (New York: Collier Books, 1968).

12. Paul Rosenblatt, *Bitter, Bitter Tears: Nineteenth-century Diaries and Twentieth-century Grief Theories* (Minneapolis: University of Minnesota Press, 1983).

13. Nin, *Novel of the Future*, 161–62.

14. Gilligan, *In a Different Voice*, 19.

15. Albert E. Stone, ed., *The American Autobiography* (Englewood Cliffs, N.J.: Prentice-Hall, 1981), 7.

16. The papers of Emily E. Hawley Gillespie and her family are in the manuscript collection of the Iowa State Historical Society, Iowa City, Iowa.

17. See editors' introductory essays in C. Vann Woodward, ed., *Mary Chesnut's Civil War* (New Haven: Yale University Press, 1981), and Susan S. Arpad, ed., *Sam Curd's Diary* (Athens: Ohio University Press, 1984).

18. Daniel B. Shea, Jr., *Spiritual Autobiography in Early America* (Princeton: Princeton University Press, 1968).

19. See, for example, Catharine Beecher and Harriet Beecher Stowe's *Principles of Domestic Sciences; As Applied to the Duties and Pleasures of the Home* (1870) and Harriet Beecher Stowe's *Uncle Tom's Cabin* (1851).

10

Autopathography: Women, Illness, and Lifewriting*

~

G. Thomas Couser

Although intellectual autobiography has a long and distinguished literary history, autobiographies have tended to ignore the body and physical concerns. Illness in particular has been omitted from autobiographical writings. These silences reflect the traditional Western belief in the superiority of the mind over the body, a belief that is often expressed through associations of the intellect with masculinity and the corporeal with femininity. For this reason, G. Thomas Couser connects the omission of illness from autobiographies with the tendency to value male experiences over those of women.

Given the traditional silences in autobiography about disease, Couser applauds the recent emergence of autobiographical narratives of illness and disability, most of them written by women, as a salutary development. He calls this literature "autopathography": auto, "self" + pathos, "suffering, disease" + grapho, "to write." Autopathography offers an honest acknowledgment and assessment of the human condition as both flesh and spirit. It corrects centuries of Western over-emphasis on the mind at the expense of the body. Couser analyzes how two contemporary women writers, Barbara Webster and Nancy Mairs, use autobiography in different ways to explore the individual and cultural ramifications of the disease of multiple sclerosis.

Thomas Couser is a professor of English at Hofstra University. His most recent book is Recovering Bodies: Illness, Disability, and Life Writing *(1997). Couser's current research focuses on lifewriting and disability and the ethics of life writing.*

*From G. Thomas Couser, "Autopathography: Women, Illness, and Lifewriting," *a/b: Auto/Biography Studies* 6 (1991): 65–75. Reprinted by permission of *a/b: Auto/Biography Studies* and the author.

THE WORD "PATHOGRAPHY" first caught my attention not in its clinical context, in which it simply refers to writing about illness, such as case histories, but in a review by Joyce Carol Oates of David Roberts's recent biography of Jean Stafford. There Oates adapted the clinical term to denote—and to denigrate—what she described as "hagiography's diminished and often prurient twin, [whose] motifs are dysfunction and disaster, illnesses and pratfalls, failed marriages and failed careers, alcoholism and breakdowns and outrageous conduct" (3). According to Oates—not entirely a disinterested party, since, as a famous writer, she is sure to be a biographer's subject eventually—we are in the midst of an outbreak of diseased biography that dwells obsessively on its subjects' (psycho)pathology.

This may be true, and it may be regrettable. But we are also—and the two phenomena may be connected—in the midst of a flowering of what I call "autopathography," autobiographical narratives of illness or disability. The texts I have in mind range from journals to essays to full-life narratives, but most lie in a middle range of "single-experience" autobiographies. Disease may remain in the background, as when serious illness stimulates reassessment of a whole life; but usually it is squarely in the foreground, as when the narrative is coextensive with the illness. Among the writers I have in mind here are Emmanuel Dreuilhe (*Mortal Embrace*), Audre Lorde (*The Cancer Journals*), Nancy Mairs (*Plaintext, Remembering the Bone House,* and *Carnal Acts*), Robert Murphy (*The Body Silent*), Oliver Sacks (*A Leg to Stand On*), May Sarton (*After the Stroke*), Eileen Simpson (*Reversals*), William Styron (*Darkness Visible*), John Updike (*Self-Consciousness*), Barbara Webster (*All of a Piece: A Life with Multiple Sclerosis*), and Paul Zweig (*Departures*).

If "pathography" is for Oates a symptom of cultural pathology, the development of autopathography is for me a sign of cultural health—an acknowledgement and an exploration of our condition as *embodied* selves. One of the notable and salutary features of this recent trend is the prominence of women writers in it. Yet despite the fact that we are in the midst of intense theorizing about women's bodies, and despite signs of a new interest in literature and the body,[1] not much critical attention has been paid, as far as I am aware, to the emerging autobiographical literature of illness and disease, much of which has been written by women. I wish to speculate about lifewriting, illness, and gender in somewhat general terms, then discuss two books by women afflicted with multiple sclerosis, Barbara Webster's *All of a Piece: A Life with Multiple Sclerosi*s and Nancy Mairs's *Plaintext.*

It is obvious, upon reflection (though most of us rarely reflect upon it), that we have our being in the world, and act upon it, through our bodies and only through them. As Jonathan Miller has pointed out,

Of all the objects in the world, the human body has a peculiar status: it is not only possessed by the person who has it, it also possesses and constitutes him [*sic*]. [As a result], . . . it is hard to give an intelligible sense to the idea of a disembodied person. . . . Our body is not, [then] something we have, it is a large part of what we actually are. (14)

Though our selves and our lives are fundamentally bodily, the body has not, until recently, figured very prominently in lifewriting. This may not be surprising, because, to quote Miller again, "The immediate experience of the human body is something which we take for granted. We perceive and act with it and become fully aware of its presence only when it is injured, or when it goes wrong" (10). Exactly: injury and illness (and aging) remind us, in various unwelcome ways, that we have bodies, that we *are* bodies.

When the subjects of lifewriting are afflicted by sufficiently serious illness or disability, those conditions do find their way into the texts. But except when illness threatens life or ends it, traditional biographers usually treat it as an interruption of the life that is their proper subject. Autobiographers are better situated than biographers to report on the bodily lives of their subjects, but until recently they have seemed disinclined to do so.[2] Illness has been as studiously ignored, or repressed, in lifewriting as has the body, and for the same reasons.

Virginia Woolf has commented incisively on the discrepancy between the "facts" of life and the "fictions" of literature:

Considering how common illness is, how tremendous the spiritual change that it brings, how astonishing, when the lights of health go down, the undiscovered countries that are then disclosed, what wastes and deserts of the soul a slight attack of influenza brings to view, . . . when we think of this, as we are so frequently forced to think of it, it becomes strange indeed that illness has not taken its place with love and battle and jealousy among the prime themes of literature. Novels, one would have thought, would have been devoted to influenza; epic poems to typhoid; odes to pneumonia; lyrics to tooth-ache. But no; with a few exceptions . . . literature does its best to maintain that its concern is with the mind; that the body is a sheet of plain glass through which the soul looks straight and clear, and, save for one or two passions such as desire and greed, is null, and negligible and non-existent. On the contrary, the very opposite is true. All day, all night the body intervenes; blunts or sharpens, colours or discolours, turns to wax in the warmth of June, hardens to tallow in the murk of February. The creature within can only gaze through the pane—smudged or rosy; it cannot separate off from the body like the sheath of a knife or the pod of a pea for a single instant; it must go through the whole unending procession of changes, heat and cold, comfort and discomfort,

hunger and satisfaction, health and illness, until there comes the inevitable catastrophe; the body smashes itself to smithereens, and the
soul (it is said) escapes. But of all this daily drama of the body there is
no record. People write always of the doings of the mind; the thoughts
that come to it; its noble plans; how the mind has civilised the universe. They show it ignoring the body in the philosopher's turret; or
kicking the body, like an old leather football, across leagues of snow
and desert in the pursuit of conquest or discovery. Those great wars
which the body wages with the mind a slave to it, in the solitude of the
bedroom against the assault of fever or the oncome of melancholia, are
neglected. Nor is the reason far to seek. To look these things squarely
in the face would need the courage of a lion tamer; a robust philosophy; a reason rooted in the bowels of the earth. Short of these, this
monster, the body, this miracle, its pain, will soon make us taper into
mysticism, or rise, with rapid beats of the wings, into the raptures of
transcendentalism. (9–10)

I quote this passage at such length not just because of its extraordinary beauty, nor simply because the subtlety of its argument defies paraphrase, but because it provides at once the theory and the practice of a
body-centered prose. The long, sinuous sentences, with their pronounced, yet organically fluctuating rhythms; the intricate patterns of
antithesis and alliteration; the heavy reliance on sensuous images to convey ideas—these stylistic features enact the linguistic equivalent of the
mediation of the body, precisely what Woolf claims has been denied by
the canon. Thus, any cutting, no matter how "surgical," must implement
a privileging of idea over image, sense over sound, that the prose takes
pains to discredit. Indeed, Woolf's metaphor of the mind kicking the
body, like a football, across wastelands in pursuit of conquest, wittily
demonstrates that embodiment may lurk even in language that purports
to efface it. Her tropes and images deconstruct the valorization of mind
over matter; her style brings us literally to our senses.

Though Woolf's remarks are not concerned explicitly with lifewriting, they are certainly relevant to it.[3] Especially to the predicament of
the female autobiographer, for her account of the suppression of illness
in literature has as its subtext the domination of discourse by masculinist
assumptions. For Woolf, the valorization of health over illness is a function of the Western privileging of mind over body, the tendency to deny
the body's intervention in intellectual and spiritual life. And Woolf's
characterization of the domination of mind over body in terms of traditionally masculine, aggressive pursuits—warfare, discovery, conquest,
and even civilization (as a process, rather than a condition)—suggests
that the suppression of bodily illness as a literary subject is related to the
valorization of "male" over "female" experience. Her countercharge is

that the (masculine) canon has not dared to face the body squarely. The irony engendered by the passage is that it takes a woman to declare, not the emperor's nakedness, but his corporeality and thus his vulnerability to "feminizing" illness.

To paraphrase the title of a well-known essay by Sherry Ortner, Woolf raises the question: Is female to male as body is to mind and illness is to health? Ortner argues that the universal subordination of women is rooted in the association of women more closely than men with nature, which in turn is based on the characterization of women as more defined—and thus confined—by their anatomy, especially its reproductive capacities. Following de Beauvoir—perhaps too closely—Ortner states: "It is simply a fact that proportionately more of a woman's body, for a greater percentage of her lifetime, and at some—sometimes great—cost to her personal health, strength, and general stability, is taken up with the natural processes surrounding the reproduction of the species" (74).

Though bodily ills usually entail a degree of marginalization, this form of marginalization has been largely ignored by literary theorists—in favor of the marginalization of race, class, gender, and sexual preference. But when illness strikes women, it may echo and expose the marginalization of gender. Something like this happened to Audre Lorde, who was already marginalized by gender, race, *and* sexual preference when she was afflicted with breast cancer. Lorde did not require disease to raise her consciousness, of course; rather, her feminism enabled her to respond to breast cancer in an unorthodox way. For example, she treats the prosthetic device she is expected to "put on" after surgery as a further mutilation of her womanhood rather than the reconstruction of her identity it is supposed to be. And in *The Cancer Journals* she constructs her own racial and gender mythology with which to counter her disease.

The marginalization produced by disease is sometimes temporary, sometimes permanent; sometimes, of course, disease threatens not merely to marginalize but to obliterate the self. Multiple sclerosis lies between extremes: while it is rarely life threatening, it is always disabling. According to Nancy Mairs, the disablement can take a variety of forms:

> During its course, which is unpredictable and uncontrollable, one may lose vision, hearing, speech, the ability to walk, control of bladder and/or bowels, strength in any or all extremities, sensitivity to touch, vibrations, and/or pain, potency, coordination of movements—the list of possibilities is lengthy and, yes, horrifying. (Mairs 1986, 11)[4]

MS, then, may involve a deadening of sensation, an inability to react to external stimuli. It may also involve sensations that have no origin in the outside world; according to Barbara Webster, "moving one's head in a certain way [may produce] a sometimes severe sensation of electrical shock. [Or one may have] a sudden sensation of water pouring down the back of a leg" (37). Since it is, as Mairs reminds us, literally a failure of nerve(s), multiple sclerosis threatens to put its victims out of touch with their bodies and thus with the world. By depriving the afflicted of control over their bodies, it may alienate them from their bodies. But like any illness, it also perversely reminds the afflicted of their embodiment; the body is brought to mind precisely because the body *refuses* to mind. Multiple sclerosis, then, can radically disrupt the usual relationship among body, mind, and world.

At first reading, it may seem that Barbara Webster and Nancy Mairs adopt antithetical responses to their disease, with Webster choosing to withdraw from her own body into cerebral analysis of her condition, while Mairs struggles to retain her foothold in the world by rooting her texts in the concrete details of sensuous experience. Certainly, the writers' styles are worlds apart. While Mairs's writing is informal, candid, concrete, and playful, Webster's is formal, reserved, abstract, and impersonal. Webster's manner is intellectual, deliberate, and distanced; her organization topical and recursive rather than narrative and chronological; her focus often on society rather than on her self. For these reasons, her book may seem to acquiesce in the alienation of mind from body that MS threatens to precipitate.

However, Webster is emphatically not, to quote Woolf's sardonic description of the usual retreat from the body, "tapering into mysticism, or ris[ing] . . . into the raptures of transcendentalism" (10). Rather, she works to indicate what *her* bodily experience implies for all of us. Doing this involves challenging certain generic conventions of content and of form. For example, contrary to the reassuring testimony of most of the MS narratives Webster has read, she finds the disease affecting not just her body, but also her identity and self-image, not just her self, but her relations with others and the culture that formed her: "dealing with MS on a purely physical level was a way of avoiding the necessary conclusion that one's very self is at issue and at stake in any real adjustment" (28).

The persistent abstraction of her style may enact not a retreat from her bodily impediments, but rather her denial that MS is solely, or even primarily, a matter of physical symptoms. At the very least, her all-too-obvious symptoms cause others to react to her as *diseased* or *disabled*; like any stigmatic or stereotypical characteristic, they tend to obliterate the subject's individuality. And she readily admits that her self-perception is at times in danger of being infected by cultural stereotypes. Similarly, though the recursiveness of her book is at times frustrating, it serves to indict the comforting linearity and cozy closure found in narratives that culminate in cure or complete adjustment. Such linearity tends to deny the reality of MS, which is incurable and whose relapsing-remitting pattern tends to keep the afflicted figuratively as well as literally off balance.

To Woolf, the overlooked value of illness for the writer lies in its alteration of vision and the consequent disclosure of hitherto "undiscovered countries." Webster's diagnosis confirmed that she had, as she suspected, been living in an "undiscovered country," and it located that country on the map. By giving her condition a name, diagnosis gave it reality. As there is no definitive test for MS, diagnosis involves making connections among symptoms dissimilar in nature and widely separated in time. Because of its difficulty, diagnosis often comes years, even decades, after the first symptoms are experienced. For all these reasons, diagnosis may be epiphanic; it makes sudden sense of mysterious, intermittent, and apparently unrelated symptoms.[5] In this case, it also vindicated Webster's previous account of her symptoms (hitherto dismissed or doubted by her family and her doctors); thus, it retroactively endowed her own incipient life-narrative with authority and credibility.

But Webster's book is ultimately less concerned with her discovery of the country of the diseased than with her disclosures about the country of the "healthy," in which most of us reside most of the time. The title of her first chapter, "Wrestling with a Phantom," might have served as the title of the whole for two reasons. First, although it is a "watershed" in her life, diagnosis did not make her phantomlike disease easy to grasp, let alone to "pin down." Second, once she is officially pronounced ill, she finds herself at odds with a phantom as formidable as her hard-to-diagnose disease—cultural attitudes toward those in her situation: "disease does not fit in the American world view and, in fact, conflicts so sharply as to create a situation in which comfort requires that it not be seen. Disease is, in fact, an affront" (64).

Webster neither denies nor claims to transcend the physical facts of her condition; rather, she sets out to interrogate cultural (mis)constructions of disease. The opening scene of her book, in which she is jostled by impatient elderly American tourists at Luxor airport, stands as a paradigm of differing cultural attitudes toward disability:

> They wanted to know exactly when the flight was leaving and the answer, of course was always the same—*Insh'allah* ("God willing" or "when God wills"), which infuriated them. . . . Faced with a total inability to control what was going on, they were going to extreme lengths to foster their sense of being in control. They seemed to think that continually fighting for a place in this largely illusory line would get them to Cairo faster. My friend and I, on the other hand, having accepted that we had no control in this situation, were beginning to revel in that feeling. (2)

Though it occurred outside her country, this incident crystallized her sense of her alienation *within* her native culture. (Perhaps it afforded her special insight into her own culture *because* it happened on foreign soil.) In any case, even as it painfully reinforced her sense of disability and marginalization, this episode also enabled her to diagnose her culture's illness.

As I have suggested, Mairs's stance is very different from Webster's. Whereas Webster guards her privacy, blocking any voyeuristic impulse in her readers, Mairs is inclined to flaunt herself, exploiting voyeurism for her own purposes. Typically, rather than cloaking her condition behind a more general term ("disabled") or a euphemism ("differently abled"), she insists upon calling herself a "cripple." Closer to the "more primitive, more sensual, more obscene" language that Woolf called for (11), Mairs's style is concise, witty, ironic: "As a cripple, I swagger" (Mairs 1986, 9). Perhaps because her form of multiple sclerosis is more serious than Webster's, she is more forthright about its debilitating and demoralizing effects. In any case, her graphic description of her lurching gait emphasizes the physically disabling and cosmetically disfiguring effects of the disease:

> My shoulders droop and my pelvis thrusts forward as I try to balance myself upright, throwing my frame into a bony S. As a result of contractures, one shoulder is higher than the other and I carry one arm bent in front of me, the fingers curled into a claw. My left arm and leg have wasted into pipe-stems, and I try always to keep them covered. When I think about how my body must look to others, especially to men, to whom I have been trained to display myself, I feel ludicrous, even loathsome. (17)

The body figures far more prominently in Mairs's writing than in Webster's. But Mairs is similarly, perhaps even more acutely, aware of the cultural construction of her condition—as is evident in the last sentence quoted. Like Webster, though in different ways, Mairs tends to read her condition as culturally as well as physically determined. This is especially true of the many afflictions she suffers in addition to MS. In the final and climactic essay in *Plaintext*, "On Living Behind Bars," she catalogues ailments dating from her adolescence (well before the onset of MS): migraines, disabling menstrual cramps, colds, hay fever, rotting teeth, dizziness, nausea, and abdominal pain (129). As an adult, she also suffered from agoraphobia and from depression severe enough to result in a six-month confinement in an asylum (and several suicide attempts).[6]

In "On Keeping Women In/Out" and especially in "On Living Behind Bars," she reads her "madness"—her depression and her agoraphobia—in early adulthood as a symptom of her predicament as a woman—especially as a woman writer:

We have had to hide while menstruating, cover our heads and swaddle our bodies, lower our eyes, hold our tongues. Not by accident has the process of giving birth, perhaps the most active of human endeavors, been euphemized by a verb used always in the passive, "to be confined." Ours has been a history of confinement, in the childbed, in the crinoline, in the kitchen, even (if all other safe harbors fail) in the asylum. . . . We've known where we belong. And if we've tried to trespass over the threshold, our hearts have knocked, our mouths have gone dry and our skins damp, our lungs have shriveled, our bowels have let go. There's nothing like the symptoms of agoraphobia for keeping a woman in her place. Let me tell you. Nothing. (103)

Nothing, one is tempted to reply, but the symptoms of MS, which confines her more consistently than her agoraphobia. But Mairs is not so much concerned with the literal confinement that is increasingly her lot as with her literary confinement, the circumscription of her talent by her conditioned sense of a woman's place. Thus she hastens to add that the confinement of agoraphobia is *not* conducive to writing. On the contrary, the agora is symbolic, "any area perceived as part of the patriarchal domain. For that reason, writing causes me as much anxiety as any other incursion into masculine activity" (103). She is not safe from agoraphobia even in "a room of her own"; rather, in the space reserved for and dedicated to writing, agoraphobia may assume its most subtle and insidious form.

Although Mairs never characterizes MS as a psychosomatic or culturally caused disease, she does see a parallel between the loss of power attendant upon MS and the passivity of her position in intercourse. She wonders, "to what extent is multiple sclerosis merely the physical inscription of my way of being in the world? In sex, as in the rest of my life, I am acted upon. I am the object, not the agent. I live in the passive voice" (85). Paradoxically, however, illness may have helped to make Mairs a writer. Insofar as she discovered some of her major themes, the larger patterns of her life, in coming to terms with disease, especially with MS, her confidence, mobility, and authority as a writer have been inversely related to her physical mobility. Although writing is obviously no cure for MS, Mairs suggests that it may help to alleviate some other, more transient ills:

I have had time to translate my madness into the rituals that keep me alive as well as dying. But at least I know now that depression and agoraphobia are metaphors, codes in the cultural text in which I am embedded. Not entities. Not the inevitable fate of the woman who trespasses onto the page. I'm a writer. If I can make the change, I'm sure as hell going to revise them out of this script. (105)

Her characterization of life here in terms of a script, of disease in terms of cultural codes, does not trivialize them; rather, it serves to render her life-text more amendable, more amenable to revision. It is a strategy based in a conception of her writing as a *vital* art in the etymological sense.

According to Ortner, women have been ill situated with regard to men because they are thought to be particularly, or peculiarly, embodied. According to Woolf, illness has not been a prime literary subject in part because of a masculinist valorization of the mind over the body. If women and ill people are both marginalized in different ways, then sick women are doubly marginalized. With recent developments in autopathography, then, we have a return of the doubly, or perhaps triply, repressed—an overt, unembarrassed, unapologetic representation of the ill, female body. If illness is a literary no-man's-land, it may be, by default, a terrain available for women to map, a zone in which to rehabilitate the body as a literary subject, and a site on which to challenge the conventional domination of mind over body. By acknowledging their illnesses and exposing the cultural components of their disability— subjecting their cultures to lay diagnosis—Mairs and Webster demonstrate that "ill" women may be well equipped to reconceptualize the relation between psyche and soma, to write the life of the body as well as the life of the mind.

Notes

1. According to Elaine Scarry, "the human body is at the present moment a special site of attention and concern. As a historical phenomenon, there is nothing surprising about this: the very extremity of the skepticism about the referential capacities of language in the past decade made it almost inevitable that at the moment when language was finally reconnected to the world, the primary site of reconnection would be not just this or that piece of material ground but the most extreme locus of materialization, the live body. The body is both continuous with a wider material realm that includes history and nature, and also discontinuous with it because it is the reminder of the extremity of risks entailed in the issue of reference" (xx–xxi).

2. An exception might be the subgenre of athletes' autobiographies, which is of course dominated by males. But here the focus is not so much on the body as on the sport, or even the career of the athlete. In any case, this genre tends to characterize the body as submissive to the will, an efficient tool, rather than to reflect on it as a medium of selfhood.

3. Woolf does not in her essay—or elsewhere, as far as I know—leave a full or detailed record of the daily drama of her body. Her essay is about being ill, not about her being ill. But her "Sketch of a Life" begins with her disturbing sense of shame about her own body, and the roots of that shame in her having been sexually abused as a child.

4. Typically, she adds, "One may also lose one's sense of humor."

5. Because it depends on the establishment of relationships among disparate and discrete events, diagnosis, itself a major life-event, may encourage the habit of seeing large-scale patterns. In any case, Mairs describes her own writing in terms

equally apt for the process of diagnosing MS: "Only recently have I begun to concatenate my experiences into patterns distinct from the narrative ground in which they are embedded: This process I call essay-writing" (Mairs 1986, 127).

6. The relation between MS and depression, if any, is unclear. Mairs puts it this way: "I am immobilized by acute attacks of depression, which may or not be physiologically related to MS but are certainly its logical concomitant" (Mairs 1986, 13). It is worth noting that before MS is diagnosed, its victims are often diagnosed as clinically depressed. Webster was referred to a psychiatrist; and, caught in a diagnostic double-bind, she reluctantly agreed to see him: "The fact that I would not admit that I was clinically depressed (and I think in retrospect it is clear that I was not) confirmed them in their belief that I was. . . . I found the whole situation very depressing indeed, and it was difficult to maintain a sense of integrity in the face of all this disapproval and certainty" (8).

Works Cited

Dreuilhe, Emmanuel. *Mortal Embrace: Living with AIDS*. Translated by Linda Coverdale. New York: Hill, 1988.

Lorde, Audre. *The Cancer Journals*. N.p.: Spinsters, 1980.

Mairs, Nancy. *Carnal Acts: Essays*. New York: Harper, 1990.

———. *Plaintext*. Tucson: University of Arizona Press, 1986.

———. *Remembering the Bone House: An Erotics of Place and Space*. New York: Harper, 1989.

Miller, Jonathan. *The Body in Question*. New York: Random House, 1978.

Murphy, Robert. *The Body Silent*. New York: Holt, 1987.

Oates, Joyce Carol. "Adventures in Abandonment." Review of *Jean Stafford: A Biography*, by David Roberts. *New York Times Book Review*, August 28, 1988, 3, 33.

Ortner, Sherry B. "Is Female to Male as Nature Is to Culture?" In *Woman, Culture, and Society*, edited by Michelle Zimbalist Rosaldo and Louise Lamphere, 67–87. Stanford: Stanford University Press, 1974.

Sacks, Oliver. *A Leg to Stand On*. New York: Summit, 1984.

Sarton, May. *After the Stroke: A Journal*. New York: Norton, 1988.

Scarry, Elaine. Introduction. In *Literature and the Body: Essays on Populations and Persons*, edited by Elaine Scarry, vii–xxvii. Baltimore: Johns Hopkins University Press, 1988.

Simpson, Eileen. *Reversals*. Boston: Houghton, 1979.

Styron, William. *Darkness Visible: A Memoir of Madness*. New York: Random House, 1990.

Updike, John. *Self-Consciousness: Memoirs*. New York: Knopf, 1989.

Webster, Barbara. *All of a Piece: A Life with Multiple Sclerosis*. Baltimore: Johns Hopkins University Press, 1989.

Woolf, Virginia. "On Being Ill." In *"The Moment" and Other Essays*, 9–23. New York: Harcourt, 1948.

Zweig, Paul. *Departures*. New York: Harper, 1986.

IV Women's Autobiography from the Early Modern Period to the Present: Sample Texts

These excerpts from women's lifewriting reflect the diverse life experiences and writing styles that comprise the category "women's autobiography." For example, Margaret Lucas Cavendish served as a maid of honor to Queen Henrietta Maria in seventeenth-century England, while Harriet Jacobs worked as a slave in nineteenth-century America. Not surprisingly, these writers' different historical moments and social positions led them to produce accounts that vary tremendously in focus and tone. At the same time, however, similar themes recur in the four autobiographical pieces, just as the critical selections in this volume suggest. All of the autobiographers write about their relationships with others, for instance, and arrive at deeper understandings of themselves through such interactions. Perhaps most important, these selections demonstrate that women have had to surmount social, economic, or psychological barriers in order to write, but have nonetheless developed an autobiographical tradition of their own.

11

Seventeenth Century: From *A True Relation of My Birth, Breeding, and Life**

~

Margaret Lucas Cavendish,
Duchess of Newcastle

Margaret Lucas Cavendish, Duchess of Newcastle (1623[?]–1673), was a literary pioneer, the first woman in England to publish an autobiography. The youngest child of a wealthy country family, she served Queen Henrietta Maria as a maid of honor and accompanied the queen into exile in France when the tide turned against the royalists in the English civil war. There she met and married William, Marquis (later Duke) of Newcastle, who was thirty years older than she.

When the couple returned to England after the restoration of King Charles II, they retired from the court and Cavendish devoted her time to studying and writing, which her husband encouraged. A prolific writer in many genres, she published eleven books and two drama collections. She wrote essays, poems, letters, orations, scientific and philosophical treatises, and a science fiction tale. Fascinated by "natural philosophy," Cavendish was the first woman in England to write about science. One of her finest works, a life of her husband, was an important contribution to the development of biography in England. Although the range of her learning was wide, she was an undisciplined writer, and the quality of her work was uneven.

Cavendish cultivated a flamboyant public persona, probably in part to compensate for her debilitating shyness. She dressed in extravagant costumes that she designed herself, sometimes outfitting her servants similarly and even decorating her coach to match.

*From Margaret Lucas Cavendish, Duchess of Newcastle, A True Relation of My Birth, Breeding, and Life in Natures Pictures Drawn by Fancies Pencil to the Life (London, 1656, microfilm collections wing, N855-1575: 38 and N856-611:10), 369–71, 373–75, 378–79, 382–91. Reprinted courtesy of University Microfilms International.

When she visited London her coach was mobbed by curious crowds eager to see "Mad Madge." Hostile contemporaries ridiculed Cavendish for her eccentricities, partly because of her attire but also for her boldness in publishing at a time when women were not supposed to possess, much less exhibit, intelligence. Her autobiography, written while she and her husband were in exile on the Continent during the civil wars, was appended to a collection of tales published in 1656.

As for my breeding, it was according to my Birth, and the Nature of my Sex, for my Birth was not lost in my breeding, for as my Sisters was or had been bred, so was I in Plenty, or rather with superfluity; Likewise we were bred Virtuously, Modestly, Civilly, Honorably, and on honest principles: as for plenty, we had not only, for Necessity, Conveniency, and Decency, but for delight and pleasure to a superfluity; 'tis true, we did not riot, but we lived orderly; for riot, even in Kings Courts, and Princes Palaces, brings ruin without content or pleasure, when order in less fortunes shall live more plentifully and deliciously than Princes, that lives in a Hurlie Burlie. . . .

As for our garments, my Mother did not only delight to see us neat and cleanly, fine and gay, but rich and costly; maintaining us to the height of her Estate, but not beyond it; for we were so far from being in debt, before these wars, as we were rather before hand with the world; buying all with ready money, not on the score. . . .

[L]ikewise we were bred tenderly, for my Mother Naturally did strive, to please and delight her children, not to cross or torment them, terrifying them with threats, or lashing them with slavish whips, but instead of threats, reason was used to perswade us, and instead of lashes, the deformities of vices was discovered, and the graces, and vertues were presented unto us. [A]lso we were bred with respectfull attendance, every one being severally waited upon, and all her servants in generall used the same respect to her children, (even those that were very young) as they did to her self, for she sufferd not her servants, either to be rude before us, or to domineer over us, which all vulgar servants are apt, and ofttimes which some have leave to do. . . . [S]he never sufferd the vulgar Serving-men, to be in the Nursery amongst the Nurss Maids, lest their rude love-making might do unseemly actions, or speak unhandsome words in the presence of her children, knowing that youth is apt to take infection by ill examples, having not the reason of distinguishing good from bad, neither were we sufferd to have any familiaritie with the vulgar servants, or conversation: yet caused us to demean ourselves with an humble civillity towards them, as they with a dutifull respect to us, not because they were servants were we so reserv'd, for many Noble Persons are forc'd to serve through necessitie, but by reason the vulgar sort of servants, are as ill bred as meanly born, giving children ill examples, and worse counsel.

As for tutors, although we had for all sorts of Vertues, as singing, dancing, playing on Musick, reading, writing, working, and the like, yet we were not kept strictly thereto, they were rather for formalitie than benefit, for my Mother cared not so much for our dancing and fidling, singing and prating of severall languages; as that we should be bred virtuously, modestley, civilly, honourably, and on honest principles.

As for my Brothers, of which I had three, I know not how they were bred, first, they were bred when I was not capable to observe, or before I was born; likewise the breeding of men were after different manner of wayes from those of women: but this I know, that they loved Virtue, endeavour'd Merit, practic'd Justice, and spoke Truth; they were constantly Loyal, and truly Valiant. . . .

But sometime after this War began; I knew not how they lived, for though most of them were in *Oxford*, wherein the King was, yet after the Queen went from *Oxford*, and so out of *England*, I was parted from them. . . . [W]hen the Queen was in *Oxford*, I had a great desire to be one of her Maids of Honour, hearing the Queen had not the same number she was used to have, whereupon I wooed and won my Mother to let me go, for my Mother being fond of all her Children, was desirous to please them, which made her consent to my request. But my Brothers and Sisters seem'd not very well pleas'd, by reason I had never been from home, nor seldome out of their sight; for though they knew I would not behave my self to their, or my own dishonour, yet they thought I might to my disadvantage, being unexperienced in the World, which indeed I did, for I was so bashfull when I was out of my Mothers, Brothers, and Sisters sight . . . that when I was gone from them I was like one that had no Foundation to stand, or Guide to direct me, which made me afraid, lest I should wander with Ignorance out of the waies of Honour, for that I knew not how to behave my self.

Besides, I had heard the World was apt to lay aspersions even on the innocent, for which I durst neither look up with my eyes, nor speake, nor be any way sociable, inso much as I was thought a Natural fool; indeed I had not much Wit, yet I was not an Idiot, my Wit was according to my years; and though I might have learnt more Wit, and advanced my Understanding by living in a Court, . . . I was so afraid to dishonour my Friends and Family by my indiscreet actions, that I rather chose to be accounted a Fool, than to be thought rude or wanton. . . .

My Lord the Marquis of Newcastle did approve of those bashfull fears which many condemn'd, and would choose such a Wife as he might bring to his own humours, and not such an one as was wedded to self conceit, or one that had been temper'd to the humours of another, for which he wooed me for his Wife; and though I did dread Marriage, and shunn'd Mens companies, as much as I could, yet I could not, nor had not the power to refuse him, by reason my Affections were fix'd on him, and he was the onely Person I ever was in love with: Neither was I ashamed to own it, but gloried therein, for it was not Amorous Love, I never was infected therewith, it is a Disease, or a Passion, or both, I onely know by relation, not by experience[.] [N]either could Title, Wealth, Power or Person entice me to love; but my Love was honest and honourable, being placed upon Merit, which Affection joy'd at the fame of his Worth, pleas'd with delight in his Wit, proud of the respects he used to me, and triumphing in the affections he profest for me, which affections he hath confirmed to me by a deed of time, seal'd by constancy, and assigned by an unalterable decree of his promise, which makes me happy in despight of Fortunes frowns[.] [F]or though Misfortunes may and do oft dissolve base, wilde, loose, and ungrounded affections, yet she hath no power of those that are united either by Merit, Justice, Gratitude, Duty, Fidelity, or the like; and though my Lord hath lost his Estate, and banish'd out of his Country for his Loyalty to his King and Country, yet neither despised Poverty, nor pinching Necessity could make him break the Bonds of Friendship, or weaken his Loyal Duty to his King or Country.

[A]fter I was married some two or three years, my Lord travell'd out of *France*, from the City of *Paris*, in which City he resided the time he was there, so went into *Holland*, to a Town called *Rotterdam*, in which place he stayed some six months, from thence he returned to *Brabant*, unto the City of *Antwerpe*, which Citie we past through, when we went into *Holland*, and in that City my Lord settled himself and Family, choosing it for the most pleasantest, and quietest place to revive himself and ruined fortunes in; but after we had remained some time therein, we grew extremely necessitated, Tradesmen being there not so rich, as to trust my Lord for so much, or so long, as those in *France*. . . .

[B]ut at last necessity inforced me to return into *England*, to seek for reliefe; for I hearing my Lords Estate, amongst the rest of many more estates, was to be sold, and that the wives of the owners should have an allowance therefrom, it gave me hopes I should receive a benefit thereby. . . . [S]o over I went, but when I came there, I found their hearts as hard as my fortunes, and their Natures as cruell as my miseries, for they sold all my Lords Estate, which was a very great one, and gave me not any part thereof, or any allowance thereout, which few or no other was so hardly dealt withall. . . .

[A]fter I had been in England a year and a half, part of which time I writ a Book of Poems, and a little Book called my Phylosophicall Fancyes, to which I have writ a large addition, since I returned out of

England, besides this Book and one other: as for my Book intituled the *Worlds Ollio*, I writ most part of it before I went into England. . . . [B]eing not of a merry, although not of a froward or peevish disposition, [I] became very Melancholy, by reason I was from my Lord, which made my mind so restless, as it did break my sleeps, and distemper my health, with which growing impatient of a longer delay, I resolved to return. . . .

I made the more hast to return to my Lord, with whom I had rather be as a poor begger, than to be Mistriss of the world absented from him; yet, Heaven hitherto hath kept us, and though Fortune hath been cross, yet we do submit, and are both content with what is, and cannot be mended, and are so prepared, that the worst of fortunes shall not afflict our minds, so as to make us unhappy, howsoever it doth pinch our lives with poverty: for if Tranquility lives in an honest mind, the mind lives in Peace, although the body suffer: but Patience hath armed us, and Misery hath tried us, and finds us Fortune proof. . . .

[M]y Lord pleaseth himself with the Management of some few Horses, and exercises himself with the use of the Sword; which two Arts he hath brought by his studious thoughts, rationall experience, and industrious practice to an absolute perfection. . . . [A]lso he recreats himself with his pen, writing what his Wit dictates to him, but I pass my time rather with scribling than writing, with words than wit, not that I speak much, because I am addicted to contemplation, unless I am with my Lord, yet then I rather attentively listen to what he sayes, than impertinently speak[.]

I [was] addicted from my childhood, to contemplation rather than conversation, to solitariness rather than society, to melancholy rather than mirth, to write with the pen than to work with a needle, passing my time with harmless fancies . . . in which I take such pleasure, as I neglect my health. . . . [M]y only trouble is, lest my brain should grow barren, or that the root of my fancies should become insipid, withering into a dull stupidity for want of maturing subjects to write on[.]

[F]or I being of a lazy nature, and not of an active disposition, as some are that love to journey from town to town, from place to place, from house to house, delighting in variety of company, making still one where the greatest number is: likewise in playing at Cardes, or any other Games, in which I neither have practiced, nor have I any skill therein[.] [A]s for Dancing, although it be a gracefull art, and becometh unmarried persons well, yet for those that are married, it is too light an action, disagreeing with the gravity thereof; and for Revelling, I am of too dull a nature, to make one in a merry society; as for Feasting, it would neither agree with my humour or constitution, for my diet is for the most part sparing, as a little boyld chickin, or the like, my drink most commonly water, for though I have an indifferent good appetite, yet I do often fast, out of an opinion that if I should eate much, and exercise little, which I do, onely walking a slow pace in my chamber, whilest my thoughts run apace in my brain, so that the motions of my minde hinders the active exercises of my body: for should I Dance or Run, or Walk apace, I should Dance my Thoughts out of Measure, Run my Fancies out of Breath, and Tread out the Feet of my Numbers[.]

[B]ut because I would not bury my self quite from the sight of the world, I go sometimes abroad, seldome to visit, but only in my Coach about the Town . . . although for my part I had rather sit at home and write, or walk, as I said, in my chamber and contemplate; but I hold necessary sometimes to appear abroad, besides I do find, that severall objects do bring new materialls for my thoughts and fancies to build upon, yet I must say this in the behalf of my thoughts, that I never found them idle; for if the senses brings no work in, they will work of themselves, like silk wormes that spinns out of their own bowels; Neither can I say I think the time tedious, when I am alone, so I be neer my Lord, and know he is well[.]

[B]ut now I have declared to my Readers, my Birth, Breeding, and Actions, to this part of my Life, I mean the materiall parts, for should I write every particular, as my childish sports and the like, it would be ridiculous and tedious; but I have been honorably born and Nobly matcht, I have been bred to elevated thoughts, not to a dejected spirit, my life hath been ruled with Honesty, attended by Modesty, and directed by Truth. . . . [S]ince I have writ in general thus far of my life; I think it fit, I should speak something of my Humour, particular Practise and Disposition. [A]s for my Humour, I was from my childhood given to contemplation, being more taken or delighted with thoughts than in conversation with a society, in so much as I would walk two or three houres, and never rest, in a musing, considering, contemplating manner, reasoning with my self of every thing my senses did present, but when I was in the company of my Naturall friends, I was very attentive of what they said, or did; but for strangers I regarded not much what they said. . . .

I took great delight in attiring, fine dressing and fashions, especially such fashions as I did invent my self, not taking that pleasure in such fashions as was invented by others: also I did dislike any should follow my Fashions, for I always took delight in a singularity, even in acoutrements of habits, but whatsoever I was addicted to, either in fashions of Cloths, contemplation of Thoughts, actions of Life, they were Lawfull, Honest, Honorable and Modest. . . .

[A]s for my Disposition, it is more inclining to be melancholy than merry . . . and I am apt to weep rather than laugh, not that I do often either of them[.] [A]lso I am tender natured, for it troubles my Conscience to kill a fly, and the groans of a dying Beast strike my Soul: also where I place a particular affection, I love extraordinarily, and constantly, yet not fondly but soberly, and observingly, not to hang about them as a trouble, but to wait upon them as a servant, but this affection will take no root, but where I think or find merit, and have leave both from Divine and Morall Laws[.] [Y]et I find this passion so troublesome, as it is the only torment to my life, for fear any evill misfortune or accident, or sickness, or death should come unto them, insomuch, as I am never freely at rest[.] [L]ikewise I am gratefull, for I never received a curtesie but I am impatient, and troubled untill I can return it, also I am Chaste, both by Nature and Education, insomuch as I do abhorre an unchaste thought: likewise I am seldom angry, . . . but when I am angry, I am very angry, but yet it is soon over, and I am easily pacified. . . .

[A]nd truly I am so vain, as to be so self-conceited, or so naturally partiall, to think my friends, have as much reason to love me as another, since none can love more sincerely than I, and it were an injustice to prefer a fainter affection, or to esteem the Body more than the Minde, likewise I am neither spitefull, envious, nor malicious, I repine not at the gifts that Nature, or Fortune bestows upon others[. Yet] . . . I think it no crime to wish my self the exactest of Natures works, my thred of life the longest, my Chain of Destinie the strongest, my minde the peaceablest; my life the pleasantest, my death the easiest, and the greatest Saint in Heaven; also to do my endeavour, so far as honour and honesty doth allow of, to be the highest on Fortunes Wheele, and to hold the wheele from turning, if I can. . . . [B]ut I fear my Ambition inclines to vain glory, for I am very ambitious, yet 'tis neither for Beauty, Wit, Titles, Wealth or Power, but as they are steps to raise me to Fames Tower, which is to live by remembrance in after-ages[.]

[L]ikewise I am, that the vulgar calls, proud, not out of a self-conceit, or to flight or condemn any, but scorning to do a base or a mean act, and disdaining rude or unworthy persons, insomuch that if I should find any that were rude, or too bold, I should be apt to be so passionate, as to affront them, if I can . . . for though I am naturally bashfull, yet in such a cause my Spirits would be all on fire. [O]therwise I am so well bred, as to be civill to all persons, of all degrees, or qualities: likewise I am so proud, or rather just to my Lord, as to abate nothing of the qualitie of his Wife. . . .

Also in some cases I am naturally a Coward, and in other cases very valiant; as for example, if any of my neerest friends were in danger, I should never consider my life in striving to help them, though I were sure to do them no good, and would willingly, nay cheerfully, resign my life for their sakes: likewise I should not spare my Life, if Honour bids me dye[.] [B]ut in a danger where my Friends or my Honour is not concerned, or ingaged, but only my Life to be unprofitably lost, I am the veriest coward in Nature, as upon the Sea, or any dangerous places, or of

Theeves or fire, or the like, Nay, the shooting of a gun, although but a Pot gun, will make me start, and stop my hearing, much less have I courage to discharge one; or if a sword should be held against me, although but in jest, I am afraid. . . .

[B]ut I hope my Readers, will not think me vain for writing my life, since there have been many that have done the like, as Cesar, Ovid, and many more, both men and women, and I know no reason I may not do it as well as they: but I verily believe some censuring Readers will scornfully say, why hath this Ladie writ her own Life? since none cares to know whose daughter she was, or whose wife she is, or how she was bred, or what fortunes she had, or how she lived, or what humour or disposition she was of? I answer that it is true, but 'tis no purpose, to the Readers, but it is to the Authoress, because I write it for my own sake, not theirs; neither did I intend this piece for to delight, but to divulge, not to please the fancy, but to tell the truth, left after-Ages should mistake, in not knowing I was daughter to one Master *Lucas* of *St. Johns* neer *Colchester* in *Essex*, second Wife to the Lord Marquis of *Newcastle*, for my Lord having had two Wives, I might easily have been mistaken, especially if I should dye, and my Lord Marry again.

12

Eighteenth Century: From *A Narrative of the Life of Mrs. Charlotte Charke**

~

Charlotte Charke

Charlotte Charke (1713–1760) was the daughter of the actor, theater manager, and poet laureate Colley Cibber, himself the author of a well-known though controversial autobiography. The youngest of twelve children, she excelled at childish pranks and in a sense never outgrew them. As an adult she led a varied and colorful life. In the theatrical world, she worked as a dancer, an actress, and, finally, a puppeteer; at various times she also became a grocer, a barmaid, a valet, a conjuror's assistant, and a sausage seller. Clever and irresponsible, often a rogue and occasionally a criminal, she barreled cheerfully through life, leaving several husbands and lovers and a mounting pile of debts behind her.

Although Charke also published a play and several novels, she owes her fame to her autobiography, A Narrative of the Life of Mrs. Charlotte Charke. *She published it in 1755, hoping among other things to use it to pressure her father, who had disowned her, into a reconciliation—and financial support. Cibber, however, firmly refused.*

The selections here suggest the scope and variety of Charke's life, beginning with childish mischief and moving on to adult scrapes and difficulties. As insouciant in print as she was in life, Charke ended her autobiography with a summary of its contents, thus creating her conclusion from the material that was conventionally placed at the beginning of eighteenth-century works.

*From Charlotte Charke, *A Narrative of the Life of Mrs. Charlotte Charke*, 2d ed. (London: W. Reeve, 1759, microfilm), 11–20, 35–39, 70–71, 113–15, 270–75.

A S THE FOLLOWING HISTORY is the Product of a Female Pen, I tremble for the terrible Hazard it must run in venturing into the World, as it may very possibly suffer, in many Opinions, without perusing it; I therefore humbly move for its having the common Chance of a Criminal, at least to be properly examin'd, before it is condemn'd: And should it be found guilty of Nonsense and Inconsistencies, I must consequently resign it to its deserved Punishment; instead of being honour'd with the last Row of a Library, undergo the Indignancy of preserving the Syrup of many a choice Tart; which, when purchas'd, even the hasty Child will soon give an Instance of its Contempt of my Muse, by committing to the Flames, or perhaps cast it to the Ground, to be trampled to Death by some Thread-bare Poet, whose Works might possibly have undergone the same Malevolence of Fate. . . .

As I have promis'd to give some Account of my UNACCOUNTABLE LIFE, I shall no longer detain my Readers in respect to my Book, but satisfy a Curiosity which has long subsisted in the Minds of many: And, I believe, they will own, when they know my History, if Oddity can plead any Right to Surprize and Astonishment, I may positively claim a Title to be shewn among the Wonders of Ages past, and those to come. Nor will I, to escape a Laugh, even at my own Expence, deprive my Readers of that pleasing Satisfaction, or conceal any Error, which I now rather sigh to reflect on; but formerly, thro' too much Vacancy of Thought, might be idle enough rather to justify than condemn.

I shall now begin my Detail of the several Stages I have pass'd thro' since my Birth, which made me the last-born of Mr. *Colley Cibber*, at a Time my Mother began to think, without this additional Blessing (meaning my sweet Self) she had fully answer'd the End of her Creation, being just Forty-five Years of Age when she produc'd her last, "THO' NOT LEAST IN LOVE". Nor was I exempted from an equal Share in my Father's Heart; yet, partly thro' my own Indiscretion (and, I am too well convinc'd, from the cruel Censure of false and evil Tongues) since my Maturity, I lost that Blessing: Which, if strongest Compunction and uninterrupted Hours of Anguish, blended with Self-conviction and filial Love, can move his Heart to Pity and Forgiveness, I shall, with Pride and unutterable Transport, throw myself at his Feet, to implore the only Benefit I desire or expect, his BLESSING, and his PARDON.

But of that, more hereafter—And I hope, ere this small Treatise is finish'd, to have it in my Power to inform my Readers, my painful Separation from my once tender Father will be more than amply repaid, by a happy Interview; as I am certain neither my present or future Conduct, shall ever give him Cause to blush at what I should esteem a justifiable and necessary Reconciliation, as 'tis the absolute Ordination of the Supreme that we should forgive, when the Offender becomes a sincere and hearty Penitent. And I positively declare, were I to expire this Instant, I have no self-interested Views, in regard to worldly Matters; but confess myself a Miser in my Wishes so far, as having the transcendant Joy of knowing that I am restor'd to a Happiness, which not only will clear my Reputation to the World, in Regard to a former Want of Duty, but, at the same Time, give a convincing Proof that there are yet some Sparks of Tenderness remaining in my Father's Bosom, for his REPENTANT CHILD.

I confess, I believe I came not only an unexpected, but an unwelcome Guest into the Family, (exclusive of my Parents), as my Mother had borne no Children for some few Years before; so that I was rather regarded as an impertinent Intruder, than one who had a natural Right to make up the circular Number of my Father's Fire-Side: Yet, be it as it may, the Jealousy of me, from her other Children, laid no Restraint on her Fondness for me, which my Father and she both testified in their tender Care of my Education. His paternal Love omitted nothing that could improve any natural Talents Heaven had been pleased to endow me with; the Mention of which, I hope, won't be imputed to me as a vain Self-conceit, of knowing more, or thinking better, than any other of my Sister Females. No! Far be it from me; for as all Advantages from Nature are the favorable Gifts of the Power Divine, consequently no Praise can be arrogated to ourselves, for that which is not in ourselves POSSIBLE TO BESTOW.

I should not have made this Remark, but, as 'tis likely my Works may fall into the Hands of People of disproportion'd Understandings, I was willing to prevent an Error a weak Judgment might have run into, by inconsiderately throwing an Odium upon me, I could not possibly deserve—FOR, ALAS! ALL CANNOT JUDGE ALIKE.

As I have instanc'd, that my Education was not only a genteel, but in Fact a liberal one, and such indeed as might have been sufficient for a Son instead of a Daughter; I must beg Leave to add, that I was never made much acquainted with that necessary Utensil which forms the housewifely Part of a young Lady's Education, call'd a Needle; which I handle with the same clumsey Awkwardness a Monkey does a Kitten, and am equally capable of using the one, as Pug is of nursing the other.

This is not much to be wondered at, as my Education consisted chiefly in Studies of various Kinds, and gave me a different Turn of Mind than what I might have had, if my Time had been employ'd in ornamenting a Piece of Canvas with Beasts, Birds and the Alphabet; the latter of which I understood in *French*, rather before I was able to speak *English*.

As I have promised to conceal nothing that might raise a Laugh, I shall begin with a small Specimen of my former Madness, when I was but four Years of Age. Having, even then, a passionate Fondness for a Perriwig, I crawl'd out of Bed one Summer's Morning at *Twickenham*, where my Father had Part of a House and Gardens for the Season, and, taking it into my small Pate, that by Dint of a Wig and a Waistcoat, I should be the perfect Representative of my Sire, I crept softly into the Servants-Hall, where I had the Night before espied all Things in Order, to perpetrate the happy Design I had framed for the next Morning's Expedition. Accordingly I paddled down Stairs, taking with me my Shoes, Stockings, and little Dimity Coat; which I artfully contrived to pin up, as well as I could, to supply the Want of a Pair of Breeches. By the Help of a long Broom, I took down a Waistcoat of my Brother's, and an enormous bushy Tie-wig of my Father's, which entirely enclos'd my Head and Body, with the Knots of the Ties thumping my little Heels as I marched along, with slow and solemn Pace. The Covert of Hair in which I was concealed, with the Weight of a monstrous Belt and large Silver-hilted Sword, that I could scarce drag along, was a vast Impediment in my Procession: And, what still added to the other Inconveniences I laboured under, was whelming myself under one of my Father's large Beaver-hats, laden with Lace, as thick and broad as a Brickbat.

Being thus accoutred, I began to consider that 'twould be impossible for me to pass for Mr. *Cibber* in Girl's Shoes, therefore took an Opportunity to slip out of Doors after the Gardener, who went to his Work, and roll'd myself into a dry Ditch, which was as deep as I was high; and, in this Grotesque Pigmy-State, walked up and down the Ditch bowing to all who came by me. But, behold, the Oddity of my Appearance soon assembled a Croud about me; which yielded me no small Joy, as I conceived their Risibility on this Occasion to be Marks of Approbation, and walked myself into a Fever, in the happy Thought of being taken for the 'Squire.

When the Family arose, 'till which Time I had employ'd myself in this regular March in my Ditch, I was the first Thing enquir'd after, and miss'd; 'till Mrs. *Heron*, the Mother of the late celebrated Actress of that Name, happily espied me, and directly call'd forth the whole Family to be Witness of my State and Dignity.

The Drollery of my Figure rendered it impossible, assisted by the Fondness of both Father and Mother, to be angry with me; but, alas! I was borne off on the Footman's Shoulders, to my Shame and Disgrace, and forc'd into my proper Habiliments. . . .

During my Residence in the Family, I grew passionately fond of the Study of Physick; and was never so truly happy, as when the Doctor employed me in some little Offices in which he durst intrust me, without Prejudice to his Patients.

As I was indulged in having a little Horse of my own, I was frequently desired to call upon one or other of the neighbouring Invalids, to enquire how they did; which gave me a most pleasing Opportunity of fancying myself a Physician, and affected the Solemnity and Gravity which I had often observed in the good Doctor: Nor am I absolutely assured, from the significant Air which I assumed, whether some of the weaker Sort of People might not have been persuaded into as high an Opinion of my Skill as my Cousin's, whose Talents chiefly were adapted to the Study of Physick. To do him Justice, he was a very able Proficient; and, I dare say, the Loss of him in *Hertfordshire*, and some Part of *Essex*, is not a little regretted, as he was necessary to the Rich, and tenderly beneficent to the Poor.

At the Expiration of two Years his Lady died, and I was remanded Home, and once again sent to our Country-House at *Hillingdon*; where I was no sooner arrived, than I persuaded my fond Mother to let me have a little Closet, built in an Apartment seldom used, by Way of Dispensatory. This I easily obtained, and summoned all the old Women in the Parish to repair to me, whenever they found themselves indisposed. I was indeed of the Opinion of *Leander* in *The Mock Doctor*, that a few physical hard Words would be necessary to establish my Reputation; and accordingly had recourse to a *Latin* Dictionary, and soon gathered up as many Fragments as served to confound their Senses, and bring 'em into a high Opinion of my Skill in the medicinal Science.

As my Advice and Remedies for all Disorders were designed as Acts of Charity, 'tis not to be imagined what a Concourse of both Sexes were my constant Attendants; though I own, I have been often obliged to refer myself to *Salmon*, *Culpepper*, and other Books I had for that Purpose, before I was able to make a proper Application, or indeed arrive at any Knowledge of their Maladies. But this Defect was not discovered by my Patients, as I put on Significancy of Countenance that rather served to convince them of my incomparable Skill and Abilities.

Fond as I was of this learned Office, I did not chuse to give up that of being Lady of the Horse, which delicate Employment took up some Part of my Time every Day; and I generally served myself in that Capacity, when I thought proper to pay my Attendance on the believing Mortals, who entrusted their Lives in my Hands. But Providence was extreamly kind in that Point; for though, perhaps, I did not actual Good, I never had the least Misfortune happen to any of the unthinking, credulous Souls who relied on me for the Restoration of their Healths, which was ten to one I had endangered as long as they lived.

When I had signified my Intention of becoming a young Lady *Bountiful*, I thought it highly necessary to furnish myself with Drugs, etc. to carry on this notable Design; accordingly I went to *Uxbridge*, where was then living an Apothecary's Widow, whose Shop was an Emblem of that described in *Romeo and Juliet*. She, good Woman, knowing my Family, entrusted me with a Cargo of Combustibles, which were sufficient to have set up a Mountebank for a Twelvemonth; but my Stock was soon exhausted, for the silly Devils began to fancy themselves ill, because they knew they could have Physick for nothing, such as it was. But, Oh! woeful Day! the Widow sent in her Bill to my Father, who was intirely ignorant of the curious Expense I had put him to; which he directly paid, with a strict Order never to let Doctor *Charlotte* have any farther Credit, on Pain of losing the Money so by me contracted.

Was not this sufficient to murder the Fame of the ablest Physician in the Universe? However, I was resolved not to give up my Profession; and, as I was deprived of the Use of Drugs, I took it into my Head, to conceal my Disgrace, to have recourse to Herbs: But one Day a poor old Woman coming to me, with a violent Complaint of rheumatick Pains and a terrible Disorder in her Stomach, I was at a dreadful Loss what Remedies to apply, and dismissed her with an Assurance of sending her something to ease her, by an inward and outward Application, before she went to Bed.

It happened that Day proved very rainy, which put it into my strange Pate to gather up all the Snails in the Garden; of which, from the heavy Shower that had fallen, there was a superabundant Quantity. I immediately fell to work; and, of some Part of 'em, with coarse brown Sugar, made a Syrup, to be taken a Spoonful once in two Hours. Boiling the rest to a Consistence, with some green Herbs and Mutton Fat, I made an Ointment; and, clapping conceited Labels upon the Phial and Gallipot, sent my Preparation, with a joyous Bottle of Hartshorn and *Sal Volatile* I purloined from my Mother, to add a Grace to my Prescriptions.

In about three Days Time the good Woman came hopping along, to return me Thanks for the extream Benefit she had received; intreating my Goodness to repeat the Medicines, as she had found such wonderful Effects from their Virtues.

But Fortune was not quite kind enough to afford me the Means of granting her Request at that Time; for the friendly Rain, which had enabled me to work this wonderful Cure, was succeeded by an extream Drought, and I thought it highly necessary to suspend any further Attempts to establish my great Reputation, 'till another watry Opportunity offered to furnish me with those Ingredients, whose sanative Qualities had been so useful to her Limbs and my Fame: I therefore dismissed her with a Word of Advice, not to tamper too much; that as she was so well recovered, to wait 'till a Return of her Pains; otherwise a too frequent Use of the Remedy might possibly lose its Effect, by being applied without any absolute necessity. With as significant an Air as I could assume, I bid her besure to keep herself warm, and DRINK NO MALT LIQUOR; and, that if she found any Alteration, to send to me.

Glad was I when the poor Creature was gone, as her harmless Credulity had rais'd such an invincible Fit of Laughter in me, I must have died on the Spot by the Suppression, had she staid a few Minutes longer....

I took it into my Head to dive into TRADE. To that End, I took a Shop in *Long-Acre*, and turn'd Oil-woman and Grocer.

This new Whim proved very successful, for every Soul of my Acquaintance, of which I have a numerous Share, came in Turn to see my mercantile Face; which carried in it as conceited an Air of Trade as it had before in Physick, and I talk'd of myself and other DEALERS, as I was pleased to term it. The Rise and Fall of Sugars was my constant Topick; and Trading, Abroad and at Home, was as frequent in my Mouth as my Meals. To compleat the ridiculous Scene, I constantly took in the Papers to see how Matters went at *Bear-Key*; what Ships were come in, or lost; who, in our Trade, was broke; or who advertised Teas at the lowest Prices: Ending with a Comment upon those Dealers, who were endeavouring to under-sell us; shrewdly prognosticating their never being quiet, 'till they had rendered the Article of Tea a meer Drug; and THAT I, AND MANY MORE OF THE BUSINESS, should be obliged entirely to give it up. An Injury to Traffick in general! that must be allowed.

I must beg Leave, gentle Reader, to tell you, that my Stock perhaps did not exceed ten or a dozen Pounds at a Time of each Sort; but that furnished me with as much Discourse, as if I had the whole Lading of a Ship in my Shop. Then, as to Oils, to be sure the famous *Nobbs*, and Fifty more, were not to be put in Competition with mine for their Excellence; and, though I seldom kept above a Gallon of a Sort in the House, I carried on the Farce so far as to write to Country Chapmen to deal with me. . . .

As Misfortunes are ever the mortifying Parents of each other, so mine were teeming, and each new Day produced fresh Sorrow: But as if the very Fiends of Destruction were employed to perpetrate mine, and that my real Miseries were not sufficient to crush me with their Weight, a poor, beggarly fellow, who had been sometimes Supernumerary in *Drury-Lane* Theatre, and Part-writer, forged a most villainous Lye; by saying, I hired a very fine Bay Gelding, and borrowed a Pair of Pistols, to encounter my Father upon *Epping-Forest*; where, I solemnly protest, I don't know I ever saw my Father in my Life: That I stopped the Chariot, presented a Pistol to his Breast, and used such Terms as I am ashamed to insert; threaten'd to blow his Brains out that Moment, if he did not deliver——Upbraiding him for his Cruelty in abandoning me to those Distresses he knew I underwent, when he had it so amply in his Power to relieve me: That since he would not use that Power, I would force him to a Compliance, and was directly going to discharge upon him; but his Tears prevented me, and, asking my Pardon for his ill Usage of me, gave me his Purse with threescore Guineas, and a Promise to restore me to his Family and Love; on which I thank'd him, and rode off.

A likely Story, that my Father and his Servants were all so intimidated, had it been true, as not to have been able to withstand a single stout Highwayman, much more a Female, and his own Daughter to! However, the Story soon reached my Ear, which did not more enrage me on my own Account, that the impudent, ridiculous Picture the Scoundrel had drawn of my Father, in this supposed horrid Scene. The Recital threw me into such an agonizing Rage, I did not recover it for a Month; but, the next Evening, I had the Satisfaction of being designedly placed where this Villain was to be, and, concealed behind a Screen, heard the Lye re-told from his own Mouth.

He had no sooner ended, than I rushed from my Covert, and, being armed with a thick oaken Plank, knocked him down and without speaking a Word to him; and, had I not been happily prevented, should, without the least Remorse, have killed him on the Spot. I had not Breath enough to enquire into the Cause of his barbarous Falshood, but others, who were less concerned than myself, did it for me; and the only Reason he assigned for his saying it, was, *He meant it as a Joke*, which considerably added to the Vehemence of my Rage: But I had the Joy of seeing him well caned, and obliged to ask my Pardon on his Knees——Poor Satisfaction for so manifest an Injury! . . .

'Tis generally the Rule to put the Summary of Books of this Kind at the Beginning, but as I have, through the whole Course of my Life, acted in Contradiction to all Points of Regularity, beg to be indulged in a whimsical Conclusion of my Narrative, by introducing that last, which I will allow should have been first. As for Example:

This Day, *April* 19, 1755, is published the Eighth and last Number of *A Narrative of the Life of Mrs.* CHARLOTTE CHARKE, with a Dedication from and to myself: *The properest Patroness I could have chosen*, as I am most likely to be tenderly partial *to my poetical Errors, and will be as bounteous in the Reward as we may reasonably imagine my Merit may claim.*

This Work contains, 1*st*, A notable Promise of entertaining the Town with *The History of* HENRY DUMONT, *Esq; and Miss* CHARLOTTE EVELYN; but, being universally known to be an odd Product of Nature, was requested to postpone that, and give an Account of myself, from my Infancy to the present Time.

2*dly*, My natural Propensity to a Hat and Wig, in which, at the Age of four Years, I made a very considerable Figure in a Ditch, with several other succeeding mad Pranks. An Account of my Education at *Westminster. Why did not I make a better Use of so happy an Advantage!*

3*dly*, My extraordinary Skill in the Science of Physick, with a Recommendation of the necessary Use of Snails and Gooseberry Leaves, when Drugs and Chymical Preparations were not comeatable.

My natural Aversion to a Needle and profound Respect for a Curry-Comb, in the Use of which I excelled *most young Ladies in* Great-Britain, My extensive Knowledge in Gardening; not forgetting *that necessary Accomplishment for a young Gentlewoman*, in judiciously discharging a Blunderbuss or a Fowling-Piece. My own, and the lucky Excape of Life, when I run over a Child at *Uxbridge*.

4*thly*, My indiscreetly plumping into the Sea of Matrimony and becoming a Wife, before I had the proper Understanding of a reasonable Child. An Account of my coming on the Stage. My uncommon Success there. *My Folly in leaving it.* My Recommendation of my Sister *Marples* to the Consideration of every Person who chuses to eat an elegant Meal, or chat away a few Moments with a humourous, good-natured, elderly Landlady. My turning Grocer, with some *wise Remarks* on the Rise and Fall of Sugars and Teas. An unfortunate Adventure, in selling a Link. A short Account of my Father and Mother's Courtship and Marriage.

5*thly*, A faithful Promise to prefer a Bill in *Chancery* against my Uncle's Widow, who has artfully deprived his Heirs at Law of a very considerable Fortune.——N. B. *The old Dame may be assured I will be as good as my Word.*——My keeping a grand Puppet-Shew, and losing as much Money by it as it cost me. My becoming a Widow, and being afterwards privately married, *which, as it proved, I had better have let alone.* My going into Mens Cloaths, in which I continued many Years; the Reason of which I beg to be excused, as it concerns no Mortal *now living*, but myself. My becoming a second Time a Widow, which drew on me inexpressible Sorrows, that lasted upwards of twelve Years, and the unforeseen Turns of Providence, by which I was constantly extricated from them. An unfortunate Interview with a fair Lady, who would have made me Master of herself and Fortune, if I had been lucky enough to have been in Reality what I appeared.

6*thly*, My endeavouring at a Reconciliation with my Father. His sending back my Letter in a Blank. His being too much governed by Humour, but more so by her whom Age cannot exempt from being *the lively Limner of her own Face*; which she had better neglect a little, and pay Part of that Regard to what she ought to esteem THE NOBLER PART, and must have an Existence *when her painted Frame is reduced to Ashes*.

7*thly*, My being Gentleman to a certain Peer; after my Dismission, becoming *only an Occasional Player*, while I was playing at *Bo-peep with the World.* My turning Pork-Merchant; broke, through the inhuman Appetite of a hungry Dog. Went a Strolling. Several Adventures, during my Peregrination. My Return, and setting up an Eating-House in *Drury-Lane*; undone again, by pilfering Lodgers. Turning Drawer, at St. *Mary-la-Bonne*. An Account of my Situation there. Going to the *Hay-Market*

Theatre with my Brother. His leaving it. Many Distresses arising on that Account. Going a Strolling a second Time, and staying near nine Years. Several remarkable Occurrences, while I was Abroad; particularly, my being sent to G—— Jail, for being an Actor; which, to do *most Strolling-Players* Justice, they ought not to have the Laws enforced against them on that Score, *for a very substantial Reason*. My settling in *Wales*, and turning Pastry-Cook and Farmer. Made a small Mistake, in turning Hog-Merchant. Went to the Seat of Destruction, called *Pill*. Broke, and came away. Hired myself to a Printer at *Bristol*, to write and correct the Press. Made a short Stay there. Vagabondized again, and last *Christmas* returned to *London*, where I hope to remain as long as I live.

I have now concluded my Narrative, from my Infancy to the Time of my returning to *London*; and, if those who do me the Honour to kill Time by the Perusal, will seriously reflect on the manifold Distresses I have suffered, they must think me wonderfully favoured by Providence, in the surprizing Turns of Fortune, which has often redeemed me from the devouring Jaws of total Destruction, when I have least expected it.

13

Nineteenth Century: From *Incidents in the Life of a Slave Girl**

~

Harriet Jacobs

Harriet Jacobs (1813–1897) was born the daughter of a South Carolina planter and lived as a slave until 1842, when she escaped to the North. She did not publish her autobiography, however, until almost two decades later. Active in the abolitionist movement and busy caring for a white family's children, Jacobs squeezed work on her manuscript into the evening hours. She wrote in the style of sentimental fiction popular during the nineteenth century, and her text espouses the virtues of modesty, chastity, and domesticity that would have been familiar to her mostly white, female readers. At the same time, she also challenges that sentimental script. For example, she writes about sexuality at a time when the topic would have been off-limits in both conversation and writing, particularly for women. And Jacobs's text clearly critiques the ways that patriarchy and chattel slavery work in tandem.

This selection was taken from Incidents in the Life of a Slave Girl, *which was first published in 1861 under the pseudonym Linda Brent. Jacobs's narrative offers a unique perspective on slavery, because it is one of the few such personal narratives written by a woman. For example, her autobiography contains five chapters devoted exclusively to women's experiences under slavery, and this is one of them. Thematically, this selection illustrates Winifred Morgan's argument about the focus on relationships throughout* Incidents in the Life of a Slave Girl *(see Chapter 5). Here the author details the conflict between herself and her owner, Dr. Flint, over her desire to marry a free black man. While the master-slave relationship offers only exploitation, those ties that Jacobs forms with her lover and other family members give her the strength to resist Flint's abuse and to dream of freedom.*

*From Harriet Jacobs, *Incidents in the Life of a Slave Girl* (Boston: Published for the author, 1861, microfilm), 58–66.

WHY DOES THE SLAVE ever love? Why allow the tendrils of the heart to twine around objects which may at any moment be wrenched away by the hand of violence? When separations come by the hand of death, the pious soul can bow in resignation, and say, "Not my will, but thine be done, O Lord!" But when the ruthless hand of man strikes the blow, regardless of the misery he causes, it is hard to be submissive. I did not reason thus when I was a young girl. Youth will be youth. I loved, and I indulged the hope that the dark clouds around me would turn out a bright lining. I forgot that in the land of my birth the shadows are too dense for light to penetrate. A land

> Where laughter is not mirth; nor thought the mind;
> Nor words a language; nor e'en men mankind.
> Where cries reply to curses, shrieks to blows,
> And each is tortured in his separate hell.

There was in the neighborhood a young colored carpenter; a free born man. We had been well acquainted in childhood, and frequently met together afterwards. We became mutually attached, and he proposed to marry me. I loved him with all the ardor of a young girl's first love. But when I reflected that I was a slave, and that the laws gave no sanction to the marriage of such, my heart sank within me. My lover wanted to buy me; but I knew that Dr. Flint was too wilful and arbitrary a man to consent to that arrangement. From him, I was sure of experiencing all sorts of opposition, and I had nothing to hope from my mistress. She would have been delighted to have got rid of me, but not in that way. It would have relieved her mind of a burden if she could have seen me sold to some distant state, but if I was married near home I should be just as much in her husband's power as I had previously been,—for the husband of a slave has no power to protect her. Moreover, my mistress, like many others, seemed to think that slaves had no right to any family ties of their own; that they were created merely to wait upon the family of the mistress. I once heard her abuse a young slave girl, who told her that a colored man wanted to make her his wife. "I will have you peeled and pickled, my lady," said she, "if I ever hear you mention that subject again. Do you suppose that I will have you tending *my* children with the children of that nigger?" The girl to whom she said this had a mulatto child, of course not acknowledged by its father. The poor black man who loved her would have been proud to acknowledge his helpless offspring.

Many and anxious were the thoughts I revolved in my mind. I was at a loss what to do. Above all things, I was desirous to spare my lover the insults that had cut so deeply into my own soul. I talked with my grandmother about it, and partly told her my fears. I did not dare to tell her the worst. She had long suspected all was not right, and if I confirmed her suspicions I knew a storm would rise that would prove the overthrow of all my hopes.

This love-dream had been my support through many trials; and I could not bear to run the risk of having it suddenly dissipated. There was a lady in the neighborhood, a particular friend of Dr. Flint's, who often visited the house. I had a great respect for her, and she had always manifested a friendly interest in me. Grandmother thought she would have great influence with the doctor. I went to this lady, and told her my story. I told her I was aware that my lover's being a free-born man would prove a great objection; but he wanted to buy me; and if Dr. Flint would consent to that arrangement, I felt sure he would be willing to pay any reasonable price. She knew that Mrs. Flint disliked me; therefore, I ventured to suggest that perhaps my mistress would approve of my being sold, as that would rid her of me. The lady listened with kindly sympathy, and promised to do her utmost to promote my wishes. She had an interview with the doctor, and I believe she pleaded my cause earnestly; but it was all to no purpose.

How I dreaded my master now! Every minute I expected to be summoned to his presence; but the day passed, and I heard nothing from him. The next morning, a message was brought to me: "Master wants you in his study." I found the door ajar, and I stood a moment gazing at the hateful man who claimed a right to rule me, body and soul. I entered, and tried to appear calm. I did not want him to know how my heart was bleeding. He looked fixedly at me, with an expression which seemed to say, "I have half a mind to kill you on the spot." At last he broke the silence, and that was a relief to both of us.

"So you want to be married, do you?" said he, "and to a free nigger."

"Yes, sir."

"Well, I'll soon convince you whether I am your master, or the nigger fellow you honor so highly. If you *must* have a husband, you may take up with one of my slaves."

What a situation I should be in, as the wife of one of *his* slaves, even if my heart had been interested!

I replied, "Don't you suppose, sir, that a slave can have some preference about marrying? Do you suppose that all men are alike to her?"

"Do you love this nigger?" said he, abruptly.

"Yes, sir."

"How dare you tell me so!" he exclaimed, in great wrath. After a slight pause, he added, "I suppose you thought more of yourself; that you felt above the insults of such puppies."

I replied, "If he is a puppy I am a puppy, for we are both of the negro race. It is right and honorable for us to love each other. The man you call a puppy never insulted me, sir; and he would not love me if he did not believe me to be a virtuous woman."

He sprang upon me like a tiger, and gave me a stunning blow. It was the first time he had ever struck me; and fear did not enable me to control my anger. When I had recovered a little from the effects, I exclaimed, "You have struck me for answering you honestly. How I despise you!"

There was silence for some minutes. Perhaps he was deciding what should be my punishment; or, perhaps, he wanted to give me time to reflect on what I had said, and to whom I had said it. Finally, he asked, "Do you know what you have said?"

"Yes, sir; but your treatment drove me to it."

"Do you know that I have a right to do as I like with you,—that I can kill you, if I please?"

"You have tried to kill me, and I wish you had; but you have no right to do as you like with me."

"Silence!" he exclaimed, in a thundering voice. "By heavens, girl, you forget yourself too far! Are you mad? If you are, I will soon bring you to your senses. Do you think any other master would bear what I have borne from you this morning? Many masters would have killed you on the spot. How would you like to be sent to jail for your insolence?"

"I know I have been disrespectful, sir," I replied; "but you drove me to it; I couldn't help it. As for the jail, there would be more peace for me there than there is here."

"You deserve to go there," said he, "and to be under such treatment, that you would forget the meaning of the word *peace*. It would do you good. It would take some of your high notions out of you. But I am not ready to send you there yet, notwithstanding your ingratitude for all my kindness and forbearance. You have been the plague of my life. I have wanted to make you happy, and I have been repaid with the basest ingratitude; but though you have proved yourself incapable of appreciating my kindness, I will be lenient towards you, Linda. I will give you one more chance to redeem your character. If you behave yourself and do as I require, I will forgive you and treat you as I always have done; but if you disobey me, I will punish you as I would the meanest slave on my plantation. Never let me hear that fellow's name mentioned again. If I ever know of your speaking to him, I will cowhide you both; and if I catch him lurking about my premises, I will shoot him as soon as I would a dog. Do you hear what I say? I'll teach you a lesson about marriage and free niggers! Now go, and let this be the last time I have occasion to speak to you on this subject."

Reader, did you ever hate? I hope not. I never did but once; and I trust I never shall again. Somebody has called it "the atmosphere of hell"; and I believe it is so.

For a fortnight the doctor did not speak to me. He thought to mortify me; to make me feel that I had disgraced myself by receiving the honorable addresses of a respectable colored man, in preference to the base proposals of a white man. But though his lips disdained to address me, his eyes were very loquacious. No animal ever watched its prey more narrowly than he watched me. He knew that I could write, though he had failed to make me read his letters; and he was now troubled lest I should exchange letters with another man. After a while he became weary of silence; and I was sorry for it. One morning, as he passed through the hall, to leave the house, he contrived to thrust a note into my hand. I thought I had better read it, and spare myself the vexation of having him read it to me. It expressed regret for the blow he had given me, and reminded me that I myself was wholly to blame for it. He hoped I had become convinced of the injury I was doing myself by incurring his displeasure. He wrote that he had made up his mind to go to Louisiana; that he should take several slaves with him, and intended I should be one of the number. My mistress would remain where she was; therefore I should have nothing to fear from that quarter. If I merited kindness from him, he assured me that it would be lavishly bestowed. He begged me to think over the matter, and answer the following day.

The next morning I was called to carry a pair of scissors to his room. I laid them on the table, with the letter beside them. He thought it was my answer, and did not call me back. I went as usual to attend my young mistress to and from school. He met me in the street, and ordered me to stop at his office on my way back. When I entered, he showed me his letter, and asked me why I had not answered it. I replied, "I am your daughter's property, and it is in your power to send me, or take me, wherever you please." He said he was very glad to find me so willing to go, and that we should start early in the autumn. He had a large practice in the town, and I rather thought he had made up the story merely to frighten me. However that might be, I was determined that I would never go to Louisiana with him.

Summer passed away, and early in the autumn Dr. Flint's eldest son was sent to Louisiana to examine the country, with a view to emigrating. That news did not disturb me. I knew very well that I should not be sent with *him*. That I had not been taken to the plantation before this time, was owing to the fact that his son was there. He was jealous of his son; and jealousy of the overseer had kept him from punishing me by sending me into the fields to work. Is it strange that I was not proud of these protectors? As for the overseer, he was a man for whom I had less respect than I had for a bloodhound.

Young Mr. Flint did not bring back a favorable report of Louisiana, and I heard no more of that scheme. Soon after this, my lover met me at the corner of the street, and I stopped to speak to him. Looking up, I saw my master watching us from his window. I hurried home, trembling with fear. I was sent for, immediately, to go to his room. He met me with a blow. "When is mistress to be married?" said he, in a sneering tone. A shower of oaths and imprecations followed. How thankful I was that my lover was a free man! that my tyrant had no power to flog him for speaking to me in the street!

Again and again I revolved in my mind how all this would end. There was no hope that the doctor would consent to sell me on any terms. He had an iron will, and was determined to keep me, and to conquer me. My lover was an intelligent and religious man. Even if he could have obtained permission to marry me while I was a slave, the marriage would give him no power to protect me from my master. It would have made him miserable to witness the insults I should have been subjected to. And then, if we had children, I knew they must "follow the condition of the mother." What a terrible blight that would be on the heart of a free, intelligent father! For *his* sake, I felt that I ought not to link his fate with my own unhappy destiny. He was going to Savannah to see about a little property left him by an uncle; and hard as it was to bring my feelings to it, I earnestly entreated him not to come back. I advised him to go to the Free States, where his tongue would not be tied, and where his intelligence would be of more avail to him. He left me, still hoping the day would come when I could be bought. With me the lamp of hope had gone out. The dream of my girlhood was over. I felt lonely and desolate.

Still I was not stripped of all. I still had my good grandmother, and my affectionate brother. When he put his arms round my neck, and looked into my eyes, as if to read there the troubles I dared not tell, I felt that I still had something to love. But even that pleasant emotion was chilled by the reflection that he might be torn from me at any moment, by some sudden freak of my master. If he had known how we loved each other, I think he would have exulted in separating us. We often planned together how we could get to the north. But, as William remarked, such things are easier said than done. My movements were very closely watched, and we had no means of getting any money to defray our expenses. As for grandmother, she was strongly opposed to her children's undertaking any such project. She had not forgotten poor Benjamin's sufferings, and she was afraid that if another child tried to escape, he would have a similar or a worse fate. To me, nothing seemed more dreadful than my present life. I said to myself, "William *must* be free. He shall go to the north, and I will follow him." Many a slave sister has formed the same plans.

14

Twentieth Century: From *All of a Piece: A Life with Multiple Sclerosis**

~

Barbara D. Webster

Barbara D. Webster's All of a Piece: A Life with Multiple Sclerosis
*(1989) is one of the contemporary autobiographies that G. Thomas
Couser analyzes in his essay on autopathography (see chapter 10).
It took fourteen years of accelerating symptoms before Webster finally received an accurate diagnosis of her disease. Bounced
around among a number of insensitive physicians and even an abu-
sive one, dismissed as a neurotic and bullied into psychiatric treatment, she faced family, friends, and a medical establishment who
continued to insist that her physical problems were imaginary. Once
her diagnosis was finally settled, however, Webster faced new difficulties as she began to adjust to life with a chronic illness. Not only
does multiple sclerosis (MS) have no cure, but, as Webster notes, the
most salient fact about the disease is "its unpredictability and its
uncertainty" (22).*

*Initially, Webster considered the many adjustments she was forced
to make to MS as her own individual problems. Later she began to see
how the attitudes of society toward disease and disability molded her
personal experiences. Couser's essay points out that one of Webster's
strengths as a writer is her ability to show the cultural construction of
disease; she reveals the extent to which prevailing attitudes in society
at large shape the lives of those who are chronically ill. The selections
below from Webster's autobiographical writing draw on some of her
travels in Egypt to show through contrast how a number of basic
American assumptions and values conflict with the realities of chronic
disease as individual human beings experience them.*

*From Barbara D. Webster, *All of a Piece: A Life with Multiple Sclerosis*
(Baltimore: Johns Hopkins University Press, 1989), 1–3, 14–15, 61–62, 68–75.
Reprinted by permission of Johns Hopkins University Press.

A FEW YEARS AFTER DISCOVERING that I have multiple sclerosis, I visited Egypt with a friend. There I had an experience that remains a metaphor of much of my experience with MS. We found ourselves one day at the airport in Luxor on our way to Cairo.

The word "airport" is something of a misnomer; I was reminded of an old and little-used branch railroad station. There was one room and one small ticket window. Jammed into this very hot and airless little room were hundreds of people, few of whom seemed to know what was going on. My friend and I eventually checked in for our flight to Cairo (although that, too, conveys a false impression of order and efficiency) and, by comparing our boarding passes with others, got at the end of what seemed to be the proper line.

Nothing happened. It soon became obvious that no one was going anywhere any time soon and that the line was essentially irrelevant. We spotted some empty seats and started working our way toward them through the crowd. Suddenly I was pushed hard, lost my balance, and fell. We realized that we were in the midst of a group of elderly American tourists, all with name tags, who were loudly objecting to our presence in their area and actually pushing us away. "Who do they think they are? They don't belong with us. They are pushing into our line. Why does she have a cane—there's nothing wrong with her." They were quite amazingly nasty and, in the center of this scene of very Egyptian absolute and seemingly uncontrolled chaos, had created their own bit of America. The contrast was compelling. They wanted to know exactly when the flight was leaving and the answer, of course, was always the same—*Insh'allah* ("God willing" or "when God wills"), which infuriated them. They would not yield an inch of their fiercely guarded territory.

Faced with a total inability to control what was going on, they were going to extreme lengths to foster their sense of being in control. They seemed to think that continually fighting for a place in this largely illusory line would get them to Cairo faster. My friend and I, on the other hand, having accepted that we had no control in this situation, were beginning to revel in that feeling; the mood is very catching and, after all, did it matter if we ever got to Cairo? We were more concerned with waiting, being there in some comfort, while they, faced with chaos, fought ever harder to maintain the illusion of doing something by pushing and pulling in line. And that, of course, was why there were empty seats for us.

My experience with MS is first and foremost a personal story. It is rooted in my history and my personality. Much of what I have found most difficult—and the metaphor for that is being pushed around by those rude Americans in Luxor—is a personal issue and something, no matter its source or explanation, for me to come to terms with. But it became increasingly clear to me that taken out of the context of the society I live in and the cultural framework through which meaning is created, there was limited adaptive power to be found in my personal story. The meaning of disability and chronic illness and many of the consequences of those states are socially determined. It took me a while to realize that. Initially I thought that coming to terms with having a chronic disease was an individual task, one to be undertaken in isolation. But chronic disease is not just defined by society, it is experienced through the mediating structures of society and culture.

The scene at the airport in Luxor began to seem a paradigm for me of that juxtaposition—that relationship. Me set alongside, and in, a society that gives its own sets of meaning to my experience. It was the very starkness of the contrast—that reconstruction of America set down in the midst of Egypt—that was so revealing and that allowed me to begin to see my own experience in a larger context. And it was that context, together with my own story, which ultimately provided some illumination and eased the process of coming to terms with having a chronic disease. . . .

The diagnosis of multiple sclerosis was for me a watershed—one of those events that radically transforms experience both past and future. It illuminated what had gone before and changed the terms of what was to follow. As an event, the diagnosis itself had limited meaning; it did not change my physical reality. Its importance lay in its power to transform the past, present, and future. The power of a name to alter reality is enormous.

The metaphorical power of the scene at the airport in Luxor comes alive for me through the prism of the diagnosis. Society, both before and after I received a diagnosis, shaped my experience. I was subject to other people's interpretation and judgment of my experience. People do tend to interpret reality through their own experience and view of the world and leave little room for others' worlds and other experiences of reality. For me, the primary goal was always to maintain my integrity within that interpretation. One way to do that, of course, and important in itself, is to step out of others' worlds. There is always an empty seat, as in Luxor, where one can sit and enjoy the scene. . . .

Several years passed after my diagnosis before I realized how significantly my experience was being shaped by my culture. The crystallizing event in that realization was a month spent in the Middle East. It took perhaps the combination of being in another, foreign culture and being away from my own to make clear to me the impact of culture on my experience. It was only through stepping away and coming back that I saw myself in this larger context.

I had, until this time, tended to think about what was happening to me in purely individual terms, not as unique to me, of course, but as bounded by me and my social world—me and my disease, a definable unit, something apart from the realm of culture. I had been aware of some of the social consequences, particularly the impact on those I was close to, but I had not thought clearly about the ways in which their reactions and responses as well as my own were culturally shaped or socially demanded. I think perhaps it was necessary first to identify and begin to come to terms with the more personal and immediate issues. After I returned from the Middle East, my intuitive feelings about the ways in which others had viewed and had written about their experience with MS began to achieve some clarity and form.

Once I began to think about my experience in its cultural frame, I tried in some ways to keep it to myself, to retain its individual character. Increasingly, however, the relationship between my everyday life and the set of generally shared ideas, values, and symbols that constitutes my culture (for want of a better word) became apparent. It may seem that this should have been obvious but in this context it was not—at least to me. As this happened, I began to be aware of the conflicts between my life with a chronic disease and the values of the society in which I lived.

When I was in Egypt, walking with difficulty and using a cane, strangers and passersby asked me directly, "What is wrong with you? Why do you limp? Why are you sitting there? Why are you using a cane?" Walking in a Cairo street, an old woman came up to me, put her arm on mine, pointed to the cane, and patted my hand. I was struck by this; in the United States people don't ask questions of that nature or respond openly to disability. Instead they stare at or ignore me. The open acceptance I experienced in Egypt contrasted starkly with the equally open turning away I have come to expect in this country.

A brief example: one evening, riding on the commuter bus, surrounded by people I saw every day and who always smiled and chatted, I was unable to stand up. I eventually struggled out of my seat and stumbled to the door. Not one of these friendly people offered a hand; without exception, they averted their eyes and pretended not to notice my difficulty. Disease or disability is not something we openly acknowledge, but something we turn away from (this turning away is, of course, a form of acknowledgment).

My time in Egypt had a dramatic effect on me, although I only realized its impact after I had come home. I had felt so free and easy there. I had been just who I was, limped and stumbled about, and had *no* feelings about it. People reacted to me with care and consideration but so quietly, so matter-of-factly, that I wasn't aware of these differences until I came home. In Israel, in many ways a very Western society, I was completely ignored. No one modified their normal pushing and shoving behavior for me—everyone in Israel wants to be first in line—and I was knocked about quite often. That kind of being ignored is very different from what happens here, however, because it does not seem to be reflective of aversion. It is a not-seeing, not a seeing followed by a turning away. . . .

After I returned home, I began to think about what it means to be disabled in America. What are the prevailing values and underlying assumptions of this culture and how do they affect my daily life? My experience is shaped and, in some measure, controlled by living within the frame of these assumptions, and it suddenly seemed very important to examine them more closely.

Several common assumptions come to mind, all rooted in the American ethic of self-determination: we are what we do; we have self-responsibility and autonomy; we can control our life and experience—outcomes are controllable. Illness and disease are seen as punishment; the idea exists that failure implies a defect in character and will.

What are the primary values of American culture on which these assumptions are based? Values are notoriously hard to define or measure, in part because a group's dominant values may conflict with how it lives on a daily basis. What we like to or need to think we are may not bear much relation to what we are in fact. Important symbols may encapsulate values that are not operative in daily life but that are crucially important in how we think about ourselves. Moreover, the dominant values of a group will be variously represented among individuals; there may be wide variations in beliefs, practices, expressed values. "Values" may well be the wrong word to use here, but I think it is as useful as any other concept in thinking about the impact of culture on individual experience. Values reflect common understandings and shared assumptions about the world and the nature of reality within which and through which experience is filtered.

There are four primary values that I have come to see as paramount and all-encompassing in shaping and coloring the experience of being ill in America. I think these values are basic to and underlie the working assumptions of this culture. The first, and probably the most important, is the notion that humans both do and should control nature and that control, on all levels, is always a desired outcome. The high value given to control is central to the common understanding of illness and disability in America. Second, and akin to the value given to control, is the centrality of the idea of independence and self-sufficiency. Independence is highly valued in this culture. It is both desired and seen as an achievable outcome. It is more important in terms of how we think about ourselves and in how we react to others than in the realities of our lives. Nevertheless, as one of the central ideas in this culture, the perceived autonomy of the individual is key. The third basic value is to be found in the dominance given to the future over both the present and the past. Future implies change, which in and of itself is highly valued. Change is perceived both as always possible and as a consistently desired outcome. Tomorrow will always be bigger and better. The fourth important value is activity. Doing is highly valued in American culture and doing, as opposed to being, is a primary response to almost anything.

These values and the assumptions that flow from them about the nature of reality provide a useful framework against which to think about what it means to be sick or disabled in this culture as well as about how disease is viewed. I also think that less important but inextricably entwined with these values and a significant element in what it means to be ill in this culture is a subsurface and covert belief that disease both reflects and results from an inherent imperfection or flaw in human nature.

Disease and disability do not fit easily within the American value system. There is almost total conflict. As I considered my experience in the light of these values, I began to see some faint glimmers of light illuminating the roots of the conflicts I felt. Suddenly one's experience—who it is that I am today—is radically at odds with governing assumptions about reality and life. Part of the difficulty in coming to terms with that break, that discontinuity, is that precisely because I am a part of this society, have been shaped by its values, and have grown up in a world that is bounded by these assumptions, the potential for conflict is so strong. The more I am congruent with my culture and have internalized its dominant thrust, the more conflict there will be when suddenly my experience is at odds with it. The paradox, of course, is that the greater the conflict, the less acknowledgment of it there may be and the stronger the need to overcome or at least to appear to overcome it.

It is at the intersection of this conflict—between American values and disease—that denial arises. In a situation where realities conflict, either one of them must be changed or disregarded or there must be an accommodation and adjustment to the fact of the conflict. In this context, the culture cannot be changed, nor can the fact that one has a disease. Denial is an easier response than its alternative, acceptance. Over time, however, denial is more stressful, requires more energy to maintain, and is ultimately self-defeating. My initial and primarily intuitive understanding of why hope, arising out of or leading to denial, was such a common response to MS in the books I read began to make sense as I considered this conflict between the reality of chronic disease and the primary values of American society.

One of the first things that a chronic disease such as MS forces one to realize is that nature is not controllable. Yet the belief that nature is, and should be, controllable by humankind is absolutely central to this culture. I have no control over the disease activity in my brain. In and of itself, this is hard enough to accept, but acceptance does come. That acceptance is infinitely harder to achieve, however, when the culture continually—in both small and big ways—tells me that I should be in control, that control is possible, and that accepting or believing that I am not in control is a giving up, a moral failure, and an affirmation of the fact that my nature is flawed.

The conflict between chronic disease and the value given to the future in this culture is fairly straightforward. For me, today is important. I have no way of knowing what will happen to me; the fact that I am walking today is of overriding importance to me. Change would certainly be nice, but if I rely on the possibility of change, the hope of improvement, then I fail to live fully today. Again, this society—in all its voices, books, the media, friends, family, even leftover bits of me—constantly tells me not to give up hope of change and moreover, would have me make that hope a centerpiece of my life. Certainly I hope that a cure for MS will be found, but I cannot live in that hope. Given the realities of this disease, chances are very good that the future may not be better; it may not be worse, but it is not likely to be better. Yet a very common response to disease in this culture is talk of overcoming it or of conquering it. The stories are legion about people who have "won the battle" against disease. With a chronic disease such as MS, this is not a very helpful approach.

The other aspect of this emphasis on the future that I find to be in conflict with my experience and my expectations is the notion that the future will take care of itself; again, the implication is that the future will be better than the present. My view of the future is radically different now than it was before I knew I had MS. The future has constricted and the range of possibility seems narrower. Of course, I am also rapidly becoming middle-aged, and, with age, the future does become less open-ended. This is true for everyone but is much more acute with chronic disease. I am more concerned with providing for the possibilities of the future than with hope of change and improvement.

The possibility, however remote, that I might become more disabled led me to take a large salary cut to get into the federal civil service because I felt it provided the greatest degree of employment security available for the disabled. Others urge me to take bigger career risks in the hope that all will be well and the future will take care of itself. I do not feel that I can do that. There is an element of contradiction here because while I feel I must be cognizant of the worst that might happen and prepare for that, I also feel enormous pressure to live for today, to enjoy life to its fullest while I can. The conflict for me becomes this: if I have some money, do I use it to go to Egypt while I am still able to walk or do I save it for the day when I might be unable to work? In either event, the cultural message that the future will be an improvement over the present is totally at odds with my understanding of reality.

It is certainly true that change is often feared. Nevertheless, even then there remains an underlying belief in and assumption of progress.

Things change, they progress; and whether change is welcomed or not, this is one of the most important operating assumptions of this society—of most of the Western world, for that matter. Radiating out from the extraordinary impact of Darwin's work on evolutionary processes into all areas of culture, this belief has permeated our thinking. Change, and in the form of progress, is seen as inevitable. Those with chronic disease live, on whatever level and whether perceived or not, in opposition to this assumption. The progression of disease will not be in a positive direction for the individual.

An outgrowth of this preoccupation with the future is the high value American society gives to time, per se. Time is valuable, time is money. And I can be very slow and get in people's way. On a train in Egypt, my friend and I asked the waiter what time dinner would be served. "*Insh'allah*," he replied. "OK," we said, "that's fine, we'll be in the club car." "No, no, no," he said. "You'll miss dinner." He had already shown his grave disapproval of two women sitting in the club car for any reason, much less our expressed reason—to have a drink. "We'll stay," we said, "if dinner is soon." "Oh," he said, "Soon? Dinner will be . . . *Insh'allah*." So we persisted, and every twenty minutes or so one of us would go to our car to check on dinner. The waiter each time said, "Come back, come back." We'd ask if dinner was ready and he, stretched out and smoking a cigarette in the kitchenette, would smile and say, "*Insh'allah*." I think we had dinner about three hours later. I loved every moment of Egypt. Time as time has no value there.

The emphasis on doing in this culture is equally in conflict with the experience of a chronic disease such as MS and is closely related to the high value placed on the future. Activity is prized and judgments are based on what one does. The question most often asked at a cocktail party is, "What do you do?" Similarly, "Let's do something about it" or "What are you doing about it?" are stock phrases in this culture. They reflect an understanding about the nature of reality that is widespread. Accepting that there is nothing that can be done and refusing to engage in futile attempts to change what is put one in an uncomfortable position. I hear constantly that acceptance is passive and weak; to rage and fight would be much more acceptable. Doing anything is far more acceptable than doing nothing.

These three primary values—that men and women control nature, that the future will be better, and that activity is the preferred response—are all related. Activity, doing something about it, rests on the understanding that nature can be controlled, something can always be done, and tomorrow will be better than today. Highlighting the future implies the possibility and efficacy of action.

Finally, living with chronic disease makes it impossible to continue to believe that individual autonomy and independence are possible, even

if one considers them desirable. Dependence is an all too real and potential outcome. I am not autonomous now; I am dependent on my friends
in many ways. Although I value my independence and try to maintain it,
I also try to remember that independence, in and of itself, cannot be a
central issue for me. I think this is made much more difficult by the fact
that dependence carries with it very negative overtones and, indeed, has
a negative meaning for me too. Because of this, I tend to go to great
lengths to avoid the appearance of dependence and, therefore, make my
life more difficult and complicated than it need be. Both the full implications of this issue and its complexity continue to become apparent to me.

The notion that human nature is basically flawed is, I think, connected
to the subsurface but strong belief in American culture that disease is a
manifestation of a break in the proper scheme of things and, moreover, is
a form of punishment. A common response in the face of illness or misfortune is, "What have I done to deserve this?" We do seem to think that
there must be a reason for misfortune and that this reason rests at the level
of moral cause and effect. If I accept, then, that I have a chronic disease, it
seems that I accept the imperfection of my nature. In this context, multiple
sclerosis is quite neutral when compared with AIDS, which is overtly seen
as a moral outcome and a punishment, or with cancer, which also carries
with it some of these connotations. There is a very strong undercurrent to
the effect that one gets exactly what one deserves.

On the surface, however, we think of ourselves as viewing disease
scientifically, in physical cause-and-effect terms, and it is important to
us that we do think this way. We believe that cures for all diseases are
available; it is only a question of when, and the when ultimately rests on
the degree of will and resources we devote to the task. The extraordinary
results of modern science and technology support this. A cure for cancer,
a vaccine against AIDS, will be found if only we work hard enough. We
overtly treat disease as a scientific problem to be solved. We assert that
our response to disease is untainted by moral notions of cause and effect
and is primarily rational.

We do think that there is no real distinction between our scientific
and folk notions of illness and disease. Although we profess to view disease entirely in scientific terms, we actually (if covertly) view it also in
moral terms. Disease is both a derangement of the proper relationship of
humans to nature—of humankind subjugating nature to its will—and a
reflection of that unimproved nature.

It is precisely because disease is covertly viewed as a moral outcome
that it is dealt with as a purely physical issue. If we were to acknowledge to
ourselves and to each other that we see disease in other than scientific
terms, a great many of the things we hold central would be seen as standing
on very fragile ground. Our world view, much of what it is most important

to us to affirm, would be shaken. I think that there is an enormous discrepancy between how we really think and feel about these things and how we tell ourselves we feel, how we profess to feel. Under the impact of something as personally overwhelming as the knowledge of chronic disease or disability these conflicts become apparent.

Suggested Readings

Anderson, Linda. *Women and Autobiography in the Twentieth Century: Remembered Futures.* New York: Prentice Hall, 1996. Anderson focuses on diaries, letters, fiction, and theoretical writing by prominent figures such as Virginia Woolf and Sylvia Plath and explores the way memory functions in their self-representations.

Ashley, Kathleen, Leigh Gilmore, and Gerald Peters, eds. *Autobiography and Postmodernism.* Amherst: University of Massachusetts Press, 1994. These essays link postmodern theories of the subject and analyses of autobiographies, a connection that had not been explicitly explored in previous works of autobiography criticism.

Benstock, Shari, ed. *The Private Self: Theory and Practice of Women's Autobiographical Writings.* Chapel Hill: University of North Carolina Press, 1988. The collection contains an important essay by Benstock, who argues that traditional theories of autobiography and selfhood are gendered as masculine and fail to allow for feminine models of subjectivity.

Bloom, Lynn Z., and Ning Yu. "American Autobiography: The Changing Critical Canon." *a/b: Auto/Biography Studies* 9 (1994): 167–80. This scholarly essay offers useful statistical information to show how critics of autobiography have recently begun to examine works by white women and minority writers.

Braham, Jeanne. *Crucial Conversations: Interpreting Contemporary American Literary Autobiographies by Women.* New York: Teachers College Press, 1995. Braham's analysis concentrates particularly on autobiographical writings by poets such as Adrienne Rich, Audre Lorde, and Alice Walker.

Braxton, Joanne M. *Black Women Writing Autobiography: A Tradition within a Tradition.* Philadelphia: Temple University Press, 1989. Braxton's study points to the ways in which black women's lifewriting has been ignored by critics who focus on the black male autobiography tradition beginning with the slave narrative or on white women's autobiographical texts.

Brodzki, Bella, and Celeste Schenck. *Life/Lines: Theorizing Women's Autobiography.* Ithaca, N.Y.: Cornell University Press, 1988. This wide-ranging collection covers a variety of texts and time periods from various critical approaches.

Buss, Helen M. *Mapping Our Selves: Canadian Women's Autobiography in English.* Montreal: McGill-Queen's University Press, 1993. Buss uses map-making as a metaphor to explain how nineteenth- and twentieth-century Canadian women arrived at their self-understandings.

Corbett, Mary Jean. *Representing Femininity: Middle-Class Subjectivity in Victorian and Edwardian Women's Autobiographies.* New York: Oxford University Press, 1992. Corbett analyzes texts by writers, actresses, and suffragettes.

Culley, Margo, ed. *American Women's Autobiography: Fea(s)ts of Memory.* Madison: University of Wisconsin Press, 1992. These essays address a wide range of multicultural texts, including Leslie Silko's *Storyteller* and Maxine Hong Kingston's *The Woman Warrior.*

Etter-Lewis, Gwendolyn, and Michèle Foster, eds. *Unrelated Kin: Race and Gender in Women's Lives.* New York: Routledge, 1996. This scholarly text is significant for its focus on personal narratives by women from non-Western cultures.

Evasdaughter, Elizabeth N. *Catholic Girlhood Narratives: The Church and Self-denial.* A literary scholar and former Dominican nun, Evasdaughter examines twentieth-century European and American women's texts. She argues that each writer resists attacks on her dignity that accompany living as a female child under patriarchal Catholic doctrine.

Fowler, Lois J., and David H. Fowler, eds. *Revelations of Self: American Women in Autobiography.* Albany: State University of New York Press, 1990. The editors have compiled excerpts from four nineteenth- and twentieth-century texts by political activists such as Elizabeth Cady Stanton.

Gilmore, Leigh. *Autobiographics: A Feminist Theory of Women's Self-Representation.* Ithaca, N.Y.: Cornell University Press, 1994. The text examines issues of authenticity and truthtelling as they relate to autobiography and notes that women's lifewriting is frequently viewed as being less truthful—and therefore less valuable—than writing by men.

Goldman, Anne E. *Take My Word: Autobiographical Innovations of Ethnic American Working Women.* Berkeley: University of California Press, 1996. The author takes an innovative look at cookbooks, collaborative autobiographies, and memoirs by labor organizers to examine the writers' representations of both their individual identities and their larger ethnic cultures.

Heilbrun, Carolyn. *Writing a Woman's Life.* New York: Ballantine, 1988. This classic text offers an accessible scholarly analysis of biographical writing about women's lives and women's own lifewriting, and it identifies key elements that have typically been omitted from such narratives.

Hoffmann, Leonore, and Margo Culley, eds. *Women's Personal Narratives: Essays in Criticism and Pedagogy.* New York: Modern Language

Association of America, 1985. Contributors to this volume analyze women's letters, diaries, and oral testimonies, suggest ways to approach the material as literature, and offer suggestions for integrating these frequently ignored materials into college courses.

Jelinek, Estelle, ed. *The Tradition of Women's Autobiography: From Antiquity to the Present.* Boston: Twayne, 1986. This wide-ranging text discusses everything from Egyptian tomb inscriptions to contemporary American texts. Jelinek characterizes women's autobiographical writing as nonlinear, fragmented, and focused on relationships, claims that other critics have often challenged.

———. *Women's Autobiography: Essays in Criticism.* Bloomington: Indiana University Press, 1980. Jelinek's text offers the first book-length analysis of women's lifewriting.

Kadar, Marlene, ed. *Essays on Lifewriting: From Genre to Critical Practice.* Toronto: University of Toronto Press, 1992. The collection is unique because it includes a section that explores the autobiographical elements in fictional works such as Margaret Atwood's *Cat's Eye.*

Lim, Shirley Geok-lin, ed. *Approaches to Teaching Kingston's* The Woman Warrior. New York: Modern Language Association of America, 1991. This text provides a variety of practical suggestions for understanding Kingston's frequently studied text and includes important information on Chinese history and culture.

Lionnet, Françoise. *Autobiographical Voices: Race, Gender, and Self-Portraiture.* Ithaca, N.Y.: Cornell University Press, 1989. Lionnet examines writings by African-American, Caribbean, and Mauritian women and argues that their works are indeed political, in spite of some male writers' assertions to the contrary.

Martin, Biddy. "Lesbian Identity and Autobiographical Difference[s]." In *The Lesbian and Gay Studies Reader*, edited by Henry Abelove, Michèle Aina Barale, and David M. Halperin, 274–93. New York: Routledge, 1993. This essay contrasts lesbian autobiographical writings of the seventies with those of the eighties. It argues that the earlier narratives suggest the existence of a uniform lesbian identity and experience, while the latter emphasize writers' individuality and their race, class, and gender along with sexuality.

Miller, Nancy K. "Changing the Subject: Authorship, Writing, and the Reader." In *Subject to Change* by Miller, 101–21. New York: Columbia University Press, 1988. This classic essay critiques postmodern theories that herald the death of the author and argues that women writers must claim subject positions for themselves.

Neuman, Shirley, ed. *Autobiography and Questions of Gender.* London: Frank Cass, 1991. Neuman's collection is notable because some contributors examine the relationship between masculinity and writing style, in addition to feminist critics' traditional focus on femininity and autobiography.

Otten, Charlotte F. *English Women's Voices, 1540–1700.* Miami: Florida International University Press, 1992. This anthology includes first-person narratives on a range of topics and in a variety of forms, including diaries, letters, sermons, and traditional autobiographies.

Parati, Graziella. *Public History, Private Stories: Italian Women's Autobiography.* Minneapolis: University of Minnesota Press, 1996. Parati examines twentieth-century autobiographies as the medium through which women writers come to terms with their often contradictory roles in the public and private spheres.

Personal Narratives Group. *Interpreting Women's Lives: Feminist Theory and Personal Narratives.* Bloomington: Indiana University Press, 1989. This expansive treatment of autobiography, biography, and oral history emphasizes the importance of situating women's life stories in specific historical and cultural moments.

Smith, Sidonie. *A Poetics of Women's Autobiography: Marginality and the Fictions of Self-Representation.* Bloomington: Indiana University Press, 1987. Smith's historical analysis points to a tradition of women's autobiography that stems in part from prohibitions against women's public speech.

———. *Subjectivity, Identity, and the Body: Women's Autobiographical Practices in the Twentieth Century.* Bloomington: Indiana University Press, 1993. Smith discusses representations of women's bodies in lifewriting and contextualizes her analysis by outlining the different relationships between mind and body for Western men and women in the seventeenth, eighteenth, and nineteenth centuries.

Smith, Sidonie, and Julia Watson, eds. *De-Colonizing the Subject: The Politics of Gender in Women's Autobiography.* Minneapolis: University of Minnesota Press, 1992. This collection examines texts by women from many different countries who represent a range of racial-ethnic backgrounds, and its contributors argue that the autobiographers practice "de-colonizing strategies" in the act of writing itself.

———. *Women, Autobiography, Theory: A Reader.* Madison: University of Wisconsin Press, 1998. Smith and Watson provide a comprehensive and detailed examination of feminist autobiography criticism.

Stanley, Liz. *The Auto/biographical I: The Theory and Practice of Feminist Autobiography.* Manchester: Manchester University Press, 1992. The text emphasizes the close links among autobiography, biography, and fiction, pointing to the fictionalized, or artful, nature of any self-portrait.

Wood, Mary Elene. *The Writing on the Wall: Women's Autobiography and the Asylum.* Urbana: University of Illinois Press, 1994. Wood examines the ways that women who were institutionalized as insane in nineteenth-

and twentieth-century America structured their autobiographical narratives for public consumption and challenged the authority of psychiatric professionals.